Lecture Notes in Economics and Mathematical Systems

For information about Vols. 1–156, please contact your bookseller or Springer-Verlag

Vol. 157: Optimization and Operations Research. Proceedings 1977. Edited by R. Henn, B. Korte, and W. Oettli. VI, 270 pages. 1978.

Vol. 158: L. J. Cherene, Set Valued Dynamical Systems and Economic Flow. VIII, 83 pages. 1978.

Vol. 159: Some Aspects of the Foundations of General Equilibrium Theory: The Posthumous Papers of Peter J. Kalman. Edited by J. Green. VI, 167 pages. 1978.

Vol. 160: Integer Programming and Related Areas. A Classified Bibliography. Edited by D. Hausmann. XIV, 314 pages. 1978.

Vol. 161: M. J. Beckmann, Rank in Organizations. VIII, 164 pages. 1978.

Vol. 162: Recent Developments in Variable Structure Systems, Economics and Biology. Proceedings 1977. Edited by R. R. Mohler and A. Ruberti. VI, 326 pages. 1978.

Vol. 163: G. Fandel, Optimale Entscheidungen in Organisationen. VI, 143 Seiten. 1979.

Vol. 164: C. L. Hwang and A. S. M. Masud, Multiple Objective Decision Making – Methods and Applications. A State-of-the-Art Survey. XII, 351 pages. 1979.

Vol. 165: A. Maravall, Identification in Dynamic Shock-Error Models. VIII, 158 pages. 1979.

Vol. 166: R. Cuninghame-Green, Minimax Algebra. XI, 258 pages. 1979.

Vol. 167: M. Faber, Introduction to Modern Austrian Capital Theory. X, 196 pages. 1979.

Vol. 168: Convex Analysis and Mathematical Economics. Proceedings 1978. Edited by J. Kriens. V, 136 pages. 1979.

Vol. 169: A. Rapoport et al., Coalition Formation by Sophisticated Players. VII, 170 pages. 1979.

Vol. 170: A. E. Roth, Axiomatic Models of Bargaining. V, 121 pages. 1979.

Vol. 171: G. F. Newell, Approximate Behavior of Tandem Queues. XI, 410 pages. 1979.

Vol. 172: K. Neumann and U. Steinhardt, GERT Networks and the Time-Oriented Evaluation of Projects. 268 pages. 1979.

Vol. 173: S. Erlander, Optimal Spatial Interaction and the Gravity Model. VII, 107 pages. 1980.

Vol. 174: Extremal Methods and Systems Analysis. Edited by A. V. Fiacco and K. O. Kortanek. XI, 545 pages. 1980.

Vol. 175: S. K. Srinivasan and R. Subramanian, Probabilistic Analysis of Redundant Systems. VII, 356 pages. 1980.

Vol. 176: R. Färe, Laws of Diminishing Returns. VIII, 97 pages. 1980.

Vol. 177: Multiple Criteria Decision Making-Theory and Application. Proceedings, 1979. Edited by G. Fandel and T. Gal. XVI, 570 pages. 1980.

Vol. 178: M. N. Bhattacharyya, Comparison of Box-Jenkins and Bonn Monetary Model Prediction Performance. VII, 146 pages. 1980.

Vol. 179: Recent Results in Stochastic Programming. Proceedings, 1979. Edited by P. Kall and A. Prékopa. IX, 237 pages. 1980.

Vol. 180: J. F. Brotchie, J. W. Dickey and R. Sharpe, TOPAZ – General Planning Technique and its Applications at the Regional, Urban, and Facility Planning Levels. VII, 356 pages. 1980.

Vol. 181: H. D. Sherali and C. M. Shetty, Optimization with Disjunctive Constraints. VIII, 156 pages. 1980.

Vol. 182: J. Wolters, Stochastic Dynamic Properties of Linear Econometric Models. VIII, 154 pages. 1980.

Vol. 183: K. Schittkowski, Nonlinear Programming Codes. VIII, 242 pages. 1980.

Vol. 184: R. E. Burkard and U. Derigs, Assignment and Matching Problems: Solution Methods with FORTRAN-Programs. VIII, 148 pages. 1980.

Vol. 185: C. C. von Weizsäcker, Barriers to Entry. VI, 220 pages. 1980.

Vol. 186: Ch.-L. Hwang and K. Yoon, Multiple Attribute Decision Making – Methods and Applications. A State-of-the-Art-Survey. XI, 259 pages. 1981.

Vol. 187: W. Hock, K. Schittkowski, Test Examples for Nonlinear Programming Codes. V. 178 pages. 1981.

Vol. 188: D. Bös, Economic Theory of Public Enterprise. VII, 142 pages. 1981.

Vol. 189: A. P. Lüthi, Messung wirtschaftlicher Ungleichheit. IX, 287 pages. 1981.

Vol. 190: J. N. Morse, Organizations: Multiple Agents with Multiple Criteria. Proceedings, 1980. VI, 509 pages. 1981.

Vol. 191: H. R. Sneessens, Theory and Estimation of Macroeconomic Rationing Models. VII, 138 pages. 1981.

Vol. 192: H. J. Bierens: Robust Methods and Asymptotic Theory in Nonlinear Econometrics. IX, 198 pages. 1981.

Vol. 193: J. K. Sengupta, Optimal Decisions under Uncertainty. VII, 156 pages. 1981.

Vol. 194: R. W. Shephard, Cost and Production Functions. XI, 104 pages. 1981.

Vol. 195: H. W. Ursprung, Die elementare Katastrophentheorie. Eine Darstellung aus der Sicht der Ökonomie. VII, 332 pages. 1982.

Vol. 196: M. Nermuth, Information Structures in Economics. VIII, 236 pages. 1982.

Vol. 197: Integer Programming and Related Areas. A Classified Bibliography. 1978 – 1981. Edited by R. von Randow. XIV, 338 pages. 1982.

Vol. 198: P. Zweifel, Ein ökonomisches Modell des Arztverhaltens. XIX, 392 Seiten. 1982.

Vol. 199: Evaluating Mathematical Programming Techniques. Proceedings, 1981. Edited by J.M. Mulvey. XI, 379 pages. 1982.

Vol. 200: The Resource Sector in an Open Economy. Edited by H. Siebert. IX, 161 pages. 1984.

Vol. 201: P. M. C. de Boer, Price Effects in Input-Output-Relations: A Theoretical and Empirical Study for the Netherlands 1949–1967. X, 140 pages. 1982.

Vol. 202: U. Witt, J. Perske, SMS – A Program Package for Simulation and Gaming of Stochastic Market Processes and Learning Behavior. VII, 266 pages. 1982.

Vol. 203: Compilation of Input-Output Tables. Proceedings, 1981. Edited by J. V. Skolka. VII, 307 pages. 1982.

Vol. 204: K.C. Mosler, Entscheidungsregeln bei Risiko: Multivariate stochastische Dominanz. VII, 172 Seiten. 1982.

Vol. 205: R. Ramanathan, Introduction to the Theory of Economic Growth. IX, 347 pages. 1982.

Vol. 206: M.H. Karwan, V. Lotfi, J. Telgen, and S. Zionts, Redundancy in Mathematical Programming. VII, 286 pages. 1983.

Vol. 207: Y. Fujimori, Modern Analysis of Value Theory. X, 165 pages. 1982.

Vol. 208: Econometric Decision Models. Proceedings, 1981. Edited by J. Gruber. VI, 364 pages. 1983.

Vol. 209: Essays and Surveys on Multiple Criteria Decision Making. Proceedings, 1982. Edited by P. Hansen. VII, 441 pages. 1983.

Vol. 210: Technology, Organization and Economic Structure. Edited by R. Sato and M.J. Beckmann. VIII, 195 pages. 1983.

continuation on page 269

Lecture Notes
in Economics and
Mathematical Systems

Managing Editors: M. Beckmann and W. Krelle

315

Isao Orishimo Geoffrey J. D. Hewings
Peter Nijkamp (Eds.)

Information Technology: Social and Spatial Perspectives

Proceedings of an International Conference
on Information Technology and its Impact
on the Urban-Environmental System
Held at the Toyohashi University of
Technology, Toyohashi, Japan, November 1986

Springer-Verlag
Berlin Heidelberg New York London Paris Tokyo

Editors

Professor Isao Orishimo
Professor of Economics and Knowledge-Based Information Engineering
Toyohashi University of Technology
Toyohashi 440, Japan

Professor Geoffrey J. D. Hewings
Professor of Geography and Regional Science
University of Illinois
Urbana, IL 61801 USA

Professor Peter Nijkamp
Professor of Regional Economics
Free University Amsterdam
The Netherlands

ISBN-13: 978-3-540-50158-9 e-ISBN-13: 978-3-642-48638-8
DOI: 10.1007/978-3-642-48638-8

2142/3140-543210

PREFACE

In celebration of the Tenth Anniversary of the founding of the Toyohashi University of Technology, an International Conference was held on the theme 'Information Technology and its Impact on the Urban-Environmental System' in November, 1986 in Toyohashi, Japan. The papers in this volume are drawn from those presented at the Conference. The papers are organised into three sections reflecting some of the major themes around which the conference was structured. However, there is considerable overlap of interests between the sections and substantial diversity within the sections particularly with regard to focus, methodology and conceptual framework. The diversity was intentional, reflecting as it does the incredible opportunities that the information revolution has opened up for research interests. The authors of the papers are drawn from a number of disciplinary backgrounds with, perhaps, a stronger representation by those who are active in regional science.

In addition to the diversity in scope and problem orientation, the set of scientific contributions to the analysis of potential impacts of information technology on the spatial organisation of our society, reflect the importance and pervasiveness of this rapidly emerging field. No country can afford to remain isolated here. Therefore, the dissemination of insights gathered at the Toyohashi meeting was regarded to be in the spirit of informatics itself.

The symposium itself was the joint responsibility of the Japanese Ministry of Education, Science and Culture and of the Toyohashi University of Technology. The contributors would like to acknowledge the financial assistance provided by a number of organisations who made the conference and subsequent publication possible: the Japanese Ministry of Education, Science and Culture, Toyohashi University of Technology, the Toyohashi Chamber of Commerce and Industry, the Telecommunications Advancement Foundation, the Daiko Foundation and the Nippon Telegraph and Telephone Corporation, while considerable scientific support was also given by several professional organisations, notably the Japan Section of the Regional Science Association, the International Institute for Applied Systems Analysis, the Japan Society of Information and Communications Research, the Information Processing Society of Japan, the Society of Instrument and Control Engineers in Japan, the Institute of Electronics, Information and Communication Engineers in Japan, the Operations Research Society of Japan, and the Japan Society of Civil Engineerings.

Finally, during the preparation of the symposium, Ms. Noriko Hayashi provided much appreciated assistance. We deeply regret her untimely passing last year.

Isao Orishimo
Geoffrey Hewings
Peter Nijkamp

December 1987

TABLE OF CONTENTS

INFORMATION TECHNOLOGY: SOCIAL AND SPATIAL PERSPECTIVES

Isao Orishimo, Geoffrey J.D. Hewings and Peter Nijkamp

In this prefatory overview on the theme of 'Information Technology: Social and Spatial Perspectives', we will attempt to set the papers in context and provide some guidance as to the way in which similar topics have been addressed from differing perspectives. No attempt has been made to orient the authors' work into specific themes; one of the contributions made by this volume will, we hope, be the diversity of approaches. Some of these perspectives reflect entirely new ways of exploring spatial interaction. Others combine more familiar models with new insights while there are contributions which call for modifications of existing frameworks. One fundamental insight does emerge from this work - the notion of space, spatial interaction, the costs of overcoming distance and the notions of what is moved over space will have to be reconsidered. However, as a number of authors note, the effects of information technology on spatial development are not clear; hence, these contributions may be seen as providing a set of challenges for future research.

In the first section of the book, the contributions are focussed on the link between Information Technology and Society. The papers range from very conceptual overviews of the processes involved, to specific case studies in Japan and finally, to a review of the possible effects of information technology on developing economies. Andersson's paper notes that the Research and Development era may be considered as the fourth major revolution with the potential to change, in a dramatic fashion, society in general and its functioning and interaction in particular. He introduces the notion of a 'creative region', a place in which there is a high concentration of R&D; while these regions might appear to be footloose, a priori, they are very closely tied to centres of learning that are accessible by modern means of transportation. This theme - the release of activity from familiar spatial constraints on the one hand and yet the increasing tendencies for concentration in specific types of places - provides a common thread through many of the papers in this and subsequent sections (for example, Gibson, Nijkamp and Salomon and Orishimo). Andersson's paper also presents a challenge for research to explore the growth and development processes emanating from these creative regions and the ways in which these processes have similarities with more familiar notions of the growth centre developments.

Segerstahl and Vasko also take us on a conceptual excursion, considering the effect of the information revolution on changes in economic conditions and competitiveness. They suggest the possibility of this revolution engendering some irreversible changes in our societies. Their paper raises an issue of the need to be able to measure many of the non-commodity flows now involved in the transactions among firms, flows which are much more difficult to detect in that they often involve machine-machine interactions which have no customs documents or bills of lading to facilitate detection. The role of regulation is raised here; clearly, many developing economies have turned away from the restrictive regulatory environments of the last half century to embrace a more open, market-oriented policy. What are the implications of the nature of work and leisure, the assurance of privacy concomitant with the expectations of liberal democracies? Information per se may be a difficult issue to handle as a 'good' in the traditional sense. Furthermore, the diffusion of information and information technology will require greater attention to be focussed on the spatial impacts at a variety of spatial scales - issues raised by a number of other authors. Segerstahl and Vasko also remind us of the important role which will continue to be played by multinational corporations in this spatial spread process.

Jensen, on the other hand, approaches the problem from a more philosophical perspective trying to trace the societal impacts from the standpoint of the timing of interactions and their social implications. These issues become very important as saturation of new innovations approaches 100% or an upper bound which may not achieve complete saturation. The issue here, in a communication sense, will involve the connectivity of those who may not be able to afford new systems thus creating issues of appropriate pricing mechanisms.

The next two papers focus on the Japanese experience. Kitahara describes the Information Network System (INS) being put into place. His paper focusses on the issue of the blurring of distinctions between telecommunications and data transmission, processing, storage and retrieval. However, several problems have arisen, not the least of which is the issue of standardisation especially for non person-person interaction. A familiar theme in this area is also raised - user charges and the associated problem of control and regulation. Akimaru then focusses on new information services in Japan. The problem of transmitting the Kanji characters and the attendant problem of relating the less specific Kana sounds to the written character set poses an interesting issue for which artificial intelligence may be called upon to assist. One troublesome side issue of computerised writing might be a decline in the quality of handwriting which has always assumed a much higher level of aesthetic appreciation in Japan than many western societies.

Inose begins to address the issue of what happens given an increase in availability of improvements in information. Clearly, the distinction between defence and non-defence related developments need to be considered in the light of a need to avoid the imposition of major obstacles. There is some suggestion that by looking at the developments in the context of the international division of labour, technological improvements and innovations engendered by the information revolution may not result in the large-scale unemployment effects which have been predicted by many authors. However, the question of quality of jobs needs to be considered and not a mere counting of jobs gained and jobs lost as a result of technological change.

Finally, Chatterji provides some perspectives on the impacts which are likely to be observed in the developing countries. In particular, one can point out that the higher percentages of population living in rural areas and the observed slower rate of adoption of most innovations in these areas will create a much more difficult climate for penetration. Countering this phenomenon is the fact that, for many developing countries, the prestige of owning and using high technology has often outweighed considerations of cost and expected benefits. There have been many cases in which developing countries have leapt over many generations of technological change in a very short period of time (for example, going from no extensive telephone system to one based on satellite transmission).

The second section focusses attention on information technology and society. Some years ago, Warntz discussed the problem of the 'tyranny of space', Nijkamp and Salomon essentially ask the question several decades later, namely, will the information and communication revolution lead to a greater freedom to live outside city regions? Their answer is generally negative; while the appearance of cottage industries once again has suggested movement towards a more spatially extensive and flexible workforce, their feeling is that this process is unlikely to become a dominant feature of the labour force. However, there will be an impact on the location of firms - the new developments will provide them with greater locational flexibility but that the 'adoptive capability' of a region for new technology will be the decisive factor in positioning the region for future growth. The authors claim that face-to-face contact will continue to be important and there appears to be increasing evidence that telemarketing of goods and services reduces the utility of many consumers who find the transaction process itself of value. They suggest that there may be evolving a new spatial organisation of society in which four components may be important - the creation of telecommunications, their diffusion, their adoption, and the spatial impacts per se.

Gibson extends this thinking by tackling the role that telecommunications may place on the management of firms. He agrees with Nijkamp and Salomon that face-to-face contacts will continue to be important. He provides a link with the restructuring processes which are now dominating the economies of many western societies and raises concerns about the costs of adoption (and its complement, the cost of non adoption). The impacts articulated by Andersson in an earlier paper will involve both spatial and aspatial components, one of the latter being the way in which the firm is organised managerially. The spatial impacts will be along more traditional lines - number of branches, devolution of functions and so forth. Finally, Gibson suggests that the new technology might be more influential on an individual's day-to-day interaction patterns rather than on an industry's overall patterns of flows and linkages. Like many authors, he suggests that the growth of existing centres will be promoted and thus, the decentralising potential of telecommunications may not be realised. This type of prognostication is more conservative and guarded than many of those which emanated from scholars asked to speculate about the way in which successive energy price increases in the 1970s would change the spatial form and function of urban areas.

Funck et al. focus on the influences of new information technologies on regional structure and development of urban systems in the Federal Republic of Germany. Their findings suggest that the development and location of information technology is channelled by government policies, that it is reinforced by the relative advantage of the more highly developed regions and that, in the short run, one could not expect changes in the economic status of lagging regions. The authors introduce the concept of 'innovation density' and attempt to measure its variability with reference to a set of economic and demographic variables. The findings reinforce those of Andersson - for example, emphasising the role of universities and the role of technology parks. However, the policy implications appear as difficult and as intractable as those faced by regional analysts two or three decades ago.

Boyce moves the discussion to a different spatial scale and a completely different perspective. Given the existence of navigational aid systems which could be installed in private automobiles, how could this new development be used to measure and handle the problems of congestion in urban areas? The navigational system would have to be linked with a receiving station which would be capable of processing the information and sending back updates on traffic patterns and a suggested 'optimal' route. The process would have strong implications for travel choices beyond route choices. In particular, it might influence departure time, trip frequency and even the choice of alternative modes. On a broader scale, one could only speculate about the degree to which it might influence the choice of housing, job location and travel to leisure and shopping activities. From the modelling perspective, it would make traffic congestion endogenous; furthermore, it would also provide new perspectives on the relationship between user and system optimal travel choices. For example, the system might indicate to a driver that a longer route might be preferable in order to reduce traffic congestion. Finally, traffic engineers would be able to set the signalling system to handle the actual rather than at present a set of fixed traffic flows.

The role of location theory and its interaction with information technology is explored by Beckmann. The key parameter which has been changed by information technology is the cost of overcoming distance. However, as Gibson and Nijkamp and Salomon questioned, will this make industries more footloose? Beckmann confirms their a priori expectations from a theoretical construct. In essence, the protection of local producers will be removed in favour of those at the best locations or at the most efficient locations or in favour of firms which are managed the most efficiently. Thus, one finds the coexistence of centralising and decentralising effects, the latter associated with the allocation of production to branch plants, the number of which is likely to be smaller than under conditions of free entry.

The final section of the volume deals with the development of impact models to address the issues of information changes on national, regional and urban economies. Hewings, Sonis and Jensen attempt to link two major modelling paradigms - input-output analysis and innovation/diffusion theory. In the former case, the role of structural change has not been addressed from the perspective of the process itself, while the direct and indirect effects of innovation development and adoption have not been considered. In this context, the linkage of these two approaches provides the potential for unravelling some important new insights into the growth and development aspects of information changes on regional economies.

Kohno and Mitomo provide a theoretical model to examine the impact of the INS system described by Kitahara on Japan. Their perspective parallels Beckmann's as they explore pricing considerations and the entry of competitive firms. The pricing structure reflects an aspatial perspective; the two-part tariff would be composed of a fixed monthly charge and a marginal rate which would be dependent upon the volume of usage but not according to distance over which the information was sent, stored or retrieved.

The next two papers look at utility approaches to the same problems, focussing attention on group and coalition behaviour. Seo and Sakawa examine multiple criteria decision analysis through game theory based on fuzzy multiattribute utility analysis. After constructing alternative integrated systems for existing individual communication networks, the process is conceptualised as an n-person cooperative game in which the payoff value is based on the incremental value of the fuzzy multiattribute utility function. In this context, each service is treated as a player participating in an integrated network (i.e., a coalition). Alternative outcomes are assumed via shadow prices providing inputs into the judgemental phase of the analysis. One interesting feature of their model is the way in which user benefits are assessed in terms of traffic potential through a redefinition of the gravity model. Tamura extends this work through the development of a computer aided multiobjective decision making process under risk. In particular, the non independence of decision making is explored by identifying group utility theory via aggregation of individual decision maker preferences. These are shown to be identical to those of the multiattribute utility function but are shown to be more general in that several decompositions (additive, multiplicative, bilateral and interpolated) are revealed as special cases.

The final paper focusses attention on the spatial process operating at the urban level. Orishimo first considers the relationship between information and knowledge and examines two major effects of telecommunications on urban development - changes in the characteristics of accessibility and the rapid decrease in telecommunication price. The first issue is handled in a similar way to Beckmann via traditional location theory but concerns are raised for quality of life considerations for both firms and individuals. The decrease in price effects are more difficult to assess; in essence, much of the outcome will depend on the degree to which physical movement will be replaced by increases in telecommunications. In this regard, the Alonso model could be redefined to handle the cases in which time constraints are considered to be more important and restrictive than income constraints. The paper provides some major challenges for new theoretical and empirical developments.

Evolving from these papers is the clear perception that the impact of telecommunications developments are unlikely to be trivial in their potential for changing the way in which society is organised. The considerable degree of inertia in our present system of work, leisure and consumption may not witness a dramatic transformation but the potential for major change is clearly present.

The need for the extension of existing conceptual frameworks and the development of new methods has been a consistent theme in the volume. At present, speculation dominates prediction based on firm analytical premises but there is almost universal agreement that the developments are going to require analysts of urban and regional systems to focus more of their attention on these issues.

PART A: Information Technology and Society

RESEARCH, TECHNOLOGICAL DEVELOPMENT AND STRUCTURAL CHANGE

Åke E. Andersson

1. THE FOUR LOGISTICAL REVOLUTIONS - A CONCEPTUAL DISCUSSION

Probing the future is what differentiates the historian from the social scientist. This often leads the social scientist - the economist, political scientist, geographer or regional scientist - to a disregard of historical observations. If history is included, it is often in the form of short term trend extrapolations or an econometric model generating predictions based on some historically dubious sample of data used in estimation of the model parameters.

History should be taken much more seriously, at least when the social scientist discusses structural development issues. One commendable example is the work by the economist Eli F. Heckscher, who analysed the evolution of international division of labour from a paradigm drawing both on classical economic theory and a close study of European economic history. Another example is Joseph Schumpeter.

The methodological reason is not that predictions should be based on sufficiently long time series. My reason for urging a proper blending of theory and historical observation is that fundamental structural changes are *rare phenomena*. Permanence or viability of a dynamic system requires structural stability. Social systems tend to have permanence and viability as a common characteristic (or requirement) and thus structural stability as a typical property. This implies that we have to scrutinise evolutionary evidence from data covering the globe during many centuries to really get at an understanding of the causal structures and the basic common characteristics of structural change processes. Infrequently, social systems undergo phase transitions from one stable structure to another, i.e. from one pattern (or form) to a not topologically equivalent pattern.

Although, in principle, infrequent structural changes occur and have occurred in the world economy, three clearly visible phase transitions in the period 1000-1980 are identifiable. I have chosen to call these the *three logistical revolutions*. Furthermore, I find signs of an emerging *fourth logistical revolution*, identifiable by actual divergence of some structural variables to be discussed in the sequel.

2. THE THREE LOGISTICAL REVOLUTIONS

As argued above, a revolution is a short bifurcation or phase transition in an otherwise structurally stable world. The term 'logistics' refers to the French (originally military) terminology and signifies the methods and systems used in order to efficiently control flows of materials, services, information, knowledge, etc. from sources via saddles to sinks. A logistical revolution is thus a phase transition or bifurcation of economic and social structure triggered by changes in the logistical system.

The first logistical revolution occurred in Europe in the 12th and 13th centuries and was caused by a slow but steady improvement in the transportation network connecting ports and rivers and along the coasts of northern, western and southern Europe.

In feudal Europe of 1000 AD, one of the few dynamic factors was the never ending fighting among all the small knights who controlled miniature countries all over Europe. The consequence of these fights was an almost prohibitive cost of trade and transportation through Europe. The seas were no better. Pirates, like the Saracens of the Mediterranean, controlled major throughways, and robber-knights and more chivalric knights controlled the river mouths in most other parts of Europe. As a result, sailing and land transportation technology did not develop. One natural consequence was the need to develop each little feudal country into a self-supporting, unspecialised economic region with little or no real dependence on other regions - i.e. with little trade. The typical feudal economy was a consequence of a likewise typical feudal constraint on movement. The church was one of the few exceptions to the pattern. Although a part of the feudal system, representatives of the church were permitted to move more freely than others, carrying ideas 'around the world'. Even during the worst period of fights in northern Europe - the Viking time - monks reached the centres of Viking societies with the Roman Catholic message. But the message had little economic development effect.

In the eleventh century the church started a process that led to the destruction of feudal Europe, however dependent upon feudal Europe the church had become. In 1095, Pope Urban II demanded that knights and other members of chivalric Europe sent troops to liberate the Holy Land from the Moslems. This was the first of nine organised crusades that destroyed not only the Byzantium, but most of the costly controls on trade flows through Europe. The fourth crusade in the beginning of the thirteenth century even created a new empire based on trade - that of Venice.

The most important effect was that the crusades destroyed feudal society and thereby the constraints on trade in Europe. With a new political structure with weakened nobility in Italy and Flanders, with the Viking societies destroyed in the Scandinavian region, and with the new merchant state in Venice, transportation cost had been reduced so as to permit the emergence of a new merchant class. This new merchant class primarily developed at the potential crossroads of Europe: in Tuscany, Genoa, Bruges and in trading towns at the other river mouths of northern and western Europe.

For the first time, it became economically meaningful to compare prices of all transportable commodities around Europe, to calculate the profits to be reaped. In most situations calculations were rough and ready. In most cases the price differences became successively large enough, not only to cover the transportation costs, but also to secure handsome profits, even on the riskiest of trade relations.

With the expansion of trade and the profits from it, the small trading towns started to grow into cities with specialised city employment and production. Surrounding regions, like the Tuscan region around the city of Florence, also became specialised in the production of commodities to which the region was comparatively well adapted. Bruges grew into a city of merchants, with surrounding Flanders being transformed into a region specialised in cloth production, supported by raw material imports from the British Isles. In the north of Europe, Bruges was connected to a network of sea towns, called the Hanseatic League, connecting towns like Lübeck, Hamburg, Danzig, Bergen and Visby.

By the middle of the fourteenth century, Europe had been transformed from a patch pattern of small, unspecialised, feudal, peasant societies with little trade into a network of trade regions with merchant cities and towns. One should of course be cautious of any exaggeration of the scale of these cities forming the dominant nodes of the new network. Florence, as an example, grew at approximately 1.4 per cent per year for 60 years and reached a total population of approximately 90,000 inhabitants in 1339. Venice was not much larger than 100,000 inhabitants at the same time, and the metropolis of European learning, Paris, had little more than 200,000 inhabitants. But the difference from the feudal towns was great; one of the centres of Viking society had a recorded population of less than 1,000.

With the reduction of transportation costs and the growth of trade, specialisation and the emergence of cities in Europe was followed by a nodally focussed growth of a skewed distribution of per capita income in these new cities. New power groups formed; the most spectacular case was the emergence of a new, confident merchant class in the northern Italian city states and in Flanders. The new class engaged in a regular power struggle with the feudal society and its constituent part, the church.

One way of identifying a new group is by its formation of a new culture - a new world view and new arts. Such a creative identification of the new bourgeoisie did not occur in every node of the new network. This development was focussed on a subset of centres. The two most prominent were Florence and Bruges. In Florence, one of the most remarkable cultural signs of the new era was Dante's *Divine Comedy* with its new glorification of reason and a nonclerical world view. It is also remarkable how artists like Dante Alighieri and Giotto were integrated into the politics of their society. Both were, for a period, high officials in the administration and planning of Florence.

The second logistical revolution was in a sense a *dual* logistical revolution, if the first is seen as *primal*. The first logistical revolution with the main emphasis on barter trade with a minimum of credits involved was by necessity limited in scale and geographical scope. During the 16th century, the trading network expanded progressively with ever increasing distance, time and risk problems. The money and credit network built up by private bankers was poorly adapted to the situation. A major innovation was needed to provide a new transaction system that could reap the potential real gains from the trade. Amsterdam was the city with local politicians capable of realising the value of a public banking system.

After this primary innovation, the idea soon diffused. Sweden was the first country to adopt the idea of a state guaranteed national bank, but this baby was still-born. Credit possibilities were no constraint on northern European trade. The story developed in an entirely different and successful fashion in England, where the location of a central bank was much more in need.

The third logistical revolution is what we normally call *the industrial revolution*. I prefer to call it a logistical revolution because it primarily reflected a change in organisational principles rather than an introduction of any modern industrial

The classical trade capitalist question was:

"Is there a pair of regions and a product for which

$$s_j - p_i > c_{ji} \text{ ? "}$$

where s_j = sales price in region j
p_i = purchase price in region i
c_{ji} = transport and transaction cost from region i to region j

This question was now rephrased in a much more active combined *capitalist-entrepreneur* fashion as:

"Is there a pair of regions and a complete *vertical integration logistical system* such that for an optimally selected product?"

$$\sigma_j - \sum_{k,i} \rho_{ki}\, a_{ki} > \sum_{k,ij} K_{k,ij}$$

where σ_j = maximal price of a commodity when sold in user region i
ρ_{ki} = minimal factor cost of factor k when purchased in region i
a_{ki} = cost minimising input-output ratio of input k purchased in region i
$K_{k,ij}$ = marginal (minimal) transport and transaction cost of input k, from source region i to sink region j

This is a *variational inequality* that forms the basis of the theory of interregional and international trade (Nagurney 1986).

The first group of products that were considered the new logistical era were based on the primary resources cotton, coal and iron ore. Cotton is probably the most interesting case. It was not well suited to mechanical engineering, it was an input in the textile and clothing manufacturing, and it had been an item in international trade. With the new principle of logistics, raw materials production, trade and manufacturing of cotton products grew in an almost explosive fashion, e.g. a five-fold increase of British cotton imports in thirty years before 1810. The emerging imbalances in the vertically integrated logistical system triggered migration, colonial measures, new mechanical devices, etc. to increase the size and profitability of the *cotton complex*. After the success story of cotton the idea of vertical integration from some raw material base in combination with a more or less explicit optimisation principle spread from one raw material to the other and from region to region along developing networks of sea lines, railroads and roads.

The three logistical revolutions share some common characteristics in terms of consequences. These are:

1. Rapid expansion of trade and transportation flows, specialisation and city

2. Increases in the flow of ideas and other forms of human communication.

3. Rapidly increasing and unevenly distributed wealth and income per capita.

4. Increasing political complexity due to formation of new economic power

5. Creative expansion in a subset of the expanding regions.

3. MODELLING THE LOGISTICAL REVOLUTIONS

A theory or model of logistical revolutions must capture two essential aspects of the historical phenomena recorded. First, slow and steady improvements of infrastructure and particularly networks seem to trigger a non smooth response at some critical point of time. Secondly, different networks seem to become connected to each other at other critical points of time, which often leads to remarkable improvements in the quality of existing networks. Thus e.g. a new information network can act as an *activator* for a network of railroads.

To use the Rosen (1984) metaphor:

$$u_{ij} = \frac{\partial}{\partial x_i} \frac{dz_j}{dt} > 0$$

where x_i ≐ an improvement of information link i
z_j ≐ the flow of commodities on road network link j

The fact that a slow and steady increase of road investment capital can lead to a structural effect can be approached in steps. Assume that the process starts by stochastic or locally optimised road investment plans of a given size, connecting subregions as illustrated by pictures 1-4 below.

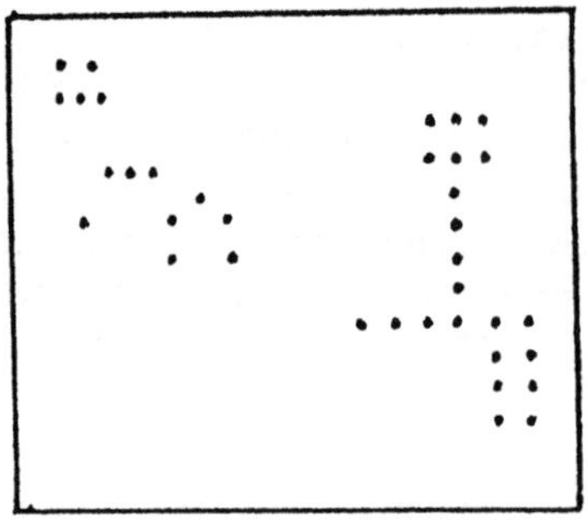

Figure 1
Disintegrated system of regions

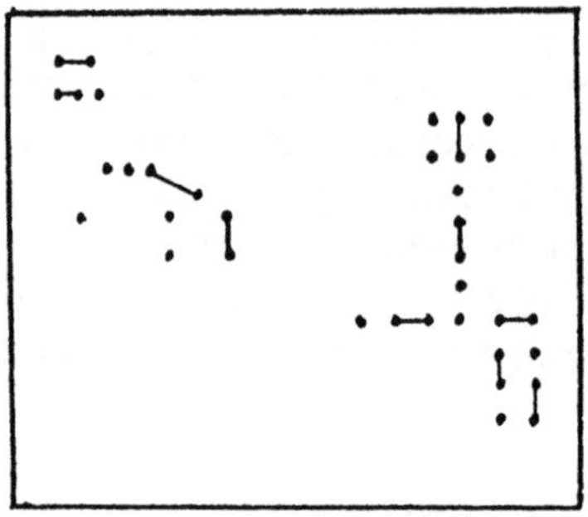

Figure 2
Pairwise integrated system of regions

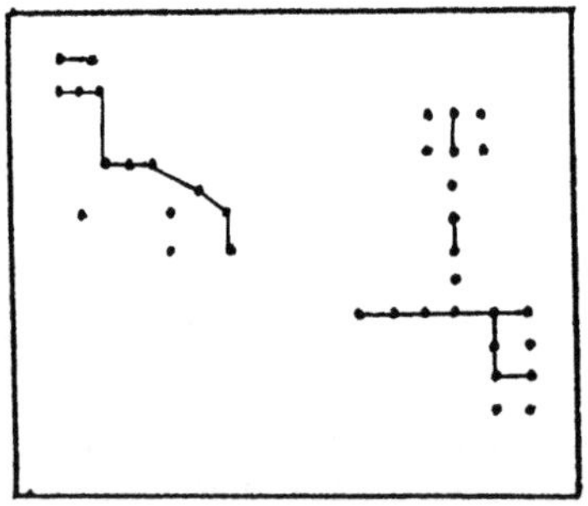

Figure 3
Partial chain integrated system of regions

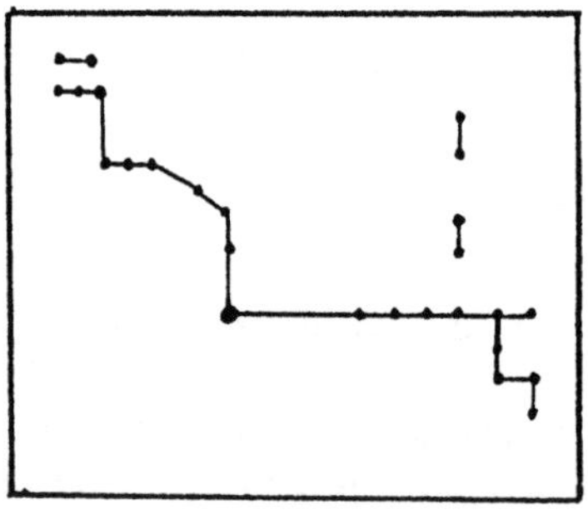

Figure 4
Full chain integrated system of regions

There is obviously a critical phase transition 23 when all the previous links are integrated into a full (although thin) network. Before and after this period partial evaluation schemes like cost-benefit procedures are acceptable as decision support models. In Figure 4 this is not possible. A full nonlinear dynamic network analysis is needed. Such an attempt is of course possible but will not be made in this context. I will rather hint in the direction of a full theory with the aid of a parable-like model.

We assume that two basically different commodities are produced in the economy. The first can be used either for consumption or for enlargement of the stock of capital, K. The second is infrastructure, on which the production takes place and is interconnected into an efficient system. The size of the infrastructure is given by G. Additions to the infrastructure most solely come from the K-sector by deducting u from the K-production output.

The production function is approximated by a Taylor-expansion

$$Q = \alpha K + \beta K^2 + \lambda K^3 + \gamma G$$

Inserting this into a capital accumulation equation we have

$$\dot{K} = T(\sigma(\alpha K + \beta K^2 + \lambda K^3 + \gamma G) - uK)$$

The accumulation of infrastructure is operating at another temporal pace or time scale with the associate time scale operator T^{-1}.

$$\dot{G} = T^{-1}(-a_1 G - a_2 G^{-1} K + bu)$$

where a_1, a_2 = depreciation rates.

If T is large, $\dot{G} = 0$ most of the time. This implies that G acts as an approximate constant in the capital accumulation equation. Solving for the temporary equilibrium of the system $\dot{K} = 0$ and thus with a given $u = \bar{u}$, we can solve for the equilibrium K:

$$\sigma(\alpha K + \beta K^2 + \lambda K^3 + \gamma \bar{G}) - \bar{u}K = 0$$

If β is close to 0, we have thus a cusp-equation with one or three equilibrium solutions. The situation can be illustrated with the following diagram:

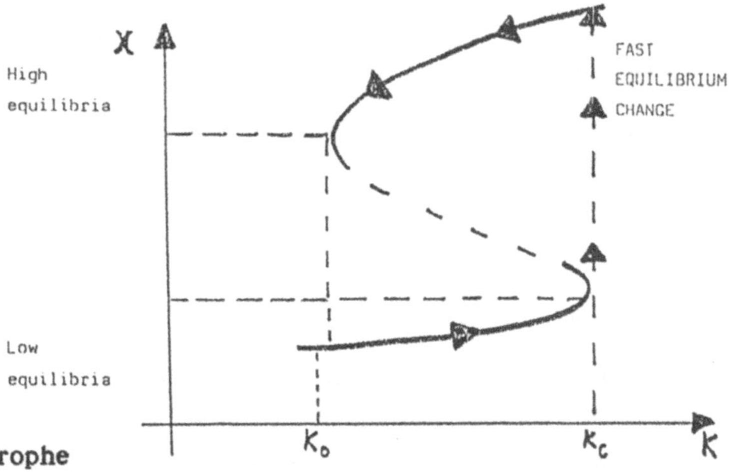

Figure 5. A cusp catastrophe

The hatched part of the S-curve is inaccessible (or unstable). Approaching low levels of $\bar{G}$ from below, only the segment E_L is accessible and signifies a low equilibrium solution, while at values of G, higher than G_C, only the segment $\bar{E}H$ is accessible and the system remains there even if G would depreciate *below* $\bar{G}_C$. The main conclusion is however that a slow, steady and marginal increase of infrastructure - occurring if $u > b^{-1}(a_1G + a_2G^{-1}K)$ - can give rise to a sudden revolutionary disequilibrium rise in the level of production until a new high equilibrium level of production is reached. Likewise a too low level of u could lead to a sudden collapse of an economy when the threshold $\bar{G}_C$ is reached from above.

4. THE FOURTH LOGISTICAL REVOLUTION

We are currently approaching the fourth logistical revolution in the United States, western Europe and Japan. The causes are the following:

. The road transportation capacity expanding into highway systems with an ever increasing number of cars and trucks.

. In every region there is an expansion of computer hardware capacity.

. These computers are steadily being connected to the telecommunications network. These telecommunications networks face bottleneck problems and are thus expanded by the use of fibre optics, computerised network control and the use of satellites.

. In all regions of the OECD system, education has produced an ever increasing number of school years per capita. In some high technology regions, the average level of schooling is now close to 12 years with a substantial part of the population having an academic education.

. The regions of knowledge and competence are being connected with each other by the rapidly expanding airline transportation system. A new knowledge network is being established on which creative ideas can be quickly exchanged by personal contacts.

Thus, we see an emerging set of networks which have had little or no impact on the structure of economies in earlier time periods. None of these networks - the highway network, the computer/telecommunications network, or the creativity/airline network - should be regarded as the dominant factor causing the fourth logistical revolution. It is rather the strong interaction between these networks that causes an increasingly higher probability of large structural change of our economies. If seen from the perspective of Rosen, there are a number of changes in links of the networks and between the networks that will activate rapid change in other parts of the generalised network.

5. SYSTEMS ECONOMIES AND RISING R&D SHARES

The standard procedure of industrial organisation during the third logistical or industrial revolution was vertical integration from a natural resource base to the market. This is now being superseded by a completely new organisational principle - systems architecture and organisation. This principle takes its starting point in a broad demand perspective. An example is the IKEA corporation. Instead of basing their production of furniture on a wood resource base, they turned the whole problem upside down and formulated the question: "What is a good home environment and how can the needs of the good home environment be efficiently satisfied by a logistical system?" IKEA then realised that creating a new home is by necessity a multi-output, multi-input, storage, transportation and communication problem. They furthermore realised that no single resource base constituted any strong impact on technological and locational decisions. Other early examples of systems oriented architecture and organisation of production are to be found in the recreation sector with corporations like Hilton, Sheraton, SAS, and Disneyland. Emerging systems organisation is to be found in the space, air, car and truck industries where the classical Detroit organisation is being superseded by networks of component producers, assembly and service plants catering to broadly defined mobility needs of firms and households.

With the emergence of systems industries, there is also an increased reliance on non material investments. In the classical vertically integrated industry there is a rather low upper limit on research and development investments. Most of these resources must be directed to an efficient transformation of raw materials into final outputs and the final outputs are rather limited in form and function by the physical and chemical properties of the few natural resource base components.

In a system organised corporation the situation is quite different. The only limit to technological research and development is given by the scope of the needs to be satisfied by the system. If seen from a Lancaster point of view, these needs can be satisfied in an infinite number of ways in which efficiency arguments are the only checks on creative activities within the corporation. A Swedish study has shown that out of the total investment of Swedish systems oriented investments, about 2/3 is allocated to non material investments, i.e. investments into new products, new production technologies, new logistical systems and market organisation. There is also a clear reorientation from process R&D to product R&D. In 1985 only 20 per cent of Swedish R&D costs were allocated to process R&D.

There is also a strong tendency to go from component control to systems control of research and development activities. In older times it was rather common to leave technological development to the component producers. Car electronics were developed by the electrical industry, and air and car engines by motor corporations, etc. Control of R&D is now progressively being moved from the component level to the systems control level. One significant example is PROMETEUS. In the PROMETEUS project most of the high tech European car industry is coordinating research and development efforts on the efficient future system of car and truck production in Europe. The communication and information industries are other examples of how decisions on research and development are centralised into a systems control of R&D strategies.

The emerging systems economy also constitutes a threat to the classical engineering education tradition. Systems architecture, organisation and control are emerging as a new scientific field. Reorganisation of engineering education in this direction can be seen at the University of California at Berkeley and at Stanford University, but a proper reorganisation of engineering education is otherwise a change to come at a later stage.

6. THE GLOBAL SYSTEM CORPORATION

Recently, a study has been made of large scale manufacturing corporations in Sweden with a subdivision into high-tech system corporations with low-tech large scale corporations. This study showed some substantial differences in research and development intensity, measured as the share of total sales revenue allocated to research and development investments. The study also showed that the reliance on exports and imports was much larger in the systems corporations than in other comparable low-tech large scale corporations. The results are given in the following table.

TABLE 1

Contact Patterns of Systems Corporations in Sweden

Corporation type/ Characteristics	R&D Int.	Export Int.	R&D Contacts USA	W.Europe	Asia
High Tech Systems Corporations	5.8%	72%	41%	43%	16%
Low Tech Large Scale Corporations	1.2%	54%	34%	59%	7%

The table shows that the high tech systems corporations are approximately five times as research and development intensive as are the low tech large scale corporations, based on the vertical integration principle. These firms are also much more dependent upon exports. Other studies of the import intensity of the high tech systems corporations have indicated that their dependence upon an international market is symmetrical between exports and imports.

Also in their research and development contact pattern in the international market there is a much stronger tendency to favour long distance contacts. The allocation of R&D contacts tends to follow the share of the *global knowledge market*. The low tech large scale corporations tend to favour contacts in western Europe and thus to cut down on the costly overseas contacts with knowledge centres. The study also indicates that *face to face* contacts are favoured in all research and development contacts. This means that telecommunications are in general not considered sufficiently efficient for communication of creative ideas and other non routine types of messages. All in all, this study indicates that the high tech systems corporations prefer locations which are *locally dense* and *globally well connected*.

7. STRUCTURAL CONSEQUENCES OF THE FOURTH LOGISTICAL REVOLUTION

The new systems organisation of production and distribution of commodities will have a number of obvious and less obvious consequences. Systems organisations means that corporations will base their production on a large number of inputs with no relation to any local natural resource base. This implies an increasing reliance on imports of components and thus of transportation. The increasing reliance on imports (and thus on exports) and on transportation also implies growing advantages of *Just in Time Planning*. In the JIT systems fast transport modes - i.e. airline and road transports - are being favoured. This leads to a general decrease in the reliance on inventories. But the Just in Time principle also means an increasing reliance on computerised telecommunications systems and networks of telecommunicating computers.

Research and development investments will be successively upgraded in the European nations. Already by 1986, Sweden superseded the United States and Japan in terms of the share of GNP allocated to research and development activities It is probable that Europe, nation by nation will reawaken to the emerging systems society and that this will first be indicated by a rapid increase in research and development activities.

The increasing reliance on creativity necessarily leads to a relocation of economic activities towards university regions like Cambridge in the UK, the Munich and Stuttgart regions in Germany and the Uppsala/Stockholm region in Sweden. These locational developments are indicative of the emerging network of primary C regions. In these C regions, which are connected to each other by the airline systems, there will be an accumulation of creative activities, communication possibilities and cultural activities. One of the greatest political problems to emerge is to get a proper connection of these primary C regions to the parts of the world in which they are embedded.

The fourth logistical revolution will not only mean advantageous development but also problems for those parts of our social structure that were shaped during the third logistical revolution. One of these problems has shown itself to the world already. Basic resource industries built on the vertical integration principle are facing serious survival problems in most parts of the economically advanced world. Not only the basic resource industries, but also the unions of employers and employees are feeling the tremors associated with a collapse of corporations based on the old economic system.

Another part of the economic system that will be hit by the fourth logistical revolution is that of public sector production. The public sector is a sector that was designed to be a natural complement to the manufacturing and other private industries of the third logistical era. The railroad services and the energy supply industries are examples of public sector production, designed to be complements to private sector production. With the internationalisation and the increasing research and development activities in the private sector, there is an obvious risk that public sector production will become obsolete on two counts. The public sector services are in practically all cases organised fully within the national borders and thus, cannot reap the benefits of internationalisation. By tradition, it has also allocated extremely small amounts of budgets to product and process research and development investments. Clear examples of the inability to adapt to the new economic era are given by the PTT corporations in different European nations and the highly subsidised national railroad authorities.

8. CONCLUSIONS

Western Europe is now approaching a new revolutionary stage of economic development. We are leaving the industrial era and approaching the fourth logistical revolution. Three different network improvements constitute the basic cause of this revolutionary structural change of our economies. An efficient road transport network interacts with the development network of telecommunicating computers and the emerging network of airports connecting centres of culture and creativity around the world.

These improving networks have generated completely new interaction patterns which have made Just in Time R&D and other systems organisation principles viable in a successively larger number of economic sectors.

Nationally organised activities are facing severe problems in this emerging new society of systems corporations located in the centres of the new network of C regions. The C region and the nation have opposing interests.

COMMUNICATION AND REGIONAL PLANNING: SOME SYSTEMIC REMARKS

Boris Segerstahl and Tibor Vasko

1. INTRODUCTION

One of the standard facts of history is that the rise of civilisations has depended on the introduction of materials that gave their names to whole epochs - the Stone Age, the Bronze Age, the Iron Age. These 'ages' derive their names from the predominant use of certain groups of metals. It is quite obvious that these labels for eras in history are based on the impact innovations in the field of metallurgy have had. A similar sequencing of history could be made using technologies for information transfer and communication for describing different eras. In this respect the work of Porat (1977) is relevant; he classified the US labour statistics to show that 53% of the working population manipulate information.

Herbert Simon (1977) is of the opinion that the emergence of the so called 'information society' is a new turning point in the intellectual history of mankind.

> "We are now in the early stages of a revolution in processing information that shows every sign of being as fundamental as the earlier energy revolution. Perhaps we should call it the Third Information Revolution. (The first produced the written language, and the second, the printed book.) This third revolution, which began more than a century ago, includes the computer but many other things as well. The technology of information comprises a vast range of processes for storing information, for copying it, for transmitting it

Not everybody is as convinced as Simon. Even if the critical voices are a minority, there is good reason to take note of their views and concerns. A well known anti-technologist, Theodore Roszak (1972) said in his book *The Citadel of Expertise* (without narrowing his criticism to the area of information technology) that:

> "Urban-Industrial society having hopelessly lost touch with life lived on a simple, more 'primitive' level, and convinced beyond question of the omnipotence of technical intelligence, can do no other than trust to ever greater numbers of experts to salvage the promise of industrialism. Accordingly, the principal business of education becomes the training of experts, for whom progressively more room is made available in government and the economy. From our desperate conviction that the endangered artificial environment is the only liveable environment, there stems the mature social form of

industrial society: the technocracy."

Roszak does not deny the fact that society has entered a stage in its development where it is totally dependent on technology for its survival. He seems however to be convinced that this is more a matter of short term survival than a matter of living through a historical stage of the type imagined by Simon. In addition Roszak is concerned about the control over technological knowledge, seeing this situation as being in conflict with the preferred overall goals of modern society. There are undoubtedly some issues involved which deserve careful analysis and evaluation. One of the key issues is the emerging conflict between technology that is of a global character and national policies that are based on national sovereignty. The growing importance of this topic is illustrated by the fact that it was the theme of a symposium organised by the National Academy of Engineering in Washington in February 1986. In this symposium Lewis M. Branscomb, former chief of IBM pointed out that:

> "... the real question is not companies challenging sovereignty, but a more complex question of synergy or conflict between global interests - of both nations and companies, and indeed many other institutions whose interests cross physical borders. This complexity is rising very fast for not only political but technological reasons."

Rene Eksl (1986) takes a more confrontational view. Under the subtitle "The cultural struggle against industrial imperialism" he expresses his pessimistic views on the issue of new technology - however without clearly indicating the specific needs for the counterbalance. This counterbalance consists in providing as much as possible for the conditions in situ, in meeting the specific expectations of local communities or of social groups with common interests, in encouraging them to be independent in running collective media, in taking advantage of the new technologies to develop creative initiatives and projects, rather than just increasing the availability of prepackaged consumer products and services.

He admits that the principle might sound simple while the concrete application of this principle to real situations can be very difficult. In addition, his view of innovations is rather conservative. In his opinion, the power of the communications industry is due less to its technological advances than to its production capacity; most technical innovations have become very old by the time they are commercialised on a large scale, and it is not their novelty which makes them invincible but the performance/cost ratio resulting from mass production.

Roszak returns to his theme in his recent book *The Cult of Information* (1986). This time his aim is more narrowly focussed on information technology and the culture emerging around it. Roszak says that:

> "...information has had a remarkable rags-to-riches career in the public vocabulary over the past forty years. It was surely among the least likely candidates to achieve the exalted status of a godword, but so it has become, and not by accident. Beginning with its esoteric redefinition by the information theorists during World War II, it has

come to be connected with a historical transition in our economic life, which unites major corporate interests, the government, the scientific establishment, and at last draws in the persuasive rhetoric of advertisers and merchandisers. If only as a unifying theme that holds so many powerful social forces together, the concept would be worth critical attention. But the Information Age has now entered the education curriculum in an aggressive and particularly insidious way which could distort the meaning of thought itself."

The debate on the character of our information society will go on for a long time. In this debate it is important to put the emergence of information technology into its societal framework and through this process indirectly touch upon a few of the concerns expressed by Roszak and other scientists who express worries about some aspects of society's development.

The technology which will form the base of our future global telecommunications network is already in existence. The basic components are satellites, fibre optic cables, digital switching systems and integration of voice, data and picture information. According to a telecommunications expert working for Philips, it is not very interesting from a business point of view to own the technical facilities as such. The main effort has to be put into providing a complete set of services which support different users' immediate needs as well as possible. The availability of services usually changes the user's behaviour. This change is not easy to identify, but it may be decisive for the diffusion of a particular innovation. For example, when long-distance direct dialling became available, their share in traffic increased as customers changed their behaviour and called long-distance more often.

On the policy side the crucial question seems to be the role and future of regulation versus deregulation and bypassing as a way to increase capacity and decrease cost for long range communication. The two most deregulated countries in the world, USA and UK, see an enormous progress in competitive new telecommunication services while, for instance, the European continent is still rigidly controlled by national PTTs that slow down the purely technical development. It is however clear that a certain amount of regulation will be the future rule in almost all countries. The question is how to avoid comparative disadvantages because of this while preserving a good overall service level. The deregulated environment has always been accused of inviting 'cream skimming' and in this way favouring uneven and undemocratic development of telecommunication services, and lead to risk averting behaviour of large regulated companies.

2. THE IMPACT OF COMMUNICATION ON SOCIETAL SERVICES

As with earlier major changes based on technological innovations, the consequences of modern information technology spread out in all directions. First, there are of course the economic consequences that follow on any innovation that increases human productivity. These consequences are without doubt easier to predict than other effects of information technology. Even the former predications, needless to say, are not easy to make. Second, there are societal consequences for the nature of work and of leisure, and the quality and content of life. Third., modern information technology will have distinctive influence on privacy and individual liberty. Fourth, there are implications for man's view of himself.

"Is information technology different from other industrial technology" is still the theme for a stimulating discussion of all the properties of information technology. Each innovation has some specific features. However, is information technology altogether different? There are many proponents of this view (Thompson 1979). They argue that among others:

- information as a good has different properties (more as a 'public good') from routine goods on the market.
- economy of scale has less relevance than in other industrial innovations.

It would, however, be false to assume that the concept of a good and economies of scale could be entirely abandoned. They have to be specified so as to accommodate the peculiarities of this technology within society. This is valid for technology as a whole - it should be accommodated with the existing material, industrial and social base of the society.

In all these studies, the immediate impact is, of course, the most readily observed. It much more difficult to predict what indirect (secondary) sequences these immediate impacts will generate.

3. DIRECT IMPACT

Economic impacts of information technology are the most obviously measurable ones. These impacts can be assumed using traditional methods which have been generated to determine the short term and long term effects of technological innovations in industry and on society as a whole. At IIASA (International Institute for Applied Systems Analysis) this has been studied in connection with videotext diffusion studies. The diffusion of telephones, radio and television shows certain regularities (Maurer and Sebestyen 1982).

The literature dealing with economic effects of technological innovations is, after several decades of intense scientific work, quite substantial. The general applicability of much of the work done is however limited due to the fact that types of innovations selected for investigation and the economic environment used as a framework are often both rather specific cases.

One of the more ambitious efforts to assess the impact of technological innovations on the basis of innovations studies has been made by Bela Gold and his colleagues. Their findings are summarised in a paper (Gold 1986). Perhaps the most important conclusion of the above mentioned paper is that many past studies on innovation neglected important differences in some cases, or over-interpreted data, usually because:

- the selected innovation provided only limited information on the diffusion process (lack of complexity);
- the studies were branch specific, and as such the message was not easily transferable (lack of generalisability over branches);
- they ignore the specific (usually favourable or hostile) economic environment (lack of generalisability over time).

From this it follows that the studies were pro innovation biased. They assumed that the more innovation the better, also that all innovation should have similar patterns and dynamics. This is not always true. It is not very easy to explain why video telephone did not spread as expected, or even why the possibility of high-fidelity was not used by the telephone companies. Some researchers (Thompson 1979) argue, for example, that what we appreciate about telephones is a common (shared) acoustic space that would be destroyed by making it wideband. This shows that here not only technical and economic determinants are at play, but also others - social or societal ones - that are of a very complex and subtle character. When it comes to the study of societal issues, and they are always complex, the warning of L. Zadeh (1973) should be remembered:

> "Essentially, our contention is that the conventional qualitative techniques of system analysis are intrinsically unsuited for dealing with humanistic systems or, for that matter, any system whose complexity is comparable to that of the humanistic system. The basis for this contention rests on what might be called the *principle of incompatibility*. Stated formally, the essence of this principle is that as the complexity of system increases, our ability to make precise and yet significant statements about its behaviour diminishes until a theshold is reached beyond which precision and significance (for relevance) becomes almost mutually exclusive characteristics."

4. INDIRECT IMPACT

Examination of the widespread application and societal impact of modern information technologies in most highly industrialised countries gives cause for concern: the different applications have not generated the expected positive social and cultural development. In many cases the new technologies have a tendency to reinforce existing structures and alliances by avoiding redistribution of resources and interconnections between different economic and social groups. France is a typical example of this tendency (Eksl 1986). As Eksl and Metayer point out in their recent pessimistic analysis of the situation in this country:

> "The global development of new telecommunications systems seems to demonstrate the hold of multinational enterprise on all societies - the efficient standardization of ideas and culture as well as technological hardware, of basic consumer goods for human survival as well as weapons which could eradicate human life."

The effect of information technology on social structures can be analysed on different levels from the interpersonal one up to the global one.

The breakdown into levels of analysis is, as Eksl and Metayer state, as arbitrary as any classification but does not indicate the complexity of communication modes of modern society. The indirect consequence of innovations may lead to difficulties (lock-ins). It is not clear how the direct impacts of information technology may lead to the revolutionary growth of the economy. We should also look into the indirect effects (Thompson 1979).

5. MORE RECENT APPROACHES TO THE DYNAMICS OF INNOVATION

Several events in technology diffusion can be explained by the 'technology-push, demand pull' concept based on the idea that: 1) there generally exists a possibility of knowing *a priori* (before the innovation process takes place) the direction in which the market is pulling the inventive activity of producers, and 2) an important part of the market 'signalling' process operates through movements in relative prices and quantities. Under this the concept of innovative process can be placed into the neoclassical framework (Dosi 1984).

These theories have numerous weaknesses, some of which are:

- they only consider a one-way causal relation, i.e. passive mechanical reactions to technical change vis a via market conditions;
- a simple forward mechanism is incapable of explaining why and when one certain innovation instead of another is taking place;
- this mechanism neglects the internal dynamics of inventive capability which is not directly related to market conditions.

It is often argued that there is not sufficient evidence to show that the needs expressed through market signalling are the prime movers of innovative activity. Market pull is a necessary, but not a sufficient, condition to explain the timing and dynamics of innovation.

Technology push theories have similar difficulties of a 'complementary' character. Over emphasis of this theory leads to a simple scheme of innovation initiation by scientific knowledge (science-technology-production) underestimating many barriers and bonds (feedbacks) between these activities.

Dosi defined a technological paradigm as a model and a 'pattern' for the solution of selected technological problems, based on selected principles derived from natural sciences and on selected material technologies. He also defined technological trajectory as the pattern of normal problem solving based on a technological paradigm. Technological paradigm embodies strong prescriptions for the directions of technological change - which alternatives to pursue and which to neglect.

As technological trajectories are explored, many new processes will come into play, speeding up or slowing down the process. There are several, sometimes unrelated, innovations that can amplify the impact of innovation and create a 'clustering' of innovations. For example, the invention of the combustion engine (but also the invention of cracking and anti-knock petrol) contributed to the expansion of the automobile industry. The property of innovations is one possible (Schumpeterian) explanation of long waves.

In 1984 an interesting book by Yakovetz, in the USSR, was published in which he structured the waves (of innovation or cycles) into four types:

- sequencing' of technology (machines) generation (for example, generations of robots);
- transfer to new directions of technology (partial technological revolution);
- periodical reproduction of fixed capital on a mass scale on the basis of the generation of new machines;
- overall (general) technological revolutionism leading to basic changes in the level of productive forces.

The impact of information falls into the last category. Each revolution adds its own part to the existing technological, economic and social base. How this part will be accommodated with the other parts is the core of the problem.

Individual cycles are structured into several phases such as start-up, contagion, maturity, obsolescence, etc. It is argued, in Yakovetz's book, that general technological revolutions can be traced back to prehistoric times.

6. INNOVATION AND REGIONAL QUESTIONS

Any major technological project or innovation and its implementation has to be embedded in the region. Usually, when this takes place the weakest points in the knowledge of innovation are exposed. One reason may be that the regional issues are linked to variables which are ill defined and difficult to quantify. Yet for the success of a particular project, these variables with societal components may be decisive. We have in mind:

- mobility of specialists;
- availability of venture capital;
- availability of risk accepting practitioners;
- established cooperation of R&D in industry with universities;
- 'infrastructure' of the particular branch;
- requirements of R&D is only the top of the iceberg, because technological links are expanding to other professions (in microelectronics, for example, it is optics, chemistry, fine mechanics, etc.);
- support of local authorities.

Positive responses in the above determinants are necessary for the diffusion of a particular innovation in a given region, and it is only wide diffusion of innovations that creates measurable macroeconomic impacts. This is one of the problems where the interest of international research and regional research overlaps.

REFERENCES

Branscomb, L.M., National and Corporate Technology Strategies in an Independent World Economy, National Academy of Engineering Symposium on World Technologies and National Soverignty, Washington DC, February 14, 1986.

Burke, J.G. and M.C. Eakin, Technology and Change, Boyd and Fraser Publishing Company, San Francisco, 1979.

Dosi, G., Technical Change and Industrial Transformation, The MacMillan Press Ltd., London, 1984.

Eksl, R., and G. Metayer, Technological modernism and social conservatism, Futures, Vol. 18, No.2, April 1986, pp. 258-273.

Gold, B., Some Empirical Perspectives of the Economic Effects of Technological Innovations, OMEGA, International Journal of Management Sciences, Vol. 14, No. 2, 1986, pp. 99-118.

Maurer, H.A., and I. Sebestyen, One-Way Versus Two-Way Videotex in Telecommunications: Some Policy Issues in: Proceedings of a Task Force Meeting, March 28-30, 1982, Budapest, Hungary, IIASA CP-82-63, International Institute for Applied Systems Analysis, Laxenburg, Austria.

Porat, M.U., The Information Economy, Definition and Measurement, Washington DC, Government Printing Office, 1977.

Roszak, T., Where the Wasteland Ends, Doubleday and Co., 1972.

Roszak, T., The Cult of Information, Pantheon Books, New York, 1986.

Simon, H.A., What Computers Mean for Man and Society, Science, Vol. 195, March 18, 1977, pp. 1186-1191.

Thompson, G.B., Memo from Mercury: Information Technology is Different, Institute for Research on Public Policy, Occasional Paper, No. 10, Montreal, Quebec, Canada, June 1979.

Yakovetz, Ti, Patterns of Scientific and Technical Progress and their Planned Use, Ekonomika, Moscow, 1984.

Zadeh, A.L., Outline of a New Approach to the Analysis of Complex Systems and Decision Processes, IEEE Transactions on Systems, Man, and Cybernetics, Vol. SMC-3, No. 1, January 1973, p. 28.

THE TELECOMMUNICATION SYSTEM IN SOCIETY

Arne Jensen

1. PRECISION IN FORECASTING

It is an often overlooked fact that stable production and stable investment are very important factors in public utilities. This requirement influences the way we make forecasts. Another neglected issue is that when 50% to 70% of the families' telephone installations have been covered we have, in fact, also carried out the expensive digging and technical installations of the remainder of the families. This means that this remaining group will get their connection to the exchange at a much lower cost than the first mentioned group of families. This fact opens, of course, possibilities for price discrimination for different groups of families - to the benefit of all groups concerned.

But even in that case we have not taken into account the special considerations to be made for the big city centres. For instance, in Denmark, outside the centre of the main city, the number of business subscribers is a rather stable part of the number of families. It is from 10% to 6% depending on the town's slow or rapid rate of growth. However, city centres have their own life as a function of the city itself with their special requirements. The highway system was an overlayer to the secondary road system and the network system for business subscribers has sometimes - for example, in Copenhagen - been an overlayer to the network for private subscribers. Thus, the time sequence of such communication networks is extremely important. And finally, current technical installations are often renewed not because they are technically obsolete, but because technical innovations make them economically obsolete. Therefore, good forecasts for long term developments are not so important as many think - as long as the development does not decline. What is important is the forecast for the construction period.

Consequently, it is more important to have reasonably good forecasts for the construction period for a system rather than for the renewal period. The heavier part of the investment in future capacity was taken care of earlier for purely economic reasons. But the desired capacity is dependent on the user rate and hence on the type of communication technology offered and this varies. In view of the previous remarks, we present some figures to illustrate these points. Most of the figures are self-evident (see Figures 1-6).

An important element which counts in almost all figures is the busy hour; the rest does not really come into consideration. The busy hour has been fixed on the basis of all the user groups. This means, therefore, that it is very important to know the individual user group's use of their telephone sets during the busy hour. In this connection, we must not forget that, for purely economic and

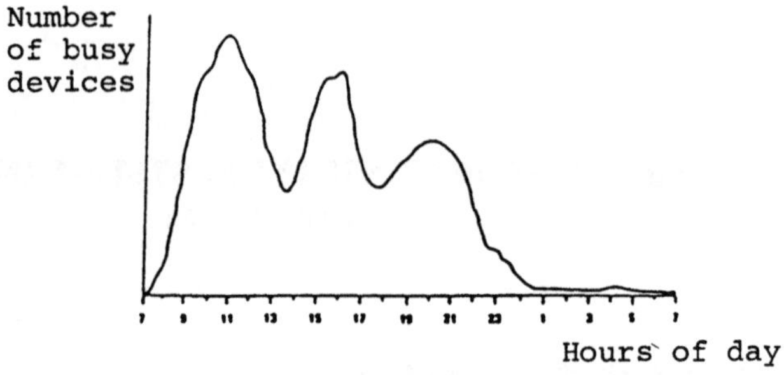

Figure 1: Traffic Variations during a day.

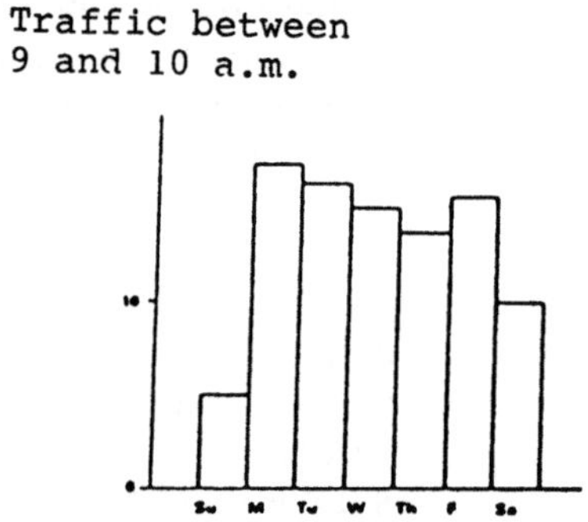

Figure 2: Traffic Variations during one week.

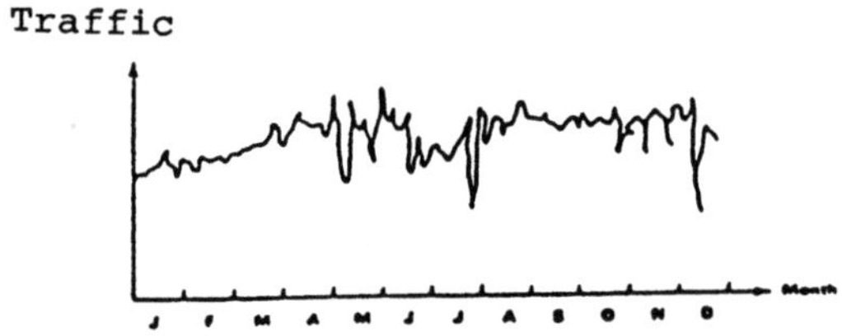

Figure 3: Seasonal Variations during one year.

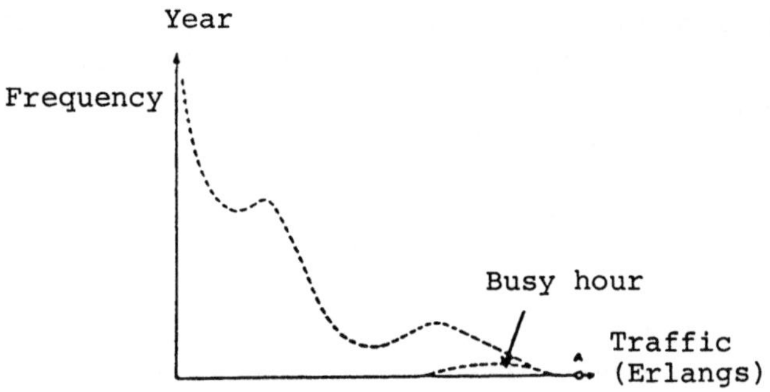

Figure 4: Variation during all 8760 hours of a year.

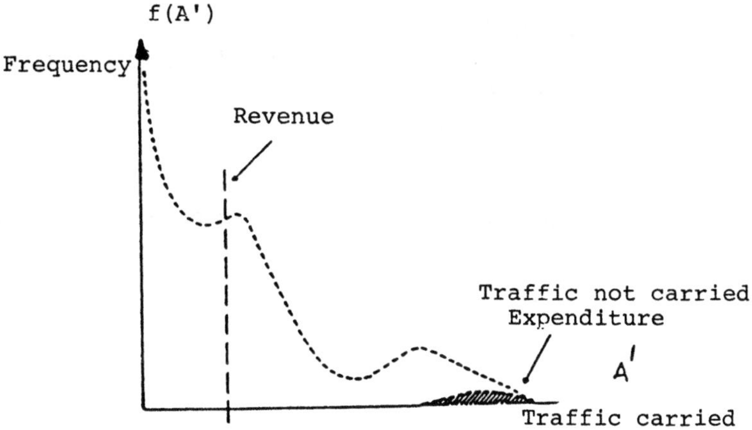

Figure 5: Variation of Traffic during an Extension Period.

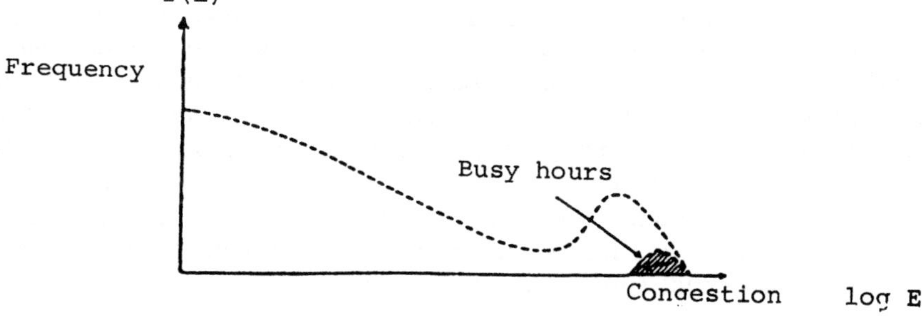

Figure 6: Variation consequences for Service: Congestion

technical reasons. large production standardisation is presently taking place. As a consequence, in order to be able to take care of the busy groups of subscribers handled by them, a great number of subscribers is connected to part of the exchanges which turn out to offer too good a service.

The mix of subscribers in many telesystems is an important factor which is often neglected. This situation may create trouble in the busy business districts. These people are often influenced by the same factors in using their telephones. They are not as independent as assumed in theory. The general dimensioning rules are often based on the assumption that there is a mixed group of subscribers with varying demands of traffic, not a group with an equal (simultaneous) demand of traffic.

In the information society we will have the chance to smooth out some of these variations, e.g., by using the same technical installations for different services with different requirements in the busy period, like, for example, sending mail through the telephone line outside the busy hour. Expenses will then only be involved for installations at the end points since transport itself can be offered free of charge by giving it a low priority for transfer from one subscriber to another. In that way, it will still be possible to maintain the idea of a fixed price for a stamp or, even more realistically, a fixed price per year for postal services.

2. COMMUNICATION SYSTEM IN SOCIETY - A PUBLIC UTILITY

2.1 Introduction

The Public Institution influences the society's national product by requiring payments for services, by imposing subsidies from and contributions to society, and by granting services. On top of this, its activities have an indirect effect on the national system via the so called multiplier effect.

The public institution has to maintain a certain economic - often linear weighted - balance between income and expense. Other socioeconomic restraints, such as staff policy and choice of technique, or the use of domestic and foreign manpower and products often have to be taken into consideration as well. All these requirements take the shape of a long series of inequality considerations. Some fulfil quality requirements, some are financially motivated, and some are motivated by requiring a smooth function of other sectors in society over time. The individual subscriber's minimum requirements of quality of the services offered on different routes have to be met.

An important issue in this picture is the overall subsidising or transfers among the various sectors of society. Some are contributors. Others are recipients. The decision whether or not, and how, is often made at a higher level in society.

The main issue in telephone systems has never been the maximisation of the company's profit. Company and subscribers have the same interests. It is characteristic of this optimisation under constraints, that the number of variables which management has to decide on is far less than the number of individual service requirements to be met. As will be seen From Table 1, the classic dimensioning rules do not deviate much from one another. The dimensioning rules for the individual groups in the teleplant seems in all cases to be characterised by the operable function:

$$F_\eta(A) = A(E_\eta(A) - E_{\eta+1}(A)) = F_1, \qquad (2.1)$$

as presented in Moe's Principle (Jensen 1950). But the norms F_1 - the level of service - depending on economic goals for administration and nation as well as the subscribers' qualitative requirements on the individual traffic routes. Dimensioning rules for direct circuit groups and protection groups can in this light be considered as part of the superior safety views for teletraffic. Not only economic views, technical possibilities and blocking probabilities, but also the risk due to overloads or technical breakdowns becomes part of this general theory.

2.2 Classical Dimensioning Rules

Molina used - as Erlang did earlier - the tail of the Poisson distribution in his dimensioning rule. The number of circuits was decided so that the tail was constant, e.g.:

$$\sum_{i=n}^{\infty} P(i) = 0.02. \qquad (2.2)$$

Christensen used an approximation for this tail, viz. the 'square root law', $n = A+2{,}3\sqrt{A}$. In engineering practice, the ability of the groups to meet overloading is often used as, e.g., in requiring blocking $B = 0.07$ at 25% overload. In Moe's Principle the last supplementary 'dollar' should have the same effect on the reduced number of lost calls no matter where it was invested in the plant. That means that

$$F_\eta = (A(E_\eta(A) - B_{\eta+1}(A)) = F_1$$

for instance, as in Denmark $F_1 = -.05$ is often used for the number of circuits.

If one wishes to split up traffic and send it in parallel along different route in an optimal way, one gets $(n+1-A(1-E))E=d$. For $d = 0.09$ the results are given in Column 'split' (Table 1). Results show that the deviation between the various old and new rules applied is very modest.

TABLE 1
Results for different dimensioning rules

A	Moe F_1=0.05 n	Molina 0.02 n	Christen-sen 2.3 n	Overload 25% B=0,07 n	Split d = 0,09 n	Blocking * Erlang in % n
4.99	10	10.6	10.3	10	10.3	1.8
11.90	20	20	19.9	19	20	1.0
27.58	40	39.3	39.7	39	40	0.6
44.18	60	59	59.5	59	59	0.4
61.2	80	79	79.2	79	79	0.3
78.7	100	98.5	99.1	99	99	0.3
96.4	120	117.5	119	-	119	0.2

* along the Moe Curve calculated by Erlang's Formula.

The interesting issue left behind is how the service level as given by the constants for these rules depends on the required goals. In practice Public Institutions - to which a service sector such as the telephone sector belongs - are subject to a special set of governing rules of a more or less formalised kind. At times such rules are just implied as a result of long stable traditions. The privileges enjoyed by Public Utilities are counterbalanaced by the obligations to grant the service in question to all members of society, on equal terms and to some extent without regard to individual cost. Also, they are counterbalanced by the fact that the financial results of an institution, its price policy and the quality of its products are subject to public regulations, often in the form of minimum requirements. Therefore, we do not often talk about maximising the financial outcome of the public institution.

The most essential issues of policy carried out by the Public Utility such as a telephone system are related to an overall goal that tries to maximise the national product for society and the Public Utility as a whole under given constraints. In this way, the Public Utilities and institutions find in a smooth way their place in society. These requirements may include a predetermined profit for the Public Utility as well as demands for minimum contributions to society and clients and a maximum draw per unit of time on the society's different resources. This influences both short term and long term investments, and often requires a smooth adaptation of the Public Utilities to changed economic and technical conditions.

Through the system of rates and greater service for the different groups of users, technical units and groups of workers, these requirements will influence the tele-activity.

A main draw has been internal subsidising of weak groups. You need to have someone to speak to and to be called by. Do not forget that it is not without interest to be called. Who is to pay? The one who is being called? The one who is calling? By tradition we collect the money from the one who is calling, but the one who is being called participates in the subsidising of the one who is calling.

Even though the communication sector so far has done without subsidies from outside, and has contributed its share to the society indirectly by meeting its requirements, one cannot in the long run forget transfers among sectors. It is characteristic of optimisation under constraints, that the number of variables which management has to decide on is far less than the number of customer groups whose individual service demands have to be met.

This means that, as far as the optimal solution is concerned, the service will be only met in a limited number of cases, (in fact, due to Zeuthen's Rule, this number is equal to the number of variables available to management). In most cases the requirements will be more than met. In other words, only a few service requirements will establish norms for the different technical groups - one dominating all others in each technical group. Only one of the communication modes it services will establish its norms for service.

Finding the specific sets or norm-establishing communication modes and their matching with the various technical groups may become a special mathematical task with (direct or indirect) political implications.

As shown by Jensen (1985) we have the following classical cases:

1. Profit Maximisation for a telephone company
2. Profit Maximisation for a telephone company with quality constraints
3. Optimisation of a telephone service by maximising the national product.

These three options lead to the following results:

1. Profit Maximisation for a Telephone Company

$$F_{\eta_\mu}(A_{.\mu}) = \frac{\alpha_2}{\alpha_1} \frac{b_\mu}{p_\mu} \qquad (2.3)$$

In other words, F depends on the ratios between the marginal cost of the group and the marginal revenue of the message transferred.

2. Profit Maximisation for a Telephone Company with Quality Constraints

$$F_{\eta_\mu}(A_{.\mu}) = \frac{\alpha_2 \, b_\mu}{\alpha_1 \left(p_{\mu\theta} + \frac{1}{\alpha} \frac{A}{s}(\mu)\right)} \qquad (2.4)$$

We notice that the changed policy has increased the marginal revenue with an additional shadow price in order to meet the quality requirements for the through traffic.

3. Optimisation of the Telephone Service by Maximising the National Product

$$F_{n_\mu}(A_\mu) = \frac{\alpha_2 \left(\lambda_2 - \frac{t_2}{\alpha_2} - \frac{\eta_1}{(1-\eta_2)} \right) b_\mu}{\alpha_1 \left[\frac{\delta g}{\delta v}(\mu) \frac{1}{\alpha_1} + \left[\lambda_0 - \frac{(1-t_1)}{\alpha_1} \right] p_\mu + \frac{1}{\mu_1} \lambda_s(\mu) \right]} \tag{2.5}$$

We notice here that the marginal cost has been modified in the light of its effect in the country and that the revenue likewise has been modified. However, the latter is also increased by the effect of the traffic in question on the national product. In other words, its importance for subscribers and society as such.

Also, effects outside the telesector have to be taken into account, even if it does not have a direct influence on the own economy of the telesectors. The individual influence of the different groups of traffic routes on standards and norms shows that a large part of our good service is the result of a rather few but important services which in all circumstances have to be met.

3. FUTURE ISSUES

The likely problems to be faced in the future are not the network connections, the distribution points for the exchanges, the transit points, etc., but the communication stations within the homes and their connection with the distribution points. Since light cables will be used between exchanges and will even reach all distribution points, there is also a need to have at these distribution points technical end point installations.

We have to take care in the following three cases:

1. Light cable connections from distribution points to the homes or to the small businesses, if there is already a telephone line
2. Light cable and/or ordinary telephone lines when there is not already a telephone line
3. The communication station at home and its interface with the different electric appliances - kitchen appliances, TV, video, personal computer, etc.

One of the critical issues to whether the end point installations in the homes are going to be a general complex interface to be used by all installations in the home, or whether each appliance is going to have its own interface. Most of this will find its solution in the process of standardisation which is going to take place over time.

Against this background it seems obvious that the realisation of plans beyond the distribution points depends to a large extent on how the transfer of mail will be solved, as automatic mail requires the establishment of an automatic communication to every home.

To the extent that there is a mix of various economic and social groups in even smaller parts of a town, the latter process is going to be a decisive factor. However, if part of the groups with limited resources in their productive age lives in separate quarters of the town, considerable delays of ordinary tele-investments may occur. Thus, the possibility of automating parts of the mail service will be considerably less, unless some citizen groups will be left out, which is usually a politically unacceptable solution. Therefore, a presumption for a good long term solution to the postal communication problem is that the telephone connection is installed in all homes in a way that it does not create financial burdens for anyone.

Oral and written communication are the backbone of our society, but not sufficient for a good description of reality as pointed out by the poet and philosopher Piet Hein in Oslo in 1986. The subsequent organisational flexibility is essential for a good utilisation of our manpower and of our resources. And this applies to homes as well as to offices. The critical phase of communication during the next 10-20 years will hence be a multi-goal situation.

It will necessarily become a mixture of technical-economic possibilities and a political willingness to provide advanced communication to all homes without access barriers. The inexpensive information storage will make it possible to differentiate the time for delivery and receipt of information and thereby strengthen the creation of social circles in tomorrow's information society as pointed out by H. Inose (1984). Thus, the capacity of tomorrow's communication system in society is going to be much better utilised. In the future, the 'unified information system', with its words, sounds and pictures will give us a needed improved description and understanding of reality, as mentioned by Piet Hein. It will then have a great impact on the Urban-Environmental systems for the benefit of man's culture.

REFERENCES

Inose, H. and R. Pierce, Information Technology and Civilization, W.H. Freeman, New York, 1984.

Jensen, A., Moe's Principle. An Econometric Investigation Intended as an Aid in Dimensioning and Managing Telephone Plant, The Copenhagen Telephone Company, Copenhagen, 1950.

Jensen, A. Traffic. Operational Research. Futurology. In Service of Research and Society, North-Holland Publishing Company, Amsterdam, New York, Oxford, 1980.

Jensen, A., 'Theory for Public Utilities Consistent with National Goals Applied to the Tele Sector', Proceedings 10th International Tele-traffic Congress, Kyoto, Japan, North-Holland Publishing Company, Amsterdam, 1985.

TELECOMMUNICATIONS IN AN ADVANCED INFORMATION SOCIETY: A JAPANESE PERSPECTIVE

Yasusada Kitahara

1. INTRODUCTION

The information communication and processing industry in our present day society has exhibited rapid development in the past thirty years. The phenomenal growth of this industry is due to the opening of a great many possibilities through the introduction of an online real time system which can electrically connect computerised *information processing* with the *telecommunications system*. The decisive factor in the industry's development was the invention of the semiconductor and the subsequent development of computers and digital technology. In particular, digital technology is now being used extensively in society because it is highly effective in reducing noise levels, upgrading the system's reliability and cutting costs: hence the current expression, *digital age*.

Special mention must be made here of Shannon (USA) who played a pioneering role in the digital age by publishing his *Mathematical Theory of Communication* in 1948. In his thesis, Shannon introduced the concept of the *bit*. He elucidated his theory of digital (not analogue) expression by using a pair of corresponding numerics, i.e., '0 or 1' or 'yes or no', and thereby built the theoretical basis for introducing the digital age.

The surprising progress in semiconductor technology has supported ongoing developments in the electronics industry, especially in the context of digital technology. The transistor which made this progress possible was invented in 1948, the same year in which Shannon published his theory. The ENIAC, the first machine that could rightly be given the name of electronic computer, was already in existence in those early days. However, the ENIAC presented a rather dim prospect for further development because it used as many as 18 thousand vacuum tubes.

The invention of the transistor was indeed a phenomenal event in that it enabled overstepping the limits set by vacuum tube-type computers and opened the way to introducing the present-day age of electronics. Specifically, semiconductor technology, with the IC as its typical product, permitted drastic cost reductions, which in turn led to the development of smaller, more sophisticated and more energy-saving equipment and subsequently gave all equipment upgraded functions and higher reliability. Semiconductor technology thus contributed inestimably to socioeconomic progress.

As a Japanese example of the development resulting from semiconductor technology, it is worth mentioning NTT's (Nippon Telegraph and Telephone

Corporation) online real time processing computer called DIPS (Denden Information Processing System). We have been working on this system for the past 15 years and during this period, which has witnessed the fast progress from ICs to VLSIs, the system has been considerably upgraded in both performance and economic efficiency, while the processing speed increased by more than seven times and the cost reduced to less than about one-thirteenth.

Despite its long history of about forty years, semiconductor technology is still showing a continued, steady growth path, with no signs of waning. For example, microelectronics technology is advancing from the micron to submicron regions, necessitating the use of electron beams and X-rays which are smaller in width than light beams. And it is foreseeable that semiconductor technology will advance even further towards the 21st century with the development of ULSI technology and molecular technologies. It is known for instance that the Bell Telephone Laboratory has already started experiments in which cerebral neurons of animals are transferred to silicon substrates.

With an advanced information society close at hand, we are now facing the need to realise high-speed transmission of an ever increasing volume of information at low cost and to minimise the distance-dependence of charges. With conventional systems using copper cables, the only plausible way to realise any sizeable cost reduction is to augment the transmission capacity. To solve such problems, an economically feasible development of new technologies is urgently called for. In 1970, Corning Glass Company of the United States succeeded in developing an optical fibre with a very low loss of only 20 Db per kilometer. In the same year the Bell Laboratories realised continuous oscillation using a semiconductor laser at room temperature. There is no doubt that these achievements greatly accelerated subsequent research and development activities.

Since that time, all research institutes throughout the world, including that of NTT, have focussed their efforts on the development of an extremely low-loss optical fibre. NTT has been making special efforts to remove impurities from and homogenise the fibre structure, and has produced a number of notable achievements including success in registering a loss of only 0.2 dB per kilometer in 1978. In 1977, we developed a novel optical fibre manufacturing method called the VAD method (the Vapor Phase Axial Disposition method), which is ideal for mass production.

On the strength of these new developments, NTT completed in February 1985 a 400 Megabit relay transmission line covering a distance of 8,400 kilometers between the northern and southern ends of the Japanese archipelago. NTT also introduced a large number of optical fibre cables in local business lines as well as in other local and trunk lines. With these improvements, we feel that we have really already entered the era of optical fibre cable communications. With the rapid advance of technology since the research into optical fibres initiated some 20 years ago, optical fibre cable communications has now become practical. It cannot yet be said, however, that we are making full use of the superb characteristics of optical fibres.

NTT is fully aware of the importance of minimising the cost of optical fibre cable communications and is developing various new systems and methods including, for example, a coherent beam transmission system. This system will be the next generation optical communications system and will enable the number of lines to be increased by more than one digit from the existing level, provide a method for inserting multiple coherent beams, and introduce a new flouride optical fibre that can reduce the loss to a level even lower than that of the quartz optical fibre. NTT is attempting to realise all of these research objectives in close collaboration with many outside organisations.

2. PHILOSOPHY AND DEVELOPMENT OF INS

2.1 Philosophy of INS

The fast progress of present day society toward an advanced information society is widening the applications of the telecommunications services. Specifically the present telephone service, which is the mainstay of the existing information communications system, is rapidly making way for computerised online real time systems and further new telecommunications services, or visual services, which will enable us to have free access to nearly 80 per cent of all information that we can read or see. Moreover, the progress in semiconductor technology will bring about a more sophisticated digital technology that will enable versatile, high quality information processing and at the same time accelerate the pace of digitisation within telecommunications services.

The conventional analogue network is neither efficient nor suitable for supplying a variety of new services such as combining audio and visual information. NTT has long felt the need for digitising the network to supply a greater variety of low cost telecommunications services, which are more user oriented, and enable less influence of distance on charges. Since 1978, NTT has advocated the establishment of a new network system, called INS (Information Network System) to meet this purpose, and has made considerable efforts to realise its implementation as one of our major business development goals.

The philosophy of INS is identical to the basic technological thought underlying the ISDN which is soon to be established by the International Telecommunication Union as an international standard. More specifically, it is aimed at unifying, on the basis of the *bit* concept, the rate systems now varying from service to service. INS will be built by making the best use of the digital and optical fibre technologies, which have recently seen rapid advancement, in order to minimise the distance-dependency charges. This can only be done on the basis of semiconductor technology which brings about higher economic efficiency, functional improvement and higher reliability.

2.2 Basic System Configuration of INS

The trend of today's technological development leaves little doubt that around 1995 when INS is completed, digital signals will account for a great part of the information flow through all network paths, regardless of the type of service.

Individual networks such as telegraph and telephone networks will also be integrated into INS. INS will basically be composed of three elements: a fundamental network having simple information transmission functions, terminal equipment, and terminal services. The following points need special attention when determining the configuration of INS.

First, attention must be paid to function allocation. Specifically, care must be taken in allocating functions between the network and the terminals for a variety of new services which are certain to be developed from growing network sophistication. In principle, NTT intends to allocate all important, necessary functions to the network and install simple, low cost terminals to provide services which are of a highly public nature. This is its basic policy for mass information services. For services in business areas, however, we know that service requirements vary from area to area and from company to company, so we plan to allocate the necessary functions to terminal equipment, including those demanded by individual enterprises. Since the choice lies with the user in both cases, any plan to offer a new type of service should be preceded by a careful survey of user needs and other conditions to ensure that all users have easy access to such new services at low cost. It is also important to design the network for open-ended expansion or optimisation because the end of the telephone age is expected to bring a drastic change in the flow of traffic and an increase in non-telephone traffic by several tens of per cent.

Second, we should exercise great care in choosing traffic and network facilities. The present network facilities are designed mainly for telephone services, and separate individual networks are built to meet other service requirements. The flow of traffic through existing network paths is dominated by man-to-man telecommunication. However, there is a strong indication that society's demands for telecommunication services will show a change from telephone to non-telephone services and that the traffic will eventually be characterised by an increasing weight of man-machine and machine-machine interactions. An extended series of technical discussions on the packet switching service and switching functions will be necessary to determine the best way to unify different traffic characteristics for network integration through digitisation.

Third, we ought to pay attention to the quality of INS service. User demands for telecommunications services will certainly be increasing and will become more diversified both functionally and qualitatively. Accordingly, the basic policy for controlling quality for various services will not only affect the user acceptability of services, but will also be pivotal in building INS. In the design of the conventional telephone network the level of quality was determined for the entire network including all terminal equipment. For INS, which is divided into terminal services and network services, it will be possible to easily determine the quality of the network side easily because only transmission services need regulation. On the terminal side, however, a variety of new quality factors must be controlled to satisfy the extensive range of user demands in the market. The quality of these new services will have to be reexamined from an entirely new view point, because the connectivity aspect (see later) will exert an important influence on the effective use of such services.

2.3 Realisation of INS

NTT is pursuing the philosophy of INS on the basis of six principles. First we intend to assure all national users free access to the network to meet their expectations for new services. For example, we are considering introducing a charging system allowing the rate to be collected from the called party or a third party, and a network routing system permitting free route selection by the user. In other words, we are planning to allocate certain network control functions to users to assure free access to various services, provided it does not cause any confusion in network operations. For this purpose, we are planning to promote upgrading the intelligent level by providing the network with databases and common channel signalling system.

Second, we aim to integrate the network by digitising it progressively with each new or additional installation and with each revision or optimisation. This is because digital technology is far more advantageous than analogue technology for reducing costs. We hope to complete the network integration by around 1992.

Third, we intend to provide amplified high speed, broad band services through the digital network for voluminous data transmission services and visual and other non-telephone services, all essential for society to progress towards a computerised information society. We believe that this plan can be materialised globally by 1990.

Fourth, we are making accelerated efforts to introduce a packet switching service because this technology is very effective in efficiently providing services with different traffic characteristics. We are also doing our utmost to develop a high speed packet switching technology which will become an important service in the future. We believe that this service will be introduced worldwide by 1990.

Fifth, to achieve high speed, low cost transmission of an ever increasing volume of information, we feel an acute need to introduce optical fibre communication technology and to use optical fibre cables instead of copper cables. We are also hoping to introduce coherent beams to realise a one-digit increase in line capacity to create an intelligent PBX and LAN. Because these improvements call for a very high level of system reliability, there will be a need for loop connection of lines including local switches and establishment of a 24-hour automatic network monitoring and switchover system. We intend to develop such loop connections and monitoring systems at the lowest possible cost.

Sixth, we are fully aware of the importance of upgrading the network to realise man-network interactions by adding knowledge processing functions, that is, various intelligent functions including AI (artificial intelligence). We intend to strengthen our technological development efforts in this direction.

As mentioned earlier, the realisation of INS depends on focussing our future research endeavours on the future development of semiconductor technology and on the introduction of advanced software technology.

2.4 Future Evolution of INS

Since NTT first advocated the philosophy of INS in 1978, it has made persistent efforts to realise this by progressively digitising the telephone network and building a pilot system providing trial services to the Mitaka-Musashino area in the western suburbs of Tokyo.

This Model System INS has been subject to a series of experiments since September 1984. Completion of ongoing experimental operations in March 1987 was followed by a second phase operation conducted in a wider area thus commencing an actual network service linking the Tokyo, Nagoya and Osaka areas. The second phase operation is aimed at collecting more data in preparation for a full scale network operation scheduled for April 1988.

Experiments using the Model System have not only attracted worldwide attention, but have also provided a number of new insights that have contributed greatly to the standardisation activities of the CCITT, the permanent organ of ITU, and have given impetus to the global research of ISDN.

We believe that international standardisation is one of the keys to successfully creating ISDN. In this context, NTT has gained experience in the Model System operations which has helped CCITT to promote its standardisation activities for user network interfaces, as well as for digital network quality and services. NTT is determined to continue efforts to support international standardisation to create a global network enabling efficient and effective communication throughout the world.

3. ASSURANCE OF TELECOMMUNICATION'S CONNECTIVITY

An important subject to be discussed is the problem of connectivity assurance. The prime objective of telecommunications system is to ensure that everyone is freely able to communicate with anyone else at any time.

Needless to say, network utilisation increases according to the widening of communicable areas. The function pertaining to the communicable range in telecommunications is called connectivity and is the most important of all functions of telecommunications system. If a telecommunications network has high connectivity in the eyes of customers, it means that the network enables anyone anywhere to communicate with anyone else or with any other kind of customer station equipment. Here, the existing telephone network can be evaluated as having very high connectivity insofar as voice communication is concerned, because it enables rapid, around-the-clock communication from any part of the world.

If the control of systems development is relaxed on the basis of the principle of free market competition, there will be a large number of versatile new systems emanating in rapid succession. However, these systems cannot be connected to each other because they use different formats, protocols and codes.

To cite a few examples of this, data communication is often impossible between different types of computers or customer station equipment, despite the fact that it has now acquired the character of an infrastructure indispensable to our day-to-day lives. Data transmission between different models of facsimile equipment is not always possible either. A well known example here is the considerable inconvenience caused to VTR users because no connection is possible between the VHS system and the Beta system. However, telephones, cassette tapes and photographic films can be interconnected or replaced with each other regardless of the manufacturer because they are all standardised, enabling them to be used freely in all countries.

An increasing number of upgraded, intelligent networks and terminal equipment will probably be developed in the future. However, neither business enterprises nor private users will be able to introduce different systems and terminals one after another. This is not just because of economic reasons but also because of human limitations in handling a number of terminals differing in the operating method. No system or terminal can be fully functional unless it is designed to interface smoothly with different models.

Free competition is certainly an important incentive in the development of the information communication and processing industry, but equally (or perhaps more) important is the promotion of standardisation through the cooperation of all manufacturers involved.

It is therefore essential that close international cooperation be promoted to assure telecommunication connectivity, and that the standardisation activities of the CCITT, ISO and IEC become successful.

4. CONCLUSION

The development of the telecommunications service industry and related technologies is an essential factor that supports the advance and growth of modern industries. We ought to realise, however, that the development of enhanced technologies invariably presupposes the availability of an enormous investment of capital as well as manpower. In particular, basic technologies and knowhow can never be developed to a very high level without years of ceaseless, untiring research endeavours and any sceptical view of such technologies or a tendency to belittle or underestimate them is prone to endanger the future of the nation involved. For sound development of an advanced information society, consistent efforts should be made in the research and development of various high technologies as well as in the efficient and effective application of such technologies to the benefit of national and international users (see Kitahara 1983).

To attain this objective, it is very important for all countries of the world to unify their efforts in order to enhance the growth of the information communication and processing industry in the widest possible spectrum; clearly, this difficult task cannot be adequately tackled without full conscientious global support and cooperation.

REFERENCES

Kitahara, Y., Information Network System - Telecommunications in the Twenty-First Century, Heinemann, London, 1983.

ASSESSMENT OF NEW INFORMATION SERVICES IN JAPAN

Haruo Akimaru

1. INTRODUCTION

Computers have been advancing on the basis of technological seeds and social needs and are providing various new information services combined with telecommunications. We are now in the advanced information society which is exerting a great influence on the humanity and society. The present chapter presents examples of new information services being developed in Japan. The chapter will contain a discussion of the issues and problems concerning the new services and technologies, and make proposals for the assessment of the impacts of the information society.

2. DEVELOPMENT OF NEW INFORMATION SERVICES

In recent years, businesses and industries have been aiming at increasing the efficiency of their organisations by using computers for their management. Versatile demands from customers also require appropriate marketing and inventory of products for which computers are essentially required. For example, for saving manpower, increasing reliability, respecting humanity, etc., the introduction of computer controlled robotics is promoted in the workplace. Furthermore, limited natural resources, such as petrol and electricity, should be efficiently utilised, which is also realised by adaptive control with computers.

The advent of computers in the middle of this century has met the above mentioned social needs and combined with telecommunications, have rapidly developed and are now widely applied in business, industry, schools, homes, etc. Hardware component devices for the computers themselves and microelectronics, represented by VLSI (Very Large Scale Integration), are now designed by computer, and the advancement of the computer promotes, in turn, a further development of the hardware itself. The ability of the computer is expanded by the software such as operating systems, application programmes, databases, etc. Such huge software resources have to be produced originally by manpower, and it needs an efficient software development environment, which is also enhanced by powerful computers. Hence, the progress of the computer results in the advancement of the hardware and software, which produces a positive feedback towards the technological seeds. Thus, the interaction between the needs and seeds produces an endless development of the information society and the C&C (Computer and Communications) technologies.

We are now in the advanced information age and many kinds of new information services are being developed by C&C technology. As illustrated in Figure 1, in

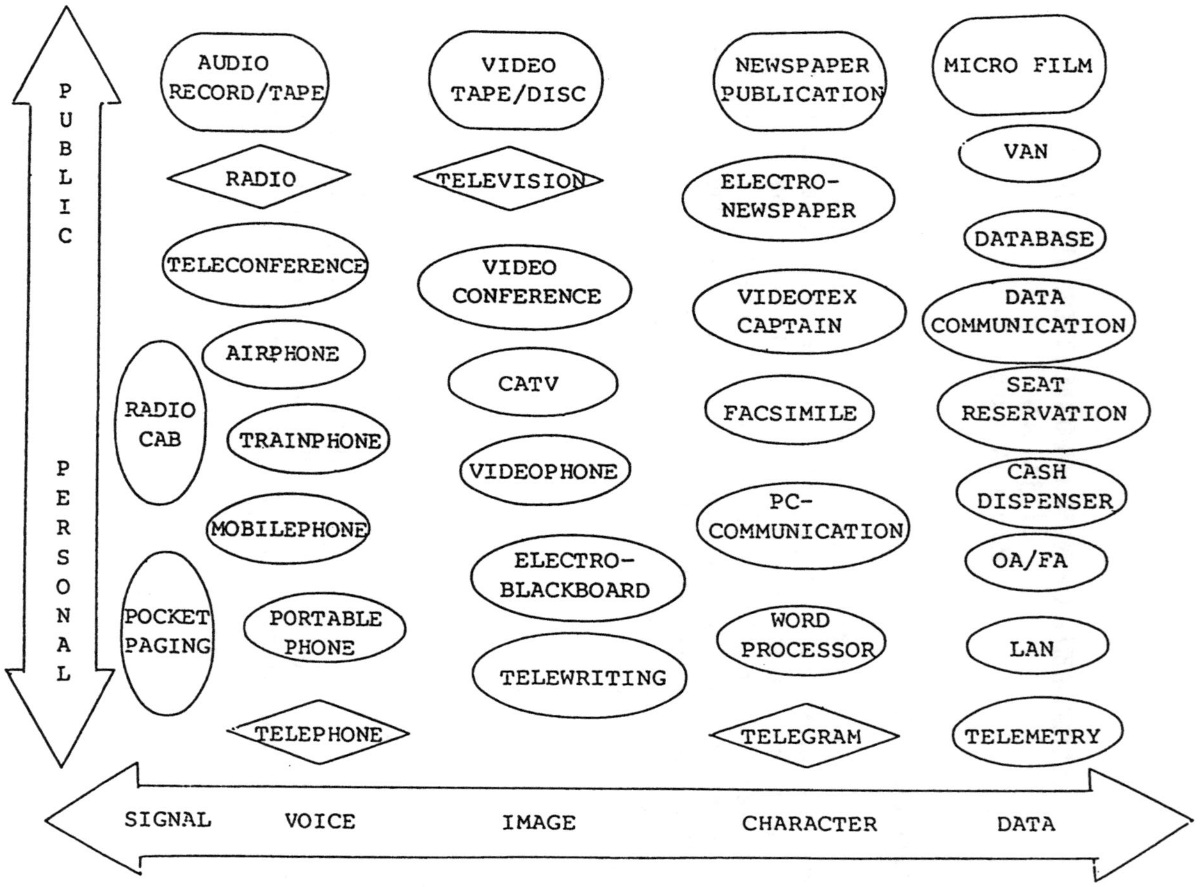

Figure 1. Development of new information services

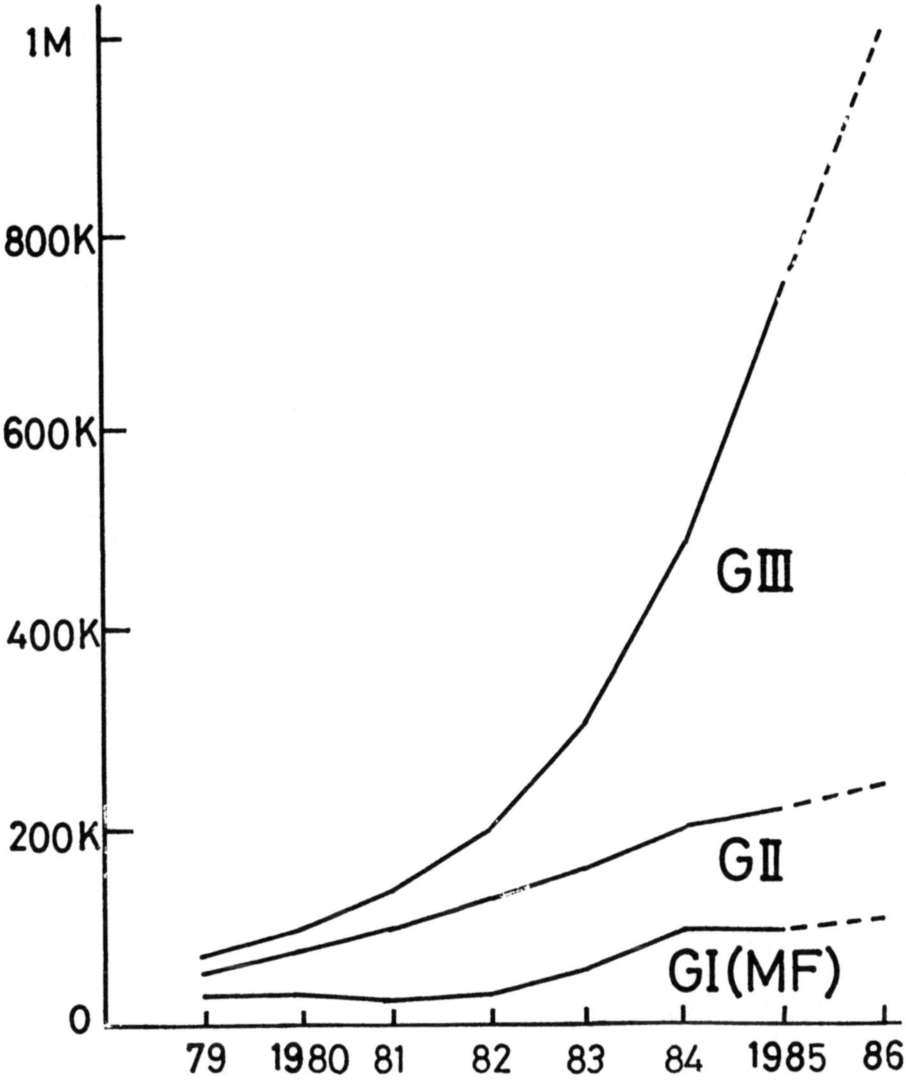

Figure 2. Facsimile installations in Japan

addition to the old media (including the telephone. telegramme. radio and television), various kinds of new media services are being introduced. Contents of information handled range from signal, voice, image, character to data. Flows of information range from person-to-person person-to-public, and public-to-public, to man-to-man, man-to-machine and machine-to-machine. The situation of a variety of new services will be similar in most advanced countries of the world. The new services are sometimes developed on a technology-oriented rather than a needs-oriented basis, and they are often provided in free competition situations. These new services increase efficiency and convenience of human activities, while at the same time, they also produce various problems for assessment of their impact on human beings.

Here, we will mainly focus attention on special features of Japanese new information services. In Japanese documents for business, science, engineering, literature, etc. Japanese characters are used, which include Chinese characters, *Kanji*, and phonetic characters *Kana*. Therefore, an essential part of the Japanese information service is oriented towards treating Japanese characters. In the sequel, we will take facsimile and Japanese word processing as examples in order to discuss the issues and problems of the new services.

3. FACSIMILE COMMUNICATIONS

3.1 International Standardisation

The facsimile can transmit documents including any characters, figures, tables, etc. For this reason, the facsimile is especially suitable for Japanese documents, and it is widely used in Japan. As shown in Figure 2, facsimile installations are rapidly growing and by the end of 1985 more than one million facsimile sets were being used in business, industry, schools, homes, etc., and they are increasing by about 50 per cent a year. The international standardisation of facsimile has been established by the CCITT (Consultative Committee of International Telegraph and Telephone), an organisation of the United Nations.

Three kinds of standard, GI, GII and GIII have been established for facsimile through an ordinary telephone line (analogue 4kHz) (see CCITT Red Book 1982). The GI type machine transmits a typical A4 document in about six minutes, with the resolution of five lines per mm by a straightforward scanning method. On the other hand, GII and GIII machines transmit the same document in about three minutes and less than one minute respectively, with the same quality by additional processing for removing the redundancy in the document in order to increase the transmission speed. These machines are sometimes referred to as 6 min., 3 min., and 1 min. facsimiles, respectively, and their prices increase according to the additional processing facilities involved. The CCITT has also established the standardisation for GIV type machines of the digital version for ISDN (Integrated Service Digital Network) applications.

Thanks to the standardisation, the facsimile has international connectivity, even despite the difference in vendors, or despite the multi-vendor environment. Usually, a higher speed machine has a downward compatibility, and thus

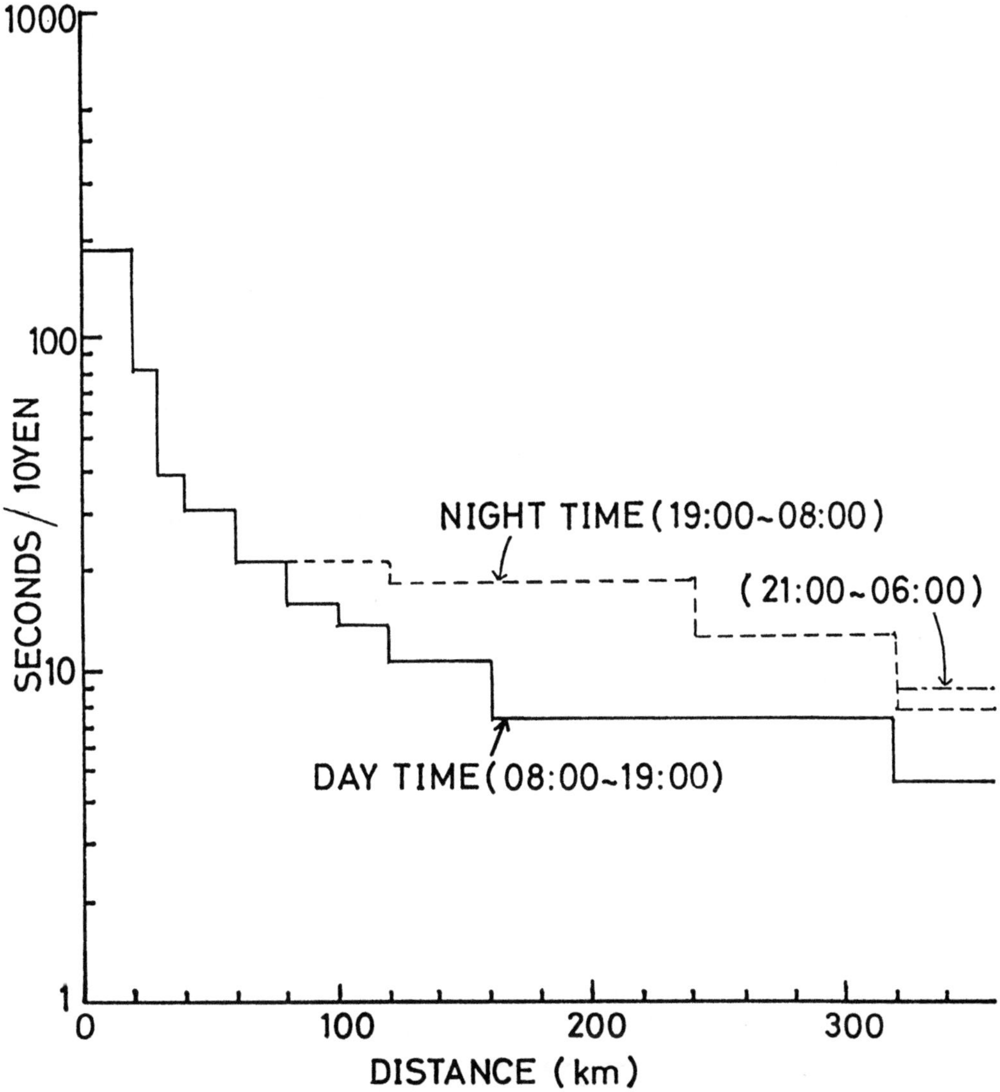

Figure 3. Japanese telephone tariff systems

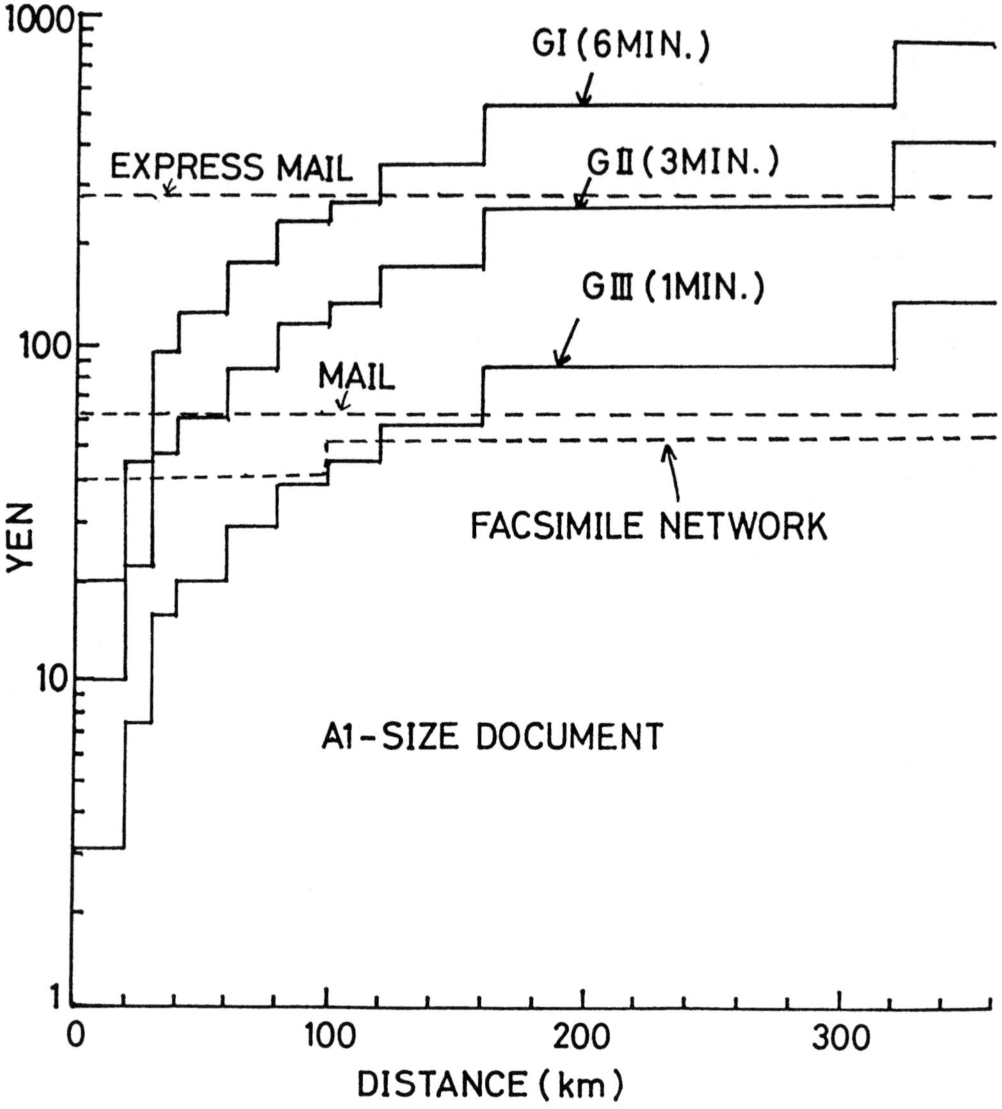

Figure 4. Facsimile tariff through Telephone Network

different speed machines can also communicate with each other. This is a reason why the facsimile communications have rapidly become popular and utilised in a wide range of applications.

3.2 Facsimile through Telephone Networks

The public telephone network in Japan is a fully automated social infrastructure containing about 50 million subscribers from coast to coast. Therefore, the facsimile communications through the telephone network is very convenient and useful for business and industrial activities, and has a high potential for a wide use. However, it is subject to the telephone tariff system which has been established for oral communication. Figure 3 shows the domestic telephone tariff system in Japan which employs a distance-time charging method. The method is based on determining the talking time (in seconds) corresponding to the unit charge (currently 10 yen, or about 8 US cents) according to the distance (in kilometers) between calling and called parties. Specifically, with 10 yen, one can talk for about 180 seconds (3 minutes) for a local call, and for 4.5 seconds for a more than 320 km call. Including these, there are, in total, 10 charging rates as illustrated.

Figure 4 shows the charges for facsimile communications for sending a typical A4 document with various types of machines. In the figures, comparisons with domestic mail are also shown. Since an advantage of the facsimile is its high speed of transmission (while the mail can send more than one page in the same postage), it might not be appropriate to simply compare them. But some indicative conclusions can be drawn. The GI machine is simple and lowest in machine cost, but more expensive than express mail (260 yen throughout the country) over 100 km. On the other hand, the GII and GII are more economical in communication cost, and in fact, the GIII is cheaper than ordinary mail (60 yen throughout the country) within 150 kilometers.

As mentioned, GII and GIII machines involve additional functions to increase the speed, and thus they are of higher cost than the GI machine. However, with the introduction of VLSI technology, the cost increment is becoming less significant. In fact, the facsimile functions are implemented in VLSI, because of the large repeatability and mass production advantages resulting from standardisation which yields a drastic cost reduction of the machines. Hence, a large part of the installations of facsimile in recent times is of the GIII type as illustrated in Figure 2. It should be noted that the standardisation contributes not only to the connectivity but also to a cost reduction of the machine, both promoting a wide distribution of the new service.

Besides the telephone network, a special facsimile network system has been developed and is now being used in Japan. This system stores original facsimile signals (analogue 4kHz) and retransmits them at a higher speed in digital form (1.5M bits/second) to save the long distance transmission cost. As shown in Figure 4, the facsimile through this network becomes cheaper than ordinary mail throughout the country. Most of the recent facsimile sets can have access to this network and may enjoy its economic service with a low additional subscription fee. The charge of this system is less dependent on distance, and it is preferred for the expansion of a uniform information society throughout the country.

3.3 Considerations on Communication Costs

As described above, the development of new information services such as the facsimile largely depends on the communication cost. In view of the nation wide development of the information society, it is ideal that the communication cost is negligible or at least independent of distance. Historically, telecommunications are distance dependent, while the mail is not or at least less dependent. For example, domestic mail postage in Japan depends only on the weight and speed (ordinary or express), and even for overseas airmail, the postage is only in the order of twice the domestic (140 yen for the US, 150 yen for Europe). The reason seems to be that the mail requires most manpower for delivery, while telecommunications need a large amount of investment and ensuing operating costs. It is not necessarily true, however, that the present telephone tariff system is based on a precise cost account basis.

The Japanese domestic telephone tariff system is more distance dependent compared with other countries. For example, the ratio of local and most distant charges is 1:40 in Japan, in contrast with 1:10 even in a larger country like the USA. The public telecommunications system in Japan has been provided by the NTT (Nippon Telegraph and Telephone Corporation) on a monopoly basis, and the tariff was sometimes controlled by the government on political grounds. Since 1985, public telecommunications have been deregulated, and several common carriers competing with the NTT appeared to provide the telecommunications services. In such a situation, the cost account basis will be promoted. On the other hand, however, the advent of satellite communications makes the transmission cost less dependent on distance. The optical fibre system provides a high speed and large capacity transmission at low cost.

In the INS (Information Network System) (see the chapter by Kitahara in this volume), a reasonable tariff system is proposed based on the digital communication system. The problem of the communication cost is an important issue in the new information services; it should not only be discussed and considered from an economic angle, but also from the viewpoint of promoting the establishment of an advanced information society that is homogeneous at a domestic and international scale.

4. JAPANESE WORD PROCESSING

4.1 Japanese Characters

As stated earlier, Japanese characters include the phonetic character *kana* and the Chinese character *Kanji* Actually, there are two kinds of Kanas, namely *Katakana* and *Hiragana*, each consisting of 48 characters with different sounds. The kanas themselves have no meaning and are used for expressing words as pronounced. The Hiragana is also used for connecting the Kanjis in Japanese sentences, and they can also express words in sounds instead of Kanjis. The Katakana may be used for stressing specific words, and even for expressing

TABLE 1
Example of Kana-Kanji Conversion

Katakana	Hiragana	Romaji	Kanji	JIS code	Idiom
サ	さ	sa	差	3A39	差異 (sai=differenc)
			査	3A3A	調査 (chousa=inquiry)
サイ	さい	sai	債	3A44	債権 (saiken=credit)
			最	3A47	最高 (saikou=highest)
			才	3A4D	才能 (sainou=talent)
			採	3A4E	採用 (saiyou=adoption)
ザイ	ざい	zai	在	3A5F	現在 (genzai=present)
			材	3A60	材料 (zairyou=material)
			財	3A62	財産 (zaisan=property)
サク	さく	saku	作	3A6E	製作 (seisaku=manufacture)
			策	3A76	政策 (seisaku=policy)
サン	さん	san	散	3B36	分散 (bunsan=variance)
			産	3B3A	生産 (seisan=production)
			算	3B3B	予算 (yosan=budget)
ザン	ざん	zan	暫	3B43	暫定 (zantei=tentative)
			残	3B44	残高 (zandaka=balance)

foreign words as pronounced. As for the number of characters, the Kanas may be considered similar to the English alphabet; to handle them by computer is not so big a problem. On the other hand, however, there are so many kinds of Kanjis that we have to have special means to treat them.

The Report of the Japanese Language Council (1981) and the Japanese Government Notification (1981) classified Kanjis in three categories:

1. Kyoiku (Educational) Kanji: 96 characters
Kanjis in this category are taught in elementary and junior high schools. They are essential for describing elementary documents and text books used in basic education.

2. Joyo (Conventional) Kanji: 1945 characters including category 1.
Characters in this category are widely used in newspapers, magazines, journals, etc. and they are almost sufficient to describe scientific and engineering papers.

3. Jinmei (Person's Name) Kanji: 166 characters
For the names of Japanese persons, sometimes special Kanjis are used. The Jinmei Kanjis are permitted for person's names as well as the Joyo Kanji.

These categories are enacted by the government and recommended for public use to promote the progress of culture and education. Besides these characters, many other Kanjis are used in proper nouns, novels, old literature, etc. In fact, we can find more than 50,000 Kanjis in Cino-Japanese dictionaries, but most of them are seldom used in daily life. Furthermore, we have simplified characters in the Joyo Kanjis instead of ancient complex Chinese characters.

For processing Japanese characters, a character code system has been standardised in the JIS (Japan Industrial Standard) (see *Handbook of Information Processing*, Japanese Standards Association, 1986), and thus the Kanjis can be processed by computers using this code system. The JIS Kanji code consists of two levels, Level 1 and Level 2, each containing 2,965 and 3,388 characters, respectively. A problem is that the levels are not consistent with the above classification. Furthermore, a modified code system for simplifying the processing is used by some vendors, and the printing industry is using another code system for their computerisation. Such various code systems cause incompatibility and complexity in applications.

In order to handle the Kanjis by computer, means are required to input and output them to and from the computers. Japanese characters can usually be expressed by a dot matrix, such as 16x16, 24x24, 32x32, and more dots. In most applications, the 24x24 dot matrix is used, examples of which can be found in Table 1. Thus, they can be provided as output on displays or printers in this way. The most difficult and important item is the input methods which will be described in greater detail in the following.

4.2 Input of Kana and Kanji

As for Kana, there are principally two methods:

(A-1) Romaji-Kana Conversion
Each Kana can be expressed by *Romaji* which is a combination of one or more alphabets, and therefore the Kana is input using a usual alphabetical keyboard by the Romaji-Kana conversion method. Hiragana and Katakana can be selected by using a shift code. By this method, a person familiar with an alphabetical typewriter can easily input Kanas in blind touching.

(A-2) Kana Keyboard
Figure 5 shows the JIS Kana keyboard in which 48 Kana characters are assigned on the keyboard with the Kana shift key. In order to use this keyboard in touch typing, one should be trained. In view of the compatibility between English and Japanese typewriting, method (A-1) is preferred, but as far as the average number of strokes is concerned, methods (A-2) is efficient.

For the Kanjis there are basically three methods:

(B-1) Character Tablet or Special Keyboard
The Kanjis are tabulated in a matrix and one character is selected by pointing. Each Kanji has sound(s) as well as meaning(s), and usually Kanjis are grouped in a tablet according to sounds. Figure 6 shows an example of the tablet which has been used for mechanical Japanese typewriting. For Kanji tele-typewriting, a special keyboard has been used in which each key contains 12 Kanjis, one of which is selected by a group of shift keys, the former operated by the right hand and latter by the left hand. This type of method is efficient for professional use, and has been used in newspaper printing, but requires special hardware and a trained operator.

(B-2) Kana-Kanji Conversion
As stated, each Kanji has sound(s) which can be expressed by Kana(s). Therefore, if one inputs Kana(s) corresponding to a specific Kanji by using method (A-1) or (A-2), then several Kanjis having that sound will be displayed, and one of them is selected. This is referred to as Kana-Kanji conversion, and has the advantage of not requiring special hardware. However, it needs the selecting operation out of several candidates, which interrupts continuous typing operation. To avoid this, the conversion is made in idiom basis which can reduce the number of alternatives. Table 1 explains the Kana-Kanji Conversion Method. Recently, by introducing syntax algorithm and AI (Artificial Intelligence) technology, the conversion is made in phrase or sentence basis which minimises the selecting operation.

(B-3) Multi-Stroke Touch Typing
The conventional keyboard has about 50 keys corresponding to alpha-numerals and symbols. By using them in a multi-stroke basis, we can input many kinds of Kanjis. Ohiwa (1983) has developed a multi-stroke inputting method in which 725 frequently used Kanjis are assigned by two strokes and another 1,800 seldom used characters by three strokes. Although this method needs special training, a person trained for three months can input about 1,000 Japanese characters per minute, which is about two times faster than method (B-2). Another advantage of this method is that the typing operation is carried out

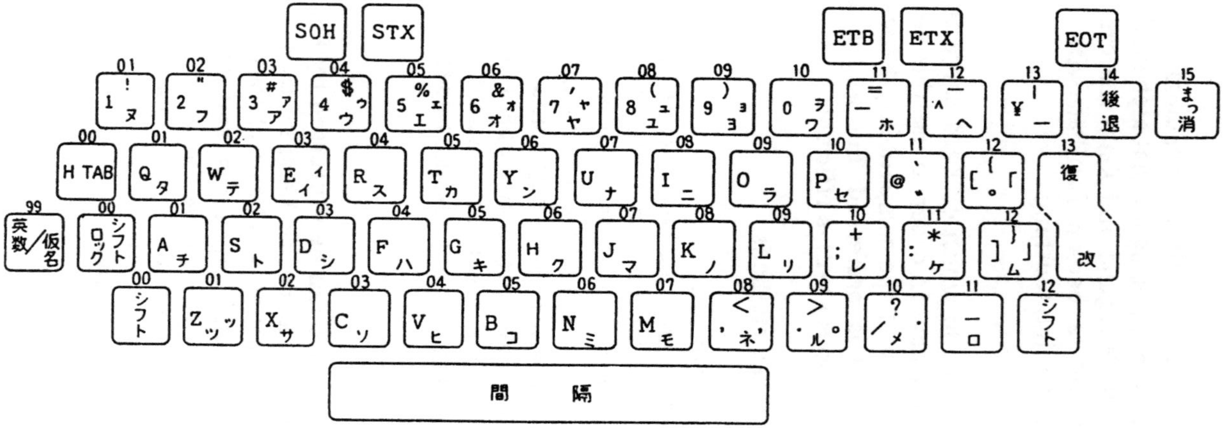

Figure 5. Layout of the JIS Kana Keyboard

Figure 6. Example of a Character Tablet

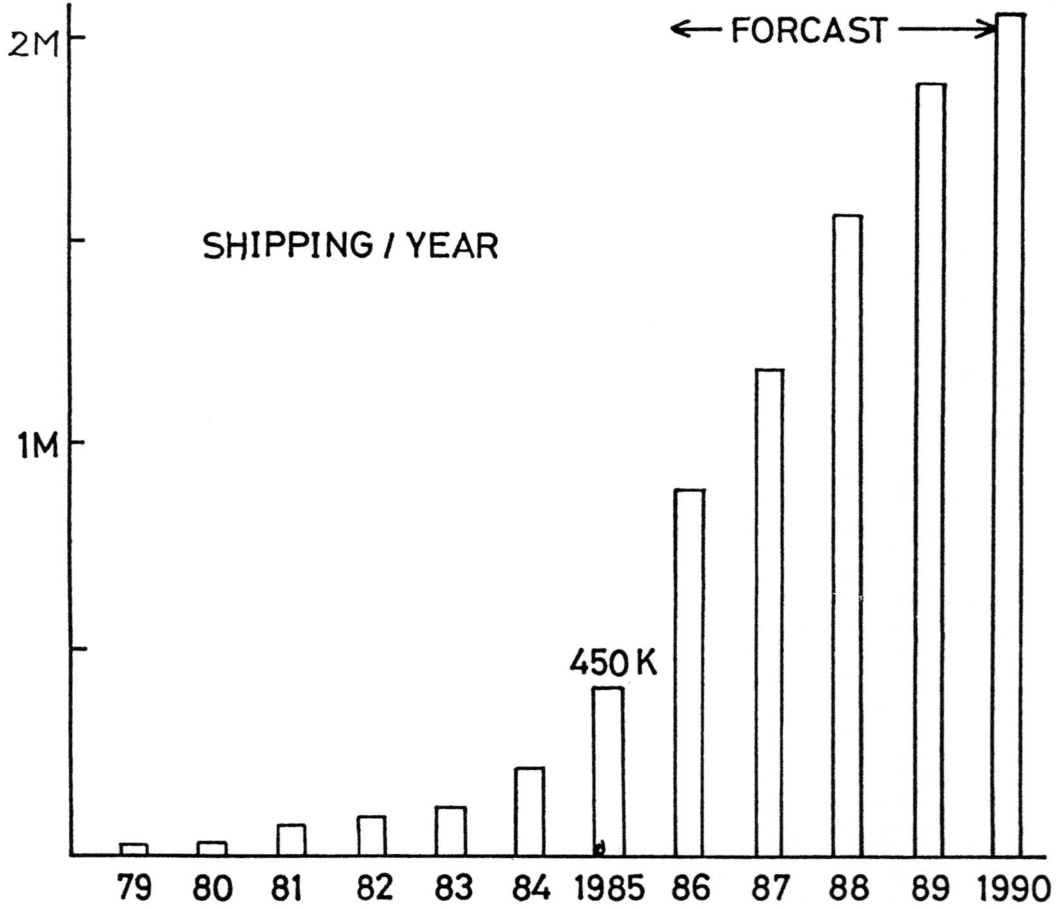

Figure 7. Production of a Japanese Word Processor

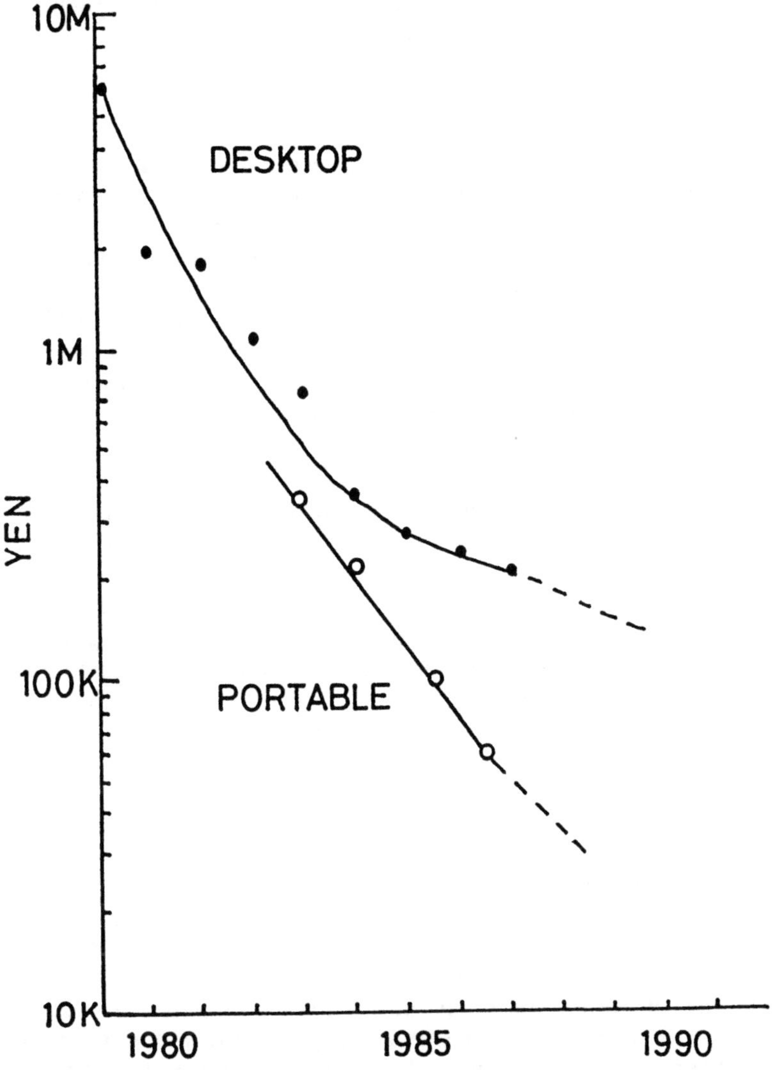

Figure 8. Price of a Japanese Word Processor

through the right hand side of the human brain, just as in English typewriting, in rhythmical action without interruptions.

4.3 Japanese Word Processors

Figure 7 shows the production trend and forecast of Japanese word processors, and Figure 8 the price trend. In the 1970s they were very expensive and of the console type, but with the advancement of hardware and software, desk-top and portable types have appeared and the price is rapidly decreasing comparable to conventional mechanical typewriters. Many kinds of Japanese word processors are now available in the market. The input methods (A-1), and (B-2) are widely used. Table 2 is part of the portable word processors and many vendors are competing with enhanced performance at lower prices. Personal computers are also used for word processing, for which various third party software packages are available on the market.

One of the most important problems with word processors is standardisation. The man-machine interfaces are different from vendor to vendor, and there is even no compatibility in document files with the same vendor. Vendors are likely to adopt their own system for distinguishing their products against those of competitors. At present, we have to learn manuals before using different types of machines, but it is desirable to be able to use them with a minimum amount of instruction like conventional typewriters. For electronic mail, word processors will be connected to communication networks, and therefore it is essential to standardise the communication protocol. We are developing an electronic mail system for Japanese characters compatible with multi-vendor machines, which are currently in an experimental phase (see Akimaru et al. 1987).

The abovementioned problem is also related to culture and education. Unlike in the US and European countries, the Japanese word processor has a great impact on the culture in this country. Reading and writing Japanese characters including Kanjis are an essential ability of the Japanese people, and a large effort is made in the learning of Kanjis in basic education in Japan. Introduction of word processors, however, might spoil the writing ability, and even if one would be able to read them, one may not be able to write, because of heavy reliance on the word processor. Moreover, there is often a limit to the kinds of Kanjis available in handy word processors. Therefore, elegant Japanese expressions cannot be made by using limited characters, which might give rise to a bad influence on Japanese literature and culture. Thus, the utilisation and standardisation of the Japanese word processor also needs to be assessed from the viewpoint of education and culture. Similar problems may occur in other countries using Kanjis or similar characters, like in China and Korea. Hence, these issues deserve discussion at an international level.

5. ASSESSMENT OF NEW SERVICES AND TECHNOLOGIES

So far, new information services have been discussed by taking examples from facsimile and word processors. It should be noted here again that the new services are provided in a free competition world. In the US, Japan and some

TABLE 2
Examples of a Portable Japanese Word Processor

Vendor	Type	Characters	Idioms	File	Printer
Casio	HW-110	3,616	10,221	ATR	16x16
	HW-700	4,409	50,000	ATR	24x24
Canon	PEN-16	2,965	14,000	ATR	16x16
	PEN-30	3,956	45,105	ATR	24x24
Sanyo	SWP-M5	3,865	70,000	ATR	24x24
Sharp	HD-50	3,751	31,000	ATR	24x24
	HD-80	4,434	50,000	ATR	24x24
Sony	HW-40	3,727	33,558	ATR	24x24
Epson	PWP-500	3,763	120,000	ICC	24x24
Toshiba	RUPO-R50	3,482	68,500	FLD	24x24
NEC	MINI-3	4,297	30,000	ATR	24x24
	MINI-7	3,636	35,000	FLD	24x24
Fujitsu	LITE-U	3,942	37,000	ATR	16x16
	LITE-K	3,942	40,000	ATR	24x24
Brother	NP-305	3,548	43,000	FLD	24x24
Matsushita	FW-7K	3,418	60,000	ATR	24x24
Ricoh	MR-5	3,668	22,000	ATR	16x16
	MR-15	3,584	38,000	ATR	24x24

ATR: Audio Tape Recorder ICC: IC Card FLD: Flexible Disk

European countries, telecommunications have been deregulated. This could promote versatile new services provided at low prices. In such a situation, however, providers have to pursue their own profit on a competitive basis which might not necessarily meet the direction of increasing human prosperity. In this context, we have to establish the criteria for assessing the new services and technologies and to provide the guidelines for their development. Here we will suggest proposals for assessment.

(1) Standardisation for Compatibility and Cost Reduction

As mentioned several times, the standardisation of new information services is important for man-machine interface, communication protocol, etc. A good example is the facsimile, for which users enjoy the universal connectivity. The standardisation also contributes to realising the functions in VLSI, which brings about a drastic cost reduction. If standardisation were premature, it would obstruct the progress of technologies but, on the other hand, if too late, it would become difficult to establish the standard. International organisations such as CCITT and ISO (International Standard Organization) contribute to the standardisation of telecommunications and computers. Academic institutions, such as the IEEE (Institute of Electrical and Electronics Engineers) in the US, are also performing such activities. Timely standardisation for the new information services and products should be promoted as national and international projects.

(2) Utilisation of Software Resources

The information services rely mostly on the software development which is originally created by human activity. Because of the lack of software manpower in view of the increasing needs, we are facing the problem of a software crisis (see also the contribution by Inose in the present volume). Means should be explored for increasing the software productivity as well as improving the development environment. In addition to these, the utilisation of software resources should be considered. Software for similar applications is being produced individually by vendors, because there is no appropriate system for protecting the property of software by means of, for example, a patent system. Although there is copyright protection, it is not effective as the patent system, which contributes mostly to the progress of technologies and industries. If we had a suitable system for protecting software by royalties, then it could be reused while wasted production of similar software could be prevented. Therefore, it is desirable to establish a system like an international treaty for patenting software property in order to encourage the utilisation of these resources on a worldwide basis.

(3) Establishment of Institutions for Assessment

As discussed, the new information services have to be assessed in view of human prosperity. In the present situation, however, the new services are mainly developed on a technology-oriented basis, and provided in a free competition world. They should be re-evaluated from the viewpoint of human prosperity and social needs, and the assessed ones would have to be developed on a need-oriented basis. Systems such as aid grants and tax reduction would encourage the development of the preferred services and technologies. The government and social institutions would have to establish such systems, as well as organisations for its evaluation and assessment, in order to promote the synergy of technology and humanity.

6. CONCLUSIONS

In the present contribution, experiences from new Japanese information services, issues on the new services and technologies and proposals on their assessment have been dealt with. It is hoped that many people in various fields are aware of such assessment problems and will discuss the new information services and technologies for achieving a prosperous information society in the 21st century.

REFERENCES

Ohiwa, H., et al., Touch Typing of Japanese Text, International Conference of Text Processing with a Large Character Set, Tokyo, 1983,

Akimaru. H. et al., A Campus Electronic Mail System Using Switching Server, Technical REport SE87-100, Institute Electro., Information and Communications Engineering, 1987.

INFORMATION TECHNOLOGY IN AN INTERNATIONAL PERSPECTIVE

Hiroshi Inose

1. INTRODUCTION

As a result of the remarkable progress in information technology, every aspect of diversified socioeconomic activities in the world has increasingly become dependent upon information. As satellites and ocean cables interconnect telecommunication and broadcasting networks of many countries, the socioeconomic activities in these countries are becoming closely knit, transcending physical distances.

As computers improve productivity in industries and save manpower through automation, labour issues are emerging at a global scale. As information technology becomes crucial for industrialised countries, competition in international market places is intensifying. And as transborder flows of information become conspicuous, concerns have been expressed about the obstacles preventing a free flow of information across national boundaries. No doubt, a new informational environment is being formed as innovation in information technology intensifies.

Obviously, one of the crucial factors for maintaining sustained economic growth, alleviating unemployment and improving quality of life is the enhancement of innovation in information technology that promotes positive adjustment of industrial structure. Considering the fact that technological innovation has been stimulated mainly by keen competition in the market place, climate for fair competition should be continuously maintained. However, in view of the fact that information technology increasingly requires enormous resources in terms of capital and manpower, international cooperation should also be promoted to the greatest possible extent.

Cooperation in this respect takes the form of international division of labour in research, development and production. For such cooperation to be established and fostered, some fundamental understanding in relevant issues seems to be necessary.

First, enterprises or sometimes countries should have sufficient understanding of the high degree of complexity, scale and diversity of modern information technologies so that they could accept the fact that any single enterprise or country, no matter how powerful, cannot tackle all information technology problems itself. Secondly, they should acknowledge the fact that any impediment which hampers the free flow of information technologies results in duplication of efforts and fragmentation of resources and thereby ends up not only weakening innovative capability of the world, but also complicates international standardisation activities. Thirdly, they should be able to understand the implications of changing technological environment, namely the diversification of end-users' needs, the emerging importance of software, the international demand and supply of knowledge-intensive labour force, and so forth.

In the following paragraphs, we will pay particular attention to the importance of the free flow of technology to promote international division of labour in research, development and production in the information technology area, and to the prospect of international division of labour in the area of software production.

2. FREE FLOW OF TECHNOLOGIES - A CRUCIAL FACTOR FOR INTERNATIONAL DIVISION OF LABOUR

Increasing competition in the area of information technology has been casting a shadow on the free exchange of ideas among scientists and technologists who belong to different organisations, enterprises, or sometimes countries. For instance, in some information technology areas, it has become increasingly difficult to distinguish non-defence technology from defence technology, or to draw a line between basic science and applied technology. As a result of this situation, various forms of protectionism are appearing on the horizon that restrict unrestricted mobility of scientists and technologists or hamper free exchange of scientific and technological knowledge.

If scientific and technological activities are split into a number of closed and isolated small elements, resources in terms of research funds and personnel will be fragmented and will result in less efficient and more duplicated efforts. Industrial specifications will become more diversified and international standardisation more difficult. Ultimately, the economic strength of the world which has emerged from rapid innovations in information technology may be weakened to a considerable extent.

Sustained economic growth and prosperity in the world has been brought about to a large extent by scientific discoveries and technological innovations which have emanated from free exchange of scientific and technological knowledge among industrialised countries. Duplication of research and development investment has been kept to a minimum. Diversification of world industrial standards has been avoided to the greatest possible extent. The United States, in particular, has been extremely successful in this regard since the 1930s when an enormous flow of extremely talented scientists and engineers emigrated from Europe to the United States, mainly due to totalitarianism and racism of the ruling Nazis. It may be clear that without the significant contributions made by immigrants and their sons, the leadership in the United Stated in science and technology would never have been established. The superiority in science and technology of the free world, centred around the US leadership, strengthened the economy and national security of the free world and thus contributed a great deal to maintaining world peace.

It is therefore crucial, not only for the United States or Europe but also for Japan to maintain and enhance unrestricted mobility of scientists and free flow of knowledge at the highest possible level. For Japan especially, whose society has a distinct monoracial structure, it is most important to encourage talented immigrants and visitors to participate in scientific programmes sponsored by public and private sectors. The impact to be brought about by the immigrants on Japanese value systems, ways of thinking and so forth will be very great. The more a country protects its knowledge, the more it becomes isolated from other scientific communities and it ends up being less competitive. Protectionism in any form should be very carefully and forcefully avoided, not only to maintain the sustained growth of the world economy, but also to enhance the national strength in science and technology.

3. SOFTWARE PRODUCTION - A PROSPECTIVE AREA FOR INTERNATIONAL DIVISION OF LABOUR

As microelectronics permeates deeper into all aspects of socioeconomic activities around the world, there will be a constant demand for an immense amount of software. It will become virtually impossible for computer manufacturers in the US, Japan and a few European countries to produce all the necessary software. Even if they could produce the volume, they could not possibly cope with the sheer diversity of the needs of the end-users unless the application software was produced on a local basis. This is why it is so important to develop an international division of labour in the software industry.

The software production in industrialised host countries that import computers should be strengthened so that they can produce diversified application software to meet endusers needs. Considering the fact that the application software is the most lucrative part of all the software needed for computers, this may not only enhance the host countries' economies but also contribute to the substantial increase of employment opportunities.

The software industry should also be encouraged in developing countries that are strengthening their higher education systems, or where highly educated people have too few opportunities in their home countries to utilise their capabilities, even though higher education is established. The unusually large proportion of Americans of Chinese origin in the field of software technology in the United States seems to suggest that Chinese people are in some way especially well suited to software production. Whatever the reason, China itself and Hong Kong, Taiwan and Singapore, and countries where overseas Chinese play an important economic role, such as Thailand, Malaysia, Indonesia and the Philippines, have a tremendous potential for software production. This is particularly true of China, and its billion people, who are all involved in the task of modernisation. While the introduction of ultramodern steel manufacturing plants, for example, will do little to augment employment, software production, which is greatly knowledge intensive as well as labour intensive, could create a vast number of jobs, and therefore is certainly 'appropriate technology'. Growth in software production can bring economic prosperity to the whole region, and through strengthening of political stability, may contribute to the wider context of world peace. It may be conceivable that the East Asian region will take the lead in this industry in the twenty-first century.

Particularly in Europe, the argument is often used that the development of computer technology only aggravates the technology gap between the advanced and developing countries and strikes a heavy blow to industry in the developing countries, which depend entirely on cheap wages, pushing unemployment up. Such claims are justified to some extent, but it must be remembered that in Hong Kong, Taiwan, Singapore and elsewhere integrated circuit assembly and production have promoted economic growth and helped to stimulate employment. The same will be true of software in these areas. Success or failure depends on the government, whether or not it undertakes effective policies for education and training, and workers themselves, whether they have the drive and diligence to accept the challenges of the new field.

The real problem lies with some of the advanced countries of Europe. They persist in the pessimistic view that microelectronics cause unemployment and tend to understress technological innovation in this field. Efforts to soothe these fears and dispel misconceptions must continue, but unless Europeans themselves recognise that microelectronics technology is their own problem and respond constructively to its implications, they themselves will be the losers. If they do not recognise the facts of what is happening and respond adequately, those developing countries which do realise the potential of software production will win in the competition. In the eighteenth century, some world powers failed to grasp the significance of the industrial revolution. Blindly continuing to rely solely on exploitation of their colonies, they eventually fell behind, becoming the cultural backwater of Europe. The microelectronics revolution today is of such immense historical significance that it too may transform the developing countries, which recognise their potential into advanced countries, and push the advanced countries that refuse to heed the challenges to the brink of disaster.

4. CONCLUDING REMARKS

What has been described is only a few of many diversified aspects to be taken into account in considering the impact of information technology upon the international environment. It is certain that at this crucial moment in time, when industrial structure is undergoing a drastic change and when solidarity among industrialised and industrialising allies is urgently called for, international cooperation through well thought out and agreed upon division of labour requires serious attention.

It should be admitted, however, that no matter how well the international division of labour in information technology is devised and will contribute to a sustained growth of the world economy, such problems as those in the international market place cannot be eradicated completely. One of the reasons is that information technology is one of many factors which affect international trade. In such instances - e.g. trade in automobiles and home video recorders - marketing policies and manufacturing skills have overridden technological capability as a major factor affecting international trade. Nevertheless, exchange of ideas and deepening of mutual understanding that could be fostered in the course of promoting international division of labour in information technology, will open the way to the harmonisation and rationalisation of international trade.

ROLE OF INFORMATION IN TECHNOLOGY TRANSFER

Manas Chatterji

1. INFORMATION AND DEVELOPMENT

The trend of economic development in the developed areas is mostly away from the extraction and fabricative activities to processing and service activities. The transformation emerges when information and knowledge are the most important variables rather than labour and capital. Production is often seen as the vehicle for moving the society from one stage to another, but it is really information and communication which make the transformation quicker and more lasting. When we look at the development process of the so called poor countries, we find that, in many cases, although considerable amounts of resources have been spent on economic development, this industrialisation process has not led to socioeconomic transformation. Many of the activities that we usually associate with the process of industrialisation did not develop, and the key sectors remained stagnant primarily due to lack of information and communication. Not only did this not create any additional employment, but it also did not contribute to the efficiency of the primary and secondary sectors.

The developing countries are mostly rural with a high degree of illiteracy. For lack of communication, millions of people are away from the mainstream of society. Information technology in the form of pre-packaged programmes can greatly remove illiteracy and form the base of a service-oriented society.

The technological revolution has been ushered in by the computer. Just as the steam engines and electricity enhanced the speed of the Industrial Revolution, the computer is now spearheading technological revolution. Information removes uncertainty. It is a product but not in the traditional sense, since even when it is sold, it remains the property of the creator. Although licensing and copyright regulation protect the right of the inventor, it is becoming increasingly difficult to guarantee this right. The computer is now being connected with telephones and telecommunication. In addition, we are now using microwave relay, satellite transmission, coaxial cables, credit cards, newspapers, teletypewriters, telephotos, teletypesetters, and telemetry. All these sources together are often called 'communications'. These developments indicate that the post-industrial society is moving to a service society.

Innovation is the basis of this technological revolution. The management of innovation, starting from the provision of capital investment for research and development, is an important subject in itself, and I do not intend to discuss it in detail here. Instead, we shall investigate the diffusion of ideas within an organisation, the relation between scientists and engineers, and the way in which people in organisations learn from each other (from scientific literature or from a technological gatekeeper). The role of published materials, formal organisation, and a project team must also be considered.

Another significant aspect of this process is the spread of technological innovation in geographical space. Although considerable effort has been made on analysing macroeconomic aspects of regional economic growth, the role of information technology in regional development is not understood. The telephone had a powerful impact in leading to the growth of large companies which were located in the major cities of the countries. It was possible, through telephone, to control economic activities at a number of points in space from a central location. The information technology has further developed, and it raises the interesting question of whether their developments will lead to decentralisation in space. Just as the concept of the steam engine has led to a wide area of application in transport and manufacturing, similarly, the computer is influencing the development of far wider use than what was originally intended.

The most interesting aspect of this computer revolution is that it is following process and product innovation. From the point of view of product innovation, it is deciding *what* goods are to be produced. Process innovation decides *how* the goods are to be produced. Any region which fails to introduce the modern innovation methods due to a variety of reasons will lose jobs through interregional competition. There will also be some displacement of jobs due to the introduction of new technology. This effect is expected to be much less than the first factor. Process innovation will also lead to some gain in new service jobs, displacing some old types. However, it is expected that the number of jobs created in new locations will be much fewer. It is true that some jobs displaced in one place and one time will be replaced by another set of jobs in another place and time. This change may take place due to the effort of a single company or through the consumer demand level in the national economy. It will, of course, be difficult to predict the spatial scale of this development. This change will have international dimensions, particularly, through the effect of multinational corporations. Although it is not difficult to anticipate which industries will be affected, it is hard to estimate interoccupational sectoral and locational linkages. The adaptive ability of a particular city or region will depend upon the economic infrastructure, entrepreneurship, and efficiency of the private and public agencies. A high-speed low-cost transmission has been developed only for a number of linked locations in space. Although it is often suggested that satellite communications will remove this discrepancy in space, it is also possible to reap these benefits from large uses. Thus the reduced communication cost will benefit the large enterprises located in the major cities. Medium and small scale enterprises will be kept outside. The benefits of the automotic switching devices will also come in stages, and the time delay will greatly affect the comparative advantage of the enterprises in medium sized enterprises. Thus, the benefits of technological development of communication will favour large cities and economically advanced areas rather than depressed areas.

In an international dimension, there is a higher level of transaction between capital cities. Peripheral countries are at a disadvantage, and the high-cost countries happen to be the poorest, since this high cost will be reflected in the profitability of the enterprise in the country.

It is true that there is abundant scope for the small scale and medium sized companies to produce information technology. Since the role of R&D in such industries is much more important compared to manufacturing, it has some advantages. Some of them are (1) reduction in the amount of fixed capital necessary for such a venture, (2) change in the market structure, namely, overlapping information processing and information transmission, and (3) the accelerated growth in the technology industry, disfavouring any particular industry from keeping the leadership for a long time. However, in this sector the market structure is so oligopolistic that any such advantages are neutralised by the more powerful market power.

The same pattern is visible in software industries. Again, the application of information technology in small scale industries and enterprises will not be realised unless it is marketed by specialists to show how it is relevant for their operations.

Although telecommunications are necessary conditions for development, they are not sufficient. Since telecommunications are international goods, quantity differences between countries will determine the development of a country's cities and regions. The most important outcome will be the development of network, switching and services. The telephone will be just another computer terminal and part of a highly complex communication system. The introduction of the fibre optics cable, although it reduced the cost of transmission, has formed the intercity rather than intracity communication link. But whereas the higher density inner city cost may be lower, the population in that area is poorer. Thus, the benefits of lower cost will depend on pricing policy regulations and on public policy.

Technical constraints shift with time. Presently current technology is still making considerable growth in circuit complexity. Technical advances happen in either the revolutionary mode or the evolutionary mode. A revolution is in the order of the invention of a vacuum tube or a transistor. The evolutionary mode is in the order of technical growth from a transistor to an Integrated Circuit Chip.

Microprocessors arrange machines to compute, store information, and sense and control outputs. The microprocessors make machines faster, safer and more reliable. In the office, mircoprocessors have replaced typewriters with word processors. They now both monitor the engine performance in automobiles and control heating and air conditioning in large facilities. In electronic packaging, microprocessors replace many IC chips, thus making printed circuit layout less complex. The microprocessor is capable of many different functions which can be altered by changing a programmed IC chip. One other advantage is that microprocessor-based products can be easily serviced. Some products have built-in diagnostics.

Changes made in manufacturing are needed to accommodate the new microprocessor-based products. Workspace requirements, capital equipment costs, and overall production time are all reduced. Due to more complex devices, companies must rely on fewer, more specialised, suppliers which will subject them to delays and price increases.

Some of the advantages of microprocessor designs over mechanical parts are quicker lead times and lower financial investments. One marketing strategy is to introduce the microprocessor machines as top of the line so consumers will pay high prices for them to enable the company to get some repayment of the R&D funds. Microprocessors affect the job market for many reasons. In the short run, employment may rise due to gaining of market shares, even though fewer workers per output price are needed. Entry costs for new firms are low, as are capital requirements. Products can be designed relatively easily and inexpensively. As the industry grows, and the systems are more tailored to the consumers' needs, the entry costs will rise.

The electronics industry is frequently dependent on universities to provide research and development. As the price/performance level continues to drop, the electronics industry is penetrating other technical sectors. The university helps the electronics industry through its educational programmes and specific links between the university and companies.

It is believed that university R&D is lagging behind industry mainly due to competition for good scientists between industry and the university. Industry generally has more to offer in attractive conditions of employment. Small companies generate more jobs than the large companies. Small companies must also be more cautious of the use of R&D funds. Electronic technology leads to more structured organisation and may adversely affect upward mobility. Of course, telecommunications alone is not the only factor. Just as new technology can revive the depressed areas in developed countries, it can also help the developing countries through its transfer.

The technology transfer is greatly facilitated by the operations of the multinational corporations. Corporations augment capital, develop associated industries, and provide more foreign exchange. Of course, multinational corporations may cause damage to indigenous industries and put pressure on the availability of local capital, labour and raw materials. The profit motive of the multinationals may transform the country into a dependent state. Most of the developing countries in the world have a strong public sector, and the role of the private sector is quite limited. In fact, the role of the government, its political philosophy, and also the international political situation greatly determine the amount and nature of the technology transfer. It is well known that western countries are quite hesitant to transfer the technology to some developing countries because they are afraid that it will be transferred to the Communist block countries. Since this is a give-and-take process, the sender must be willing. Of course, this willingness is possible if the sender also benefits from such a transaction. Technology is not only machinery. It basically means knowledge which can be used to produce goods. Thus, in addition to the tangible things such as machinery, hardware, and software, means of transferring knowledge should be discussed.

In recent years, the term 'appropriate technology' has been used, since the suitability of the transfer must be judged by the existence of the market, raw materials, the production possibilities. When we consider the question of market, we must discuss it both nationally and internationally. We have to be sure that the raw materials exist within the country or can be imported without straining the foreign exchange reserve. In modern mass production technology, scale economies are very important. The size of the market will be a determining factor in deciding whether an optimum size of the industry is feasible in the receiving country. The basic problem in the less developed countries is loss of employment opportunity. Any technology which makes this unemployment situation worse will not be acceptable. However, it is always possible that the introduction of new technology may reduce the employment on one sector but increase the employment potential in others. The overall employment picture in the long term is the very point to keep in mind. Modern day high technology is also risky in terms of accidents unless the workers are properly trained. This aspect of training and management is an important ingredient in any transfer. The partnership between the received and sender is subject to the international political situation. Adverse political relationships often make the receiver country dependent on the sender for spare parts and maintenance. Seeds of innovation have a multiplier effect. Obviously, technology is most suited if it has a maximum multiplier effect.

Continuous assessment of technology not only from the point of view of technical matters but from social values is needed. This social assessment distinguishes technology transfer between rich and poor countries from that within the country. Whereas the management style of technology transfer has to be something quite new, it can build up a new spirit of entrepreneurship. It may also open up new ways to measure the magnitude of transfer and identify the different channels of transfer. The development of appropriate information systems to monitor and evaluate the effectiveness of managerial technology will motivate indigenous talent so as to induce reverse transfer. So far we have discussed the problem associated with technology transfer in terms of managerial considerations. But the use of techniques developed in management science, economics, and marketing in judging the optimum ways to perform these transactions needs to be discussed. In the second part of the paper, we shall discuss concepts and methodology in economics and management, such as production function, cost function, linear programming, econometric models, input-output analysis, diffusion models, and economics of innovation and technical change. An evaluation will be made, indicating ways in which powerful techniques can be developed. But the focus will be their relevance to technology transfer and impact in the developing countries.

Since most of the technologies are the property of the developed countries, the poor countries are very much dependent on them. However, the licensing and proprietary rights created an oligopolistic market. So if a developing country wants to produce, it also wants trading and marketing rights.

Technology is transferred in different forms - formal (direct investment, joint collaboration) and informal (meetings and people changing jobs). It may be packaged when the direct investment is associated with services. More advanced sophisticated technologies are usually more packaged than less sophisticated ones. In the initial process of industrialisation, countries tried to industrialise as quickly as possible and did not consider the cost of the project very much. Later on, they were more conscious about the importance, self-reliance, and appropriateness of the technology, so a process of learning emerged. The transaction price in such deals was hard to identify. Since in most cases intrafirm sales and technology flows were involved, it is difficult to separate the real price and the price paid for such a transaction. It may be that the cost to the receiver was quite high, but that does not mean that the produce is not worth the price. After the importation of technology, local technological capacities grew. However, due to the restrictive nature of the imported technology, the technology suffers. The use of selective technological imports to protect local technology has paid dividends in the long run, as evidenced from Japan's technological development. However, for this strategy one needs a fair degree of technological sophistication and administrative judgement. A restricted policy on importation may induce independence, reduce cost, and accelerate the learning process. Some countries have also discouraged too much packaging even to the extent of banning ownership. A national registration system has been set up in many countries, enabling registration when it meets certain criteria. A tax system with a preferential tax can also affect the desired type of technological transfer. Technology transfer is a very important means to narrow income differences between countries. However, it is becoming a game with developed countries dictating the terms and conditions of the transfer. 'Intermediate technology' is superior to primitive technology but still cheaper and simpler than advanced technology. This phrase has a bad connotative meaning of 'second best'. 'Appropriate technology' describes economic productivity by what is determined by need, and it assumes that the only development that makes sense is development of the people and their skills, by the people and for the people.

'Alternative technology', on the other hand, is a phrase describing the processes of rejecting modern technology of developed countries. Technologies should be compatible with existing culture in undeveloped countries and conducive to the evolution of more diversity in developed countries. Cultural beliefs, values and norms change relatively slowly - certainly more slowly than technology, and often more slowly than organisational strructures. Technological change is a force of social change. Structure is a product of the Appropriate Technology movement. There are many agricultural situations where it is expected that small farms and small holdings will be run by expert teams rather than by the large scale energy intensive process as it exists presently.

Transfer of Technology to developing countries involves a host of political, social and economic problems. From the point of view of economics, the problem here is to link two economic systems with different production functions with the help of transfer of knowledge. For the purposes of these linkages and diffusion, we can use some of the concepts and methodologies of economics and management. We now summarise some of them below.

2. SOME CONCEPTS AND METHODOLOGIES, OF ECONOMICS AND MANAGEMENT RELATED TO DIFFUSION

2.1 Production Function

The Cobb Douglas form of the production function is:

$$Q = AK^{\alpha}L^{\beta}. \tag{1}$$

The Cobb Douglas form can be rewritten as:

$$\frac{Q}{L} = AK^{\alpha}L^{\beta-1} = A(K/L)^{\alpha}L^{\lambda} \tag{2}$$

where Q = output; K = capital; L = labour, and

$$\lambda = \alpha + \beta - 1 = \varepsilon - 1. \tag{3}$$

In the Cobb Douglas production function, A is the efficiency constant: a higher value of A means a more efficient process and corresponds to a high value of Q.

To account for the time effect, a time trend, t, is added to the production function:

$$Q_t = f(t,K,L). \tag{4}$$

The Cobb Douglas function becomes:

$$Q_t = Ae^{\theta t}K_t^{\alpha}L_t^{\beta} \tag{5}$$

The exponential rate of technical progress, t, implies that output rises at a rate of θ per cent per annum and is not affected by changes in input. This function is Hicks-neutral since the marginal rate of substitution of K and L is unaffected (Wynn and Holden 1974).

A second approach to time-series of the Cobb Douglas production function is the use of the vintage model (Wynn and Holden 1974). This assumes capital of different vintages (or ages) of a capital:

$$Q_t(v) = Ae^{\theta v}K_t^{\alpha}(v)\,L_t^{\beta}(v) \tag{6}$$

The vintages, v, explain capital of a certain age. This capital contains equipment with specific efficiencies, and the capital has a specific cost of capital.

Using the Cobb Douglas production function:

$$Q_t = Ae^{\lambda t}K_tC_t^{\beta}L_t^{1-\beta} \tag{7}$$

where

Q_t = output
C_t = capital
L_t = labour
K_t = $\Sigma_i w_i R_{t-i}$ = accumulated and still productive research capital
R_t = measures investment in Research in period t
W_i connects the past research to the current knowledge
λ = rate of disembodied external technical change.

The research capital function K has three properties: "... the lag between investment in research and the actual invention of a new technique or product; the lag between invention and the development of complete market acceptance of the new product; and its disappearance from the currently utilised stock of knowledge due to changes in external circumstances and the development of superior techniques or products by competitors (depreciation and obsolescence)" (Griliches and Ringstad 1971).

2.2 CES Production Functions

The CES production function is written as:

$$V = \beta[\delta K^{-\rho} + (1-\delta)L^{-\rho}]^{-\mu/\rho}. \qquad (8)$$

In the CES production function, "... the output elasticities are not constant and $\sigma \neq 1$, but both the elasticity of scale ($\varepsilon = \mu$) and the elasticity of substitution [$\sigma = 1/(1+\rho)$] are constant." The CES production function can be rewritten as:

$$\frac{V}{L} = \beta L^{h}[\delta + (1-\delta)(K/L)^{-\rho}]^{-\mu/\rho} \qquad (9)$$

where $h = \mu - 1$ (Griliches and Ringstad 1971).

2.3 Capital and Technical Change in the CES Production Function

To make a two-level CES production function, a number of inputs must be aggregated into a single index. This must be done for all types of capital and labour. Sato (1967) concludes through an empirical study that investments can be broken into a primary stage, (determining an outlay on new asset acquisition) and a secondary stage (allocating the outlay on various types of capital). Sato's study predicts gross investments using capital of two types, structure and equipment. When using the correct proportions of capital for structure and equipment, Sato has a good fit for predicted gross investment.

2.4 Trans-log Production Function

The trans-log production function is derived from the CES production function:

$$Y = \gamma[\delta K^{-\rho} + (1-\delta)L^{-\rho}]^{-\mu/\rho}. \tag{10}$$

Elasticity of scale ($\varepsilon = \mu$) and elasticity of substitution [$\sigma = 1/(1+\rho)$] are constant. In this case, technical efficiency is measured as γ.

Taking logarithms

$$\ln Y = \ln\gamma - (\mu/\rho) f(\rho) \tag{11}$$

where

$$f(\rho) = [\delta K^{-\rho} + (1-\delta)L^{-\rho}] \tag{12}$$

A Taylor series expansion around $\rho = 0$ gives:

$$f(\rho) \simeq 1 f(o) + f'(o)\rho + \frac{f''(o)}{2}\rho^2.$$

This form is used in transformation of the CES production function (Griliches and Ringstad 1971).

$$\log y = \log\gamma + \frac{\mu}{2\rho}[2(\delta\ln K + (1-\delta)\ln L + \delta^2(\ln K)^2)) + 2\delta(1-\delta)(\ln L)\ln K + (1-\delta)^2(\ln L)^2]. \tag{13}$$

Accounting for technical change in the trans-log production function is approached in the same way as it is for the CES production function.

2.5 Empirical Results of the Trans-log Production Function

Griliches and Ringstad (1971) present capital and labour data for seventeen industries. Some of the industries were meat products, textiles, printing, furniture, and paper. They analysed the data using the Cobb Douglas production function and "a more general and flexible production function form". This form has the virtue that it does not impose either the constant elasticities or the homotheticity assumptions on the data.

Various techniques for solving the production function along with three types of production functions are available. Sato's study shows good correlation when investment funds are broken down into capital equipment and capital structures.

He also shows how to aggregate different types of capital into a fairly simple two-level production function. Sato's two-level production function may be expanded, giving a method for technical change to be shown in a more flexible, higher order production function, the trans-log function. The trans-log function was not shown to be much more significant than the other functions studied, but it could be, if capital were to be
He also shows how to aggregate different types of capital into a fairly simple two-level production function. Sato's two-level production function may be expanded, giving a method for technical change to be shown in a more flexible, higher order production function, the trans-log function. The trans-log function was not shown to be much more significant than the other functions studied, but it could be, if capital were to be
aggregated and technical change considered.

It was shown that there is a significant lag of time from when a capital project starts until capital is released for expenditure. So we should be careful in applying the theoretical framework for deciding industrial or public policy.

The production function can be redesigned for a regional economy. Specific regional variables can be included there. Industry and sector-wise production factors can be constructed for such sectors as electronics. Information, innovation and diffusion over space can be specifically considered. These factors can be utilised for estimating the impact of import substitution. A function involving the transfer of knowledge, technology and raw materials, i.e. some sort of an interregional production function, can be proposed.

The use of production functions in the study of research and development is one of many avenues of research possible in the area. On the micro level, the reasons of success or failure of individual projects can be investigated. Economic historians are interested in inventions, and sociologists concern themselves with indicators of development of science. Subject matter which is now popular in economics are (1) relationship between R&D and productivity, (2) R&D and market structure, (3) relationship between patents and R&D, (4) R&D and firm size, (5) R&D and patent application, (6) R&D, innovation and technical change, (7) industrial location and R&D, and (8) use of stock market value as the indicator of success of R&D.

In recent years, there has been a considerable amount of research activity in the field of research and development, innovation and productivity. This research is used particularly when we consider the impact of technology transfer on productivity increase in the developing countries. Unfortunately, few theoretical studies of this linkage exist.

2.6 Models of New Product Development

There are some models in new product development which have been successfully used in product adoption. They have the potential for being restructured for use in technology transfer.

(1) The Bass model is the base for the model with an accelerated rate of new product diffusion:

$$\frac{dS(t)}{dt} = [p+q\frac{S(t)}{S^*}][S^*-S(t)]. \qquad (14)$$

where S^* is the total number of firms eligible to adopt the innovation
- $S(t)$ is the cumulative number of adopters
- p is the coefficient of external influence
- q is the coefficient of internal influence

When considering the help of government sponsored demonstration programmes to accelerate diffusion, the Bass model is rewritten. Therefore,

$$\frac{dS(t)}{dt} = [p+q^*T(t)]\,[S^*-S(t)] \qquad (15)$$

where $T(t) - S(t) + A(t)$

$q^* = q/S^*$

$A(t)$ is the cumulative number of government sponsored programmes at time t. It is assumed that the government will set up C demonstration programmes; there $(A(\infty)) = C$.

Equation (15) can be further broken down by making

$$\frac{dS(t)}{dt} - \frac{dS_1(t)}{dt} + \frac{dS_2(t)}{dt}$$

It is assumed p and q do not change due to number of government sponsored programmes.

Therefore:

$$\frac{dS_1(t)}{dt} - \frac{q}{S^*} A(t)\,[S^*-S(t)] \qquad (16)$$

and

$$\frac{dS_1(t)}{dt} - \frac{q}{S^*} A(t)\,[S^*-S(t)] \qquad (17)$$

The maximisation of

$$\frac{dS(t)}{dt}$$

happens when $A(t)$ becomes as large as possible, as soon as possible.

In this case, it does not pay to delay the support of demonstration programmes. The initial support is the most important. Any delay can be improved by

Studies have shown that the perceptions of the potential adopters toward innovations' attributes affect the rate of adoption. The Coleman, Shariff and Ramanathan (1976) model uses the following assumptions; the population of adopters remains constant over time, all numbers eventually adopt, the diffusion process comes from a constant source, and the impact of this source is the same on all nonadopters. The rate of adoption, from the Coleman model is:

$$\frac{da(t)}{dt} = \beta_1 (N-a(t)) \quad (18)$$

After integrating

$$a(t) = N-(N-a_o)e^{-\beta_1 t}$$

Where B_1 is a constant, N is the total population.

The only cases where the Coleman model is valid is when the influence comes from sources other than the adopted population. Examples are sales people, consultant recommendations, advertisements, articles in periodicals, etc. The assumptions of the Dodd model (19) are as follows: the population of adopters remains constant over time, all members eventually adopt, the population mixes homogeneously, adopters will adopt after seeing others using the innovation, adoption rate is dependent on both the number who adopted and the proportion of the maximum adopters who have not yet adopted, and the probability of any two individuals meeting is equal. The rate of adoption for the Dodd Model is:

$$\frac{da(t)}{dt} - \beta_2 \left(\frac{N-a(t)a(t)}{N}\right) \quad (19)$$

After integration and setting boundary condition, $t-0$, $a(t-0)-a_0$,

$$a(t) = \frac{N}{1+\left(\frac{N-a_o}{a_o}\right)e^{-\beta_2 t}} \qquad N \geq a_0 > 0$$

This model will result in an S shaped function. The Dodd model is limited by not considering impersonal sources of information important in adopter decision making.

The Generalised model assumes adoption decisions are made by both impersonal sources and contact with prior adopters. The rate of adoption is given by

$$\frac{da(t)}{dt} = \beta_1 [N-a(t)] + \beta_2 a(t) \frac{[N-a(t)]}{N}. \tag{20}$$

After integration and setting boundary conditions, t+0, a(t-0)-a,

$$a(t) = N \frac{\left(1-\phi\left(\frac{\beta_1}{\beta_2}\right)e^{-(B_1+B_2)t}\right)}{\left(1+\phi\left(\frac{\beta_1}{\beta_2}\right)e^{-(B_1+B_2)t}\right)} \tag{21}$$

where B_1 and B_2 are constants, and

$$\phi = \frac{N-a_0}{N(\frac{B_1}{B_2})+a_0} \qquad N \geq a_0 > 0 .$$

The three models discussed above all hold the adoption population constant. In high technology areas, where the price of goods drops due to technical innovations and new market entries of firms, the potential for increased adopters becomes greater. Another reason for changes in the adopter population is

The three models can be rewritten to show a variable adopter population:

To summarise, the Coleman Model is

$$\frac{da(t)}{dt} = B_1 [N(t) - a(t)] \tag{22}$$

where,

$$a(t) = [A_1 + B_1 \int N(t) e^{\beta_1 t} dt] e^{\beta_1 t}$$

Dodd Model

$$\frac{da(t)}{dt} = B_2 [\frac{N-(t)-a(t)}{N(t)}] a(t)$$

Generalised Model

$$\frac{1}{a(t)} = [A_2 + B_2 \int \frac{e^{\beta_2 t}}{N(t)} dt] e^{\beta_2 t}$$

Models of new product development combined with the material in production function research and econometrics offer a new avenue of modelling of technology transfer. It can be supplemented by Hagerstrand (1967) type of spatial diffusion models available in the literature of statistical geography.

A model relating the present levels of achievement between the leader (in this case developed country) and follower is now discussed. The model is described with differential equations. The equation yields a solution of the level of proficiency of the follower as a function of time, given initial levels of technology for the leader and the follower, and constants relating to the rate of development for both and the rate of technology transfer between them.

The basic model studied shows an S shaped curve relating time and level of technology proficiency. The S curve is explained by three stages. The first stage, the curve, follows an exponential path. In the beginning it is generally flat. In the second stage, the curve deviates from the exponential due to limitations or constraints (technical, economic, etc.) on the innovation. The curve approaches the limit asymptotically in the third stage.

Technology transfer for a follower differs from the leader in time, but still follows the S curve. In Phase 1, the follower may not have production supplies, tools, or skilled personnel to make a fast rate of technical progress. The external sources of technology are available, but the follower is constrained from progressing at the same rate as the leaders.

In the learning phase, the follower begins to "catch up" with the leader, and the gap is reduced. During this learning stage, the role of technology transfer is the most important. In the third stage, the gap between the leader and the follower is substantially reduced or closed. Generally this happens far in the future.

One of the assumptions for the quantitative model is that the leader develops independently from the follower. Let X be as a function of the technical proficiency $x = f(p)$. It is assumed that the leader's technical proficiency increased linearly with time, $dX_L/dt = K_L$. This becomes:

$$X_L(t) = x^{o}_L + K_L t \qquad (23)$$

The simplest function representing X and p is $X = \ln p$.

The rate of technical progress for the follower is

$$\frac{dX_f}{dt} = K_f + f_1(X_f) f_2(X_L, X_f) \qquad (24)$$

The function, $f_1(X_f)$ is a nonlinear step function that has a value of zero for small values of X_f and a finite constant value for other values of X.

The function, $f_2(X_L, X_f) = (X_L - X_f)$ (25)

shows the gap between the technical proficiencies between the leader and the follower. The simplest type of gap is straight subtraction.

We can solve for X_f, with a substitution of

$$X_L = X_L^0 + K_L t \quad (26)$$

and knowing that

$$\frac{dx_f}{dt} = K_t X_f = K_f + K_t X^0 L + K_t K_L t \text{ and } f_1 (x_f) = K_t \quad (27)$$

This non-homogeneous equation has both a homogeneous solution

$$X^H = Ce^{-K_t t}, \quad (28)$$

and a particular solution $X^p = A + B_t$

$$X_f = X^p X^H$$

The solution is:

$$X_f(t) = X_L^0 + K_L t - (K_L - K_f)/(K_t - [X_L(0) - \frac{(K_L - K_f}{K_t}]e^{-K_t t} \quad (29)$$

The initial gap is represented as

$$X_L(0) - X_f(0)$$

and the progress of the leader is

$$X^0{}_L + K_L t$$

The solution for the gap between the two countries is:

$$G = X_L - X_f = (K_L - K_f)\,K_t + [(X_L^0 - X_f^0) - (K_L - K_f)/K_t]e^{-K_t t} \tag{30}$$

When the initial levels are equal, we have a solution of

$(K_L - K_f)/Kt$

when t is large. It follows that the technical proficiency of the leader is:

$$X_L(t) = X^0_L + K_L t. \tag{31}$$

and the technical proficiency of the follower is

$$X_f(t) = X_L(t) - G_\infty - (G_0 - G_\infty)e^{-K_t t}$$

where

$$G_0 = X_L^0 - X_f^0$$

represents the initial gap, and

$$G_\infty = (K_L - K_f)/Kt$$

represents the eventual gap. The gap can be bridged through a learning process. The process of learning has been nicely developed in a solar photovoltaic industry study from its start in the 1950's to the end of the century. He uses the strategy of both a producer and a consumer. A producer will have to develop a product that is cheaper while still having the same or better quality than that of the alternatives. At the same time the innovation is first developed, the costs may be far above what a consumer is willing to pay. The producer may anticipate the costs to go down in the future due to the learning curve of production and innovation. The producer may not be able to acquire the learning experiences that will enable costs to drop unless some consumers find the innovation superior in its early stages. Some of the cost and performance improvements result from production improvements including skilled labour and good management, design enhancements, and better products. The learning curves can be expressed as

$$C = cN^{-a} \tag{32}$$

$$P = pN^{b} \tag{33}$$

where

$0 < a < 1$
$0 < b < 1.$
C = unit cost of production
P = unit cost of performance
N = cumulative volume of production.

Rewriting, we see that:

$$\ln C = -a \ln N + \ln c$$

$$\ln P = b \ln N + \ln p$$

The rate of cost reduction and performance improvement can be found to be related to the growth of output:

$$\frac{dc}{C} = \frac{adN}{N}$$

$$\frac{dP}{P} = \frac{bdN}{N}$$

if output grows at a constant rate, K, then dN/N = K:

$$\frac{dC}{C} = -aK$$

$$\frac{dP}{P} = bK$$

The parameters (a,b) of innovative industries generally fell between 0.2 and 0.5. This implies that a doubling of production will lower the cost by 20-50%.

Factors affecting the purchase of solar photovoltaics are alternative energy costs, per annum decline of solar photovoltaics, and energy investment tax credit. Consumers are willing to wait presently, because the cost of solar photovoltaics is expected to drop substantially.

3. CONCLUSION

The objective of this article has been to give an introduction to the information and technology transfer and the models of technology transfer that can be developed to link two economies. Obviously, considerable work needs to be done to link work being done in information science, economics, organisation behaviour, and marketing.

NOTE

This is a survey paper incorporating materials from the above references; particularly to those marked with an *. This author wishes to acknowledge this.

REFERENCES

Griliches, Z., Productivity, R&D and Basic Research at Firm Level in the 1970's, The American Economic Review, 7.1, March 1986, pp. 144-145.

Griliches, Z. (ed), R&D, Patents and Productivity, The University of Chicago Press, Chicago, 1986.

*Griliches, Z. and V. Ringstad, Economics of Scale and the Form of the Production Function, North-Holland Publishing Company, Amsterdam, 1971.

Hagerstrand, T., Innovation Diffusion as a Spatial Process, University of Chicago Press, Chicago, 1967.

*Hamilton, I. and G. Linge (eds), Industrial System, Vol. 1, John Wiley & Sons, Chichester, 1979.

Johnston, P., Appropriate Technology for Small Developing Countries, Smoothie Publications, 1975.

Jorgenson, D.W. and J.A. Stephenson, The Time Structure of Investment Behavior in United States Manufacturing, 1947-1960, The Review of Economics and Statistics, 49.1, February 1967, pp. 21-22.

Mahajan, V. and R.A. Peterson, Models for Innovation Diffusion, Sage Publications, 1985.

Sato, K., A Two-Level Constant-Elasticity-of-Substitution Production Function, Review of Economics Studies, 34, 1967, pp.207-208.

*Sharif, M.N. and K. Ramanathan, Polynomial Innovation Diffusion Models, Technological Forecasting and Social Change, Vol. 21, 1982, pp. 301-323.

Sharif, M.N. and C. Kabir, Systems Dynamics Modelling for Forecasting Multi-level Technological Substitution, Technological Forecasting and Social Change, Vol. 9, 1976, pp. 89-112.

Schumacher, E.F., Small is Beautiful, Blond & Briggs Ltd., London, 1973.

Solow, R., Technology Change and the Aggregate Production Function, Review of Economics and Statistics, Vol. 39, 1957, pp. 312-320.

Wynn, R.F. and K. Holden, An Introduction to Applied Econometric Analysis, John Wiley & Sons, New York, 1974.

PART B: Information Technology and Space

TELECOMMUNICATION AND THE TYRANNY OF SPACE

Peter Nijkamp and Ilan Salomon

1. THE TYRANNY OF SPACE

Spatial patterns of economic activity have never been static, but always in a state of flux. Both external driving forces and internal behavioural reactions of economic actors have led to a permanently changing land use and location pattern from the side of both households (H) and firms (F). Their location patterns have varied between dispersion (D) and concentration (C) in different periods of history. The resulting combinations of spatial patterns of H and F can be illustrated by means of the following 2 x 2 cross-tabular representation.

F \ H	D	C
D	I	II
C	IV	III

Cell I (dispersed locational pattern of both households and firms) relates to a primitive society based on small scale handicraft and selfsupporting economy. Cell II describes a society which is facing the first signs of urbanisation (the medieval society, e.g.), while most economic activities (agriculture, extractive activities, e.g.) are still dispersed (the Von Thunen economy). Then Cell III refers to the period of the industrial revolution marked by a concentrated pattern of both households and firms (the Weber economy). Finally, Cell IV concerns the post war period in which large scale suburbanisation and desurbanisation takes place,leading to a rise in commuting radius. These four different phases in the history of locational developments are represented by means of the arrow in the abovementioned figure. It is of course an intriguing question whether the circle will be closed, in other words, whether a circular movement of locational patterns will emerge.

It is sometimes hypothesised that the current information society with its emphasis on telecommunication may lead to a liberation of the tyranny of space, so that more deconcentrated and even dispersed patterns of location may become plausible. Therefore it may be interesting to focus attention on the information sector and its potential geographical implications.

2. THE INFORMATION SECTOR

The modern informatics sector plays an important role in the framework of both entrepreneurial decision making and public decision making and planning (at both a national and a regional or local level). In general, information is not only power, but even ammunition. Consequently, effective and efficient decision making in a modern society is strongly oriented toward the use of modern communication and information technology.

In contrast to the conventional industrial technology (mechanisation, energy transmission, electronics), it is noteworthy that the informatics sector has a highly regulating and controlling potential which makes information and telecommunication extremely appropriate instruments in a policy making context. This new development has three major features, viz. a) high speed and reliability, b) flexibility and adaptive potential, and c) organisation and communicative power. Consequently, informatics will not become a substitute for private or public decision making, but it will enhance its quality by providing complementary tools (cf. Wegener 1985). In this respect one may assume that the 'wealth of nations' (Adam Smith) will in the future be determined by the 'wealth of information'. The distribution and use of modern information and telecommunication technology will also exert a decisive impact on the distribution of welfare among regions (see also Fritsch and Ewers 1985). Free access to information and knowledge networks is therefore of paramount importance for a balanced development of a country or a global economy. Monopoly tendencies on the other hand will no doubt aggravate distributional and spatial inequalities (see Nijkamp 1987).

Given the increasing importance of information for management and decision making, it is no surprise that the information sector has grown dramatically. For instance, Naisbitt (1982) claims that approximately 60 per cent of total employment in the USA is information-oriented. Despite this growth, it is interesting to report on some disenchanting observations made by Jonscher (1983), who claims that the contribution of the information sector to final (consumer) expenditures is relatively low (approximately 7 per cent) and that it is more its turnover and substitution rate within the quaternary sector which is higher, than its absolute growth. On the other hand, the indirect productivity increases caused by the information sector may be very significant. In general, the employment generating effects of the information sector appear to be fairly modest, while the assessment of these effects is fraught with various difficulties and uncertainties. For instance, the information technology market is highly segmented and mainly composed of three different segments (see Hills 1984), viz. computers (mainframes, micros, software, etc.), telecommunications (transmission via satellites, microwaves, fibre optics, cable, videotext, etc.), and microelectronics (chips, microprocessors, etc.).

Despite many uncertainties, it is clear that the information sector has grown in importance over the past decades. For instance, the telecommunications industry absorbs already one per cent of the GNP in the OECD countries annually (see Ergas and Okayama 1984). This importance is also illustrated by Figure 1, based on Business Week (June 30, 1980, p.140). The same journal also states:

> "The old industrial society that generated wealth in the form of capital goods and manufactured products is giving way to a new society valued in terms of intangible assets, such as knowledge and information processing. In fact, for 15 years more people have been working at processing information than any other type of job." (June 30, 1980, p.102)

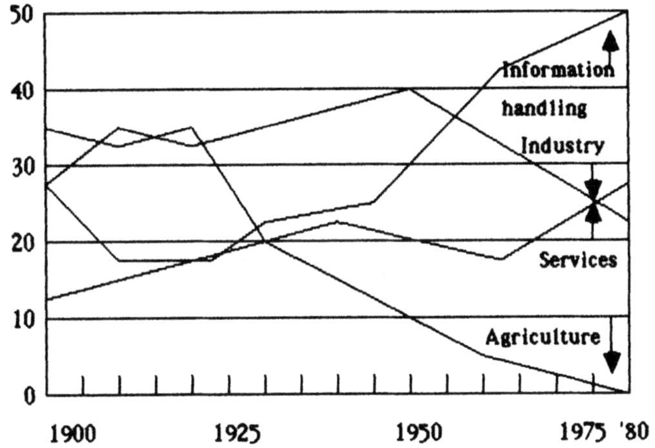

FIGURE 1: Employment trends in four US Sectors (1900-1980)

An interesting contribution to the discussion on the importance of the information technology for corporate strategy has been made by Goldhar and Jelenek (1983) who emphasise the *economies of scope* - in contrast with the economies of scale - offered by this technology. This means that the information technology allows an integration of all economic, organisational and technological functions (such as engineering and marketing) in one organisation, so that the process predictability, timely delivery, quality and efficiency can be improved without losing flexibility and variety. The capabilities of such information based systems for manufacturing processes are:

Extreme flexibility in product design and product mix, which allows for an almost unlimited variety of specific designs within a reasonable family of options, including alternative materials.

Rapid response to changes in market demand, product design and mix, output rates and equipment scheduling.

Greater control, accuracy and repeatability of processes, all of which lead to better quality products and more reliable manufacturing operations.

Reduced waste lower training and changeover costs, and more predictable maintenance costs.

Greater predictability in all phases of manufacturing operations and more information, both of which make possible more intensive management and control of the system.

Faster throughput due to better use of all machines, less in-process inventory, fewer stoppages for missing parts or materials, or machine breakdowns. Higher speeds are now made possible and economically feasible by the sensory and control capabilities of the 'smart' machines and the information management abilities of the CAM (Computer Aided Manufacture) software.

Distributed processing capability makes possible and economical the encoding of process information in easily replicable software.

The same authors also claim that the differences between traditional technology and Computer Integrated Manufacturing in factories and organisations can be indicated as follows (see Goldhar and Jelenek 1985):

Traditional technology	**Computer Integrated Manufacturing**
Centralisation	Decentralisation
Large plants	Disaggregated capacity
Balanced lines	Flexibility
Smooth flows	Inexpensive surge & turnaround ability
Standard product design	Many custom products
Low rate of change and high stability	Innovation and responsiveness
Inventory used as a buffer	Production tied to demand
'Focussed factory' as an organising concept	Functional range of repeated reorganisation
Job enrichment and enlargement	Responsibility tied to reward
Batch systems	Flow systems

Such new technologies, especially in the field of the information and telecommunication sector, may have a far reaching impact on the locational pattern of firms and hence on regional development. The modern technology offers also a large growth potential for traditional rural areas, provided these areas are connected with an information and knowledge network. Thus, the adoptive capability of a region for this new technology will be decisive for its future economic position.

Clearly, the new information technology (NIT) may also exert an impact on the mobility behaviour of people (teleshopping, teleconferencing, e.g.). The use of modern telecommunication facilities enables technically the substitution of physical commuting by telecommuting, so that more jobs may cease to require physical travel. However, the degree to which this will take place is still very much subject to speculation. This issue will be further discussed in subsequent sections.

3. TELECOMMUNICATION: DESIGN AND ADOPTION

Popular views suggest that telecommunication is a friction reducing technology, so that it may induce geographical dispersion of economic activities. Consequently, any increase in the use of telecommunications would make many activities more footloose, so that future locational patterns would become more dispersed. It is however doubtful whether this simple hypothesis can be supported from empirical facts, as the relationship between telecommunications and spatial deconcentration is rather complex (see Goddard 1980). In order to study the spatial impact of new technologies like the telecommunications sector, we may make a useful and systematic distinction between three phases of implementing such new technologies (see Stoneman 1983):

i) design and generation This phase concerns mainly the invention of a new product, production process, production system, institutional system or management system, and leads eventually to the emergence of a new technological 'regime' (see Nelson and Winter 1982).

ii) diffusion and adoption Diffusion processes of new phenomena have both a temporal and a geographical dimension (see Hagerstrand 1967, as well as Davies 1979, Dosi 1984, Kamien and Schwarz 1982, and Rogers 1983). The recent literature on this issue exhibits a wide variety of diffusion paths, depending on the parameters of the diffusion model, the initial conditions, the feedback structure of the evolutionary model, and the resistance factors from the side of potential adopters. The conventional deterministic epidemic disease model is increasingly losing its relevance, whilst it is being substituted for more behaviourally-oriented models incorporating decision uncertainty, systemic resilience and environmental complexity (see for example, the self-organisation model advocated by Prigogine 1976).

iii) effects These effects are usually multidimensional in nature, and may relate to employment effects, locational effects, environmental effects, land use effects, effects on industrial structure etc. at different geographical scales.

In conclusion, forecasting of new technologies is characterised by many uncertainties emerging inter alia from the attributes of the technology at hand (e.g. the competitive structure of the industry at hand), the intervening opportunities offered by related technologies, and the information supply regarding the potential of such new technologies. Consequently, forecasts of impacts of such technologies are in general highly stochastic by nature (see also Jimenez Montano and Ebeling 1980).

The evolutionary behaviour of new technologies like NIT has led to the emergence of various dynamic models aiming at portraying and forecasting the time trajectory of such a new technological regime. Instead of conventional cost-disease (or unbalanced growth) models for the evolutionary path of new technologies, we observe nowadays more complicated nonlinear dynamic models, based inter alia on a competitive exclusion of new technologies, or on a predator-prey approach adopted from population biology. Especially the latter type of model has recently become very popular in dynamic economic analysis, mainly due to the appealing analytic properties of the underlying Volterra-Lotka dynamics (which is mainly based on the principle of primacy of major activities).

The information sector (including telecommunications) may be one of such primate activities. In this respect, it is often claimed that the productivity rise caused by the information sector is formidable. For example, the transmission of live performances from theatres to television broadcasting represents one of the largest leaps in productivity that have ever taken place, as approximately the same amount of effort is able to offer services to millions of people watching television, instead of to a couple of thousand people visiting a theatre (see Baumol and Wolff 1984).

The growth of the information sector as a whole is in most developed countries no doubt impressive, no matter how the information sector is defined precisely (see Jonscher 1984). In this context, various models have been described to analyse the evolutionary pattern of this sector (e.g. the stochastic process control model, the disaggregate market signalling model, etc.). Whatever the contents and shape of the models aiming at portraying an uncertain future may be, it is in any case clear that a further growth in information-processing resources will have a direct impact on the growth path of telecommunications in the future. In this framework, an interesting econometric exploration based on a growth model for the relationship between R&D capital in communication, output and government expenditures in this sector has been developed by Terleckyj (1984).

In order to design a systematic analysis framework for assessing the spatial impacts of the telecommunications sector, we will use Figure 2.

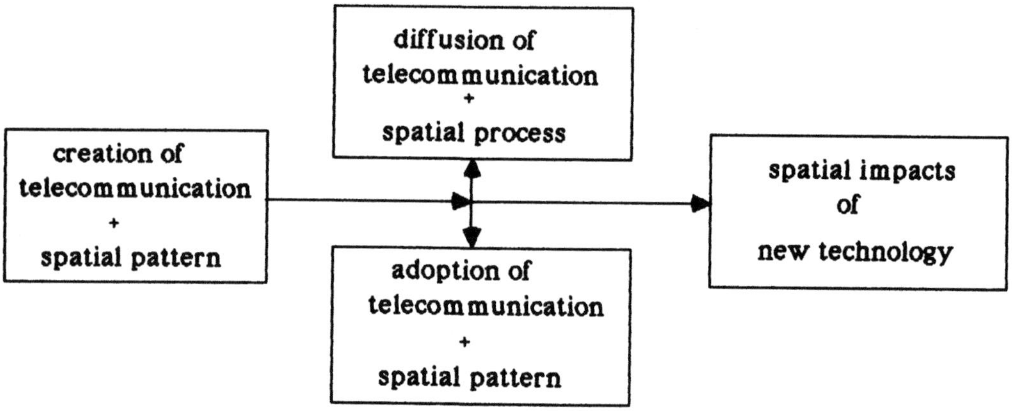

FIGURE 2: Phases in spatial impact analysis of telecommunication

The *offspring* of new technologies like telecommunications can be explained from various angles (see Nijkamp 1986). Examples are the *demand pull* hypothesis, the *depression trigger* hypothesis, and the *technology push* hypothesis. Clearly, in all three cases a distinction has to be made between the adjustment of old technologies, the introduction of new technologies, and new applications of existing technologies. In this respect the telecommunications sector is multifacetted and heterogeneous, so that some caution is needed if general statements are to be made regarding its evolution and impacts. Attributes to be considered in this respect are: speed of information transmission, quality and bandwidth of information, reliability and security, the modularity and flexibility of information transferred and the versatility of new telecommunications systems concerned.

In most countries, there appears to be an increasing need for information and hence - as a derived demand - for telecommunications services (Manski and Salomon 1985). This information need is codetermined by the rise in complexity of intertwined socioeconomic, spatial and environmental processes (see also Nijkamp and Rietveld 1984). In addition, statistical and mathematical tools, as well as suitable computer hardware and software stimulate a further increase in demand for information and hence for telecommunication services.

From a geographical viewpoint, it has to be added that the current organisation of socioeconomic life in Western countries is based on ever increasing interpersonal interactions (face-to-face contacts, business linkages, etc.) because our economies exhibit increasingly a complicated network structure. This exponential rise in the demand for interactions is hampered by the physical ability of man to fully interact at an (inter-)personal level, with many people involved.

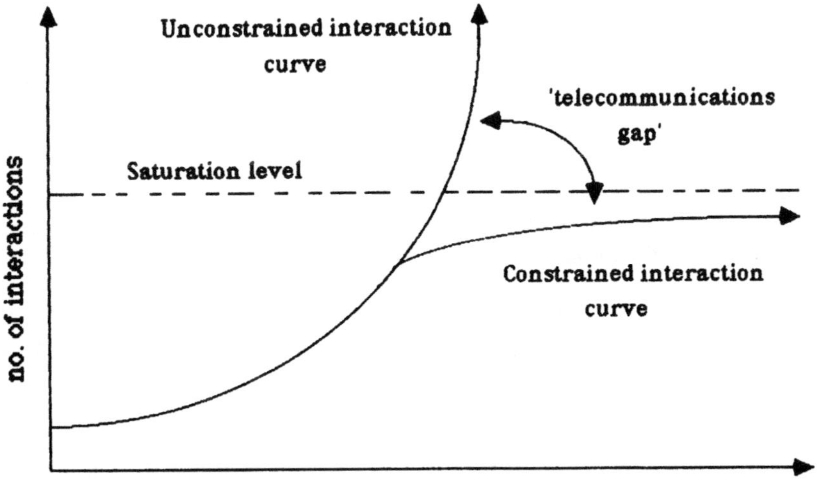

FIGURE 3: The 'Telecommunications Gap'

Therefore, telecommunication services are, to some extent, necessary in order to compensate for an exponential growth pattern in interactions. This also implies that - given a certain physical saturation level for direct human interactions - the use of telecommunications services is likely to exhibit a rapid growth in the near future (see also Figure 3). The 'telecommunications gap' reflects here essentially the increase in the use of telecommunications services caused by physical constraints of persons who have a potentially exponential growth curve for human interactions.

It is obviously an interesting question *where* these new technologies are likely to be generated. The telecommunications sector is a specific high tech sector which is strongly oriented towards the presence of a highly skilled labour force (engineers, technicians, etc.) in a given area. Thus a region may exert an incubator or 'seedbed' function, if its specific labour market configuration acts as a birthplace for such new activities (see also Malecki 1980, Nijkamp 1985). Usually, the presence of a university and advanced R&D centres is regarded as a necessary condition for such new telecommunication technologies to emerge. Thus, the geographical patterns of the telecommunications sector is not randomly distributed, but exhibits usually a strong orientation toward academic information and knowledge centres.

The *diffusion pattern* of telecommunications services is often assumed to follow a logistic growth curve over time and a distance decay curve in space. It is worth mentioning however, that constraining factors may impede such a regular trajectory. A major reason is that - in contrast to conventional thinking - telecommunications technology is not mainly supply driven: the introduction of a specific technology in this area is very much determined by constraints and by user needs and preferences. If the demand side is decisive for the introduction and acceptance of a new technology, a forecast of the temporal and spatial penetration of specific telecommunications technologies should take into account underlying behavioural factors.

Thus the supply of telecommunications diffusion may be hampered by various types of inertia and limitations of suppliers and demanders. Consequently, a conventional S-shaped growth curve and a downward bending spatial friction curve are not by definition appropriate analytical forecasting tools. Much consideration has to be given to behavioural aspects of all actors involved, thus increasing the level of uncertainty of forecasts and the use and impact of telecommunications technology.

The *adoption pattern* of telecommunication technologies reflects the demand behaviour of (potential and/or actual) users. The degree of adoption of NIT and related services depends on various factors, such as:

- the *nature* of the information that can be transmitted through the system. This is exemplified by the tendency of organisations (or some of their functions) involved in negotiation-type interactions which are not amenable to telecommunications, to prefer agglomeration economies over benefits of decentralisation (see e.g. the study by Goddard and Morris 1976 on office decentralisation in the Greater London Area).
- the *reliability* of the system, both in terms of technical performance and in terms of the security of the information.
- the relative costs of obtaining a desired level of information via alternative communication media for including face-to-face interaction (i.e. physical travel).

- the sociodemographic characteristics or organisational attributes of the adopters. In the case of households, it is generally assumed that age composition, education, income, and employment configuration are relevant, explanatory factors. In the case of organisations, the structure, the geographical pattern and the relative shares of the intra- and inter-organisational information flows are among the relevant factors. The decision to adopt a new technology is not always determined by measurable (economic) criteria but is often influenced by perceived costs and benefits, including prestige as one specific benefit (see Gold 1979, Charles 1981).

Clearly, the adoption of telecommunication services has a geographical component, not only in terms of the spatial location pattern of adopters, but also in terms of a judgement of real physical distance versus sociopsychological distance between senders and receivers of information. Perception of distance and the importance of direct face-to-face contacts are major factors in adopting a certain telecommunications technology (see Meyerowitz 1985, Korzenny 1978, Salomon 1986). Furthermore, urban agglomerations and geographical concentrations of activities may provide more stimuli for a rapid adoption of new telecommunications technologies in the household sector due to imitative behaviour caused by the 'keeping up with the Joneses' effect. Thus, the geography of adoptive behaviour has no doubt an impact on the spatial dispersion of telecommunications technologies.

The next section will be devoted to a more thorough discussion of the spatial effects of the telecommunications technology.

4. GEOGRAPHICAL IMPACTS OF TELECOMMUNICATIONS

The most publicised spatial effect of telecommunications is decentralisation. It is based on the assumption that i) telecommunications will provide a uniform distribution of information over space, and ii) that the technologies and their applications will be adopted by significant shares of a growing information-dependent market. The uniform validity of these arguments is however questionable. At present such impacts can only be identified in well defined particular contexts for specific technology applications. Only one plausible generalisation can be made, viz. that individuals and firms may enjoy greater flexibility in the locational decisions, the reason being that - given the principle of minimisation of transport costs in many location decision models - the major impact of telecommunications technologies is that it produces a different cost-distance distribution than that solely based on physical movements. While telecommunications rates are significantly less distance-sensitive than travel costs, they do exhibit greater sensitivity to the duration of telecommunication. Hence, both perceived and actual cost 'maps' are altered by the availability and use of telecommunication systems. There are numerous moderating variables which affect the spatial patterns of NIT-induced phenomena. Some major variables in this context are the scale effect, the prior geographical distribution, the demand for information, the organisational structure and the logistics. These factors will successively be discussed.

The Scale Effect

The first moderating effect can be attributed to scale. The spatial impacts of telecommunications range from the micro scale of a single building or complex (e.g. 'smart buildings'), through local, metropolitan and regional scales to the national and international scales (e.g. location of multinationals at the proximity of telecommunications facilities). While a certain effect is observed at, say the metropolitan scale, it need not be repeated at other spatial scales. For example, the decentralisation of back office activities from major metropolitan centres like New York City (Moss 1985) does not imply that one should expect a general decentralisation of back offices at local or regional scales.

The Prior Geographical Distribution of Activities and Resources

The impacts of telecommunications on the spatial distribution of activities is likely to depend on the distribution prevailing prior to the introduction of the new technology. Forces of both centralisation and decentralisation are always here at work, while inertia (or costs of transaction) and the current distribution of costs of communications and resources create a quasi-equilibrium in the locational patterns. However, a change in the costs of traversing distance for particular (information-intensive) activities relaxes some of the constraints on location or may change the relative weights of location factors (see Baki 1981, Brotchie 1984). For instance, existing firms can - as a result of the availability of telecommunications - change their pattern of activities. This would mean that they can then enter markets which were too remote prior to the change, or they can increase their interactions with other firms so as to generate new products or services.

Current trends like the decrease in environmental quality in large cities, the increase in congestion and the resulting demand for rural life styles evident in many developed countries are also affecting the probability of decentralisation of activities into non-urban regions. Yet, the desired amenities (e.g. cultural) available in cities can only partially be transmitted through NIT. In particular, the spatial distribution of labour resources illustrates this point.

The combination of the growing share of service and information activities with the availability of telecommunications may provide for a new spatial pattern of employment. On the one hand, individuals who did not participate in the labour force due to physical or social mobility constraints can now - given the option of telecommuting - engage in information related work. This opens new pools of labour for employers, e.g. housewives in the suburbs. On the other hand, it may also provide new alternatives for individuals who prefer the amenities of rural environments without being removed from the 'urban' white collar labour market. In that sense, the prior distribution of attractive environments can now be exploited more efficiently. Yet, it is worth mentioning that urban amenities exert a centralising force in attracting people to remain in urban areas and this may be in line with Holland's (1976) claim about the importance of social factors in the location of economic activities.

However, the 'flexiplace' work location, a popular concept introduced as a result of telecommunications availability, does not seem to have major impacts in terms of changing the geography of employment. Social and psychological impediment to working at home (Salomon and Salomon 1984, Shamir and Salomon 1985) along with management reluctance (Olson 1983) indicate that in the near future the 'work-at-home' application of remote work is not expected to be widely adopted. So, while 'electronic cottages' are likely to appear in many remote areas, the magnitude of the phenomenon may be expected to be limited.

The Demand for Information

As the demand for telecommunications is derived from the demand for information, firms and individuals with different demand patterns are likely to exhibit variations in their location decisions. A communications analysis can reveal the extent to which the reliance on telecommunications-based interactions is economically feasible to a firm, taking into account not only the perceived travel cost savings but also such 'softer' long term effects as changes in productivity of managers deprived from their (enjoyable) business trips (see Gold 1979).

Given the development that can be expected in the next decade or so, it is plausible that for firms having a demand for information which is largely not suitable for telecommunications transmissions, the costs of 'maintaining contact' (Pye 1977) will result in only very few relocation decisions to remote areas. The city's role as a 'transaction centre' (Gottmann 1983) will likely continue to attract economic, political and social activities.

The Organisational Structure

The suitability of various telecommunications technologies to accommodate different categories of information can result in spatial behaviour varying as a reaction to the organisational structure. Intra-organisational communications, given its nature and the probability of acquaintance between parties, are more amenable to electronic communications than inter-organisational communications. Consequently, multiplant corporations or large ones which can fragment into corporate plants, are more likely to adopt telecommunications in order to accommodate locational dispersion than single plants or small firms. Hence, the market composition will affect the extent of decentralisation attributable to telecommunications.

Logistics

Even highly information based industries - and more so high tech oriented industries involved in production rather than R&D - have a certain need for physical goods movements. The influence of this need is twofold. First, in considering the location decision, the costs of goods movement need also be considered. Second, as a second order spatial effect, the possibility of decentralisation of activities implies an increase in total vehicle movement to remote locations. This enhanced traffic can in itself create spatial impacts such as service centres, requirements for road improvements (to be paid by the public sector). etc.

Concluding Remarks

At present, there is very little empirical evidence that supports either the dispersion or the concentration hypothesis attributed to telecommunications. Hence, most forecasts are, at best, only educated speculations. Webber (1963), Mandeville (1983) and Kellerman (1984) have, in different ways suggested that these technologies are neutral and may, depending on specific contextual factors, accommodate either of the directions to change. We therefore refrain from attempting any generalisation as to the spatial impacts of NIT. Instead, forecasts should aim to identify the factors (some of which are discussed above) which affect the location decisions of particular agents, i.e. individuals' residential and workplace choices, and firms' decisions, distinguishing between different organisational structures and information dependency. Also, government intervention in the telecommunications sector, through direct investment, subsidies or regulation are to be accounted for as sometimes dominant factors in shaping the spatial impacts of these technologies.

5. A NEW SPATIAL ORGANISATION OF OUR SOCIETY?

Telecommunications will undoubtedly have certain spatial impacts resulting from the spatial variation in the generation, diffusion and adoption of new technologies. However, forecasting these impacts for policy making or private sector decision making is complicated by the above mentioned factors.

In recent years, the results of telecommunications have become spectacular due to the emergence of video transmission, telefax, teleshopping, etc. Information and communication have become key elements in industrial organisation and location. A new 'paperless' or 'wired' society is likely to emanate, so that the printing technology which has had a superior position for many centuries may lose ground. Talking and communication machines as well as artificial intelligence may be a next step, although one has to realise that - despite the technological potential - the human mind has in general only a limited capacity for adopting revolutionary innovations. In this framework, Naisbitt (1982) argues that any 'high tech' development evokes a countervailing 'high touch' development, as the alienation caused by technology forces people to compensate by increasing personal and social face-to-face contacts.

As said before, the development of informatics may potentially have an impact on the spatial patterns of economic activities of our societies. For instance, peripheral areas might get direct access to the information centres of the world or of the country concerned. On the other hand, traditional centres might perhaps reinforce their position as a 'spider' in a network, so that the role of nodal points in such a network becomes even more important. The net result of all such developments is hard to forecast, so that at best one can try to identify some prevailing trends in the field of informatics and regional development.

A special case here is the transportation sector, as the impacts of the so called telematics on the transportation system are becoming more evident. Various studies have been undertaken in the meantime to analyse the viability of telecommuting, teleshopping, and telerecreation, and so forth (see Fritsch and Ewers 1985). Although conventional wisdom suggests that telematics may lead to a reduction of physical movements as it compensates for distance friction costs ('the tyranny of space'), empirical evidence suggests so far only a very modest impact (see also Nijkamp and Salomon 1986). In the goods production, however, it is clear that telematics no doubt will have a substantial impact, witness the great influence of modern logistics on storage management and automated routing systems, including JIT (just-in-time) technologies. It turns out that in this field the use of telematics favours both geographical concentration and deconcentration, so that a dual spatial development is likely to emerge.

It is plausible that, although telecommunications will be adopted and applied in remote regions - inducing in turn some new activities in such areas - the overall pattern of activities will not be significantly different from that known today. We expect that telecommunications will never create a uniform distribution of information over space and therefore firms at remote locations are likely to be disadvantaged as compared with more centrally located facilities. Temporary departures from this general pattern may be observed in newly emerging branches which exhibit high revenues until competition arrives. The high revenues can then only temporarily offset other locational disadvantages.

Economic activities are increasingly dependent on the availability and use of reliable and up-to-date information systems. In general, the best access to such information systems can be found in nodes of a network. Consequently, there will be a tendency to a geographical orientation of firms toward nodes in a communication network. Such a multinodal geographical configuration is - to some extent - already present in the current spatial patterns of our societies (Pred 1977). Apart from specific cases, a dramatic spatial dispersion of activities is hence not likely to take place. A related point is that in nodes of a network a wide variety of polyvalent information may come together, so that firms seeking risk minimisation in terms of information gathering and availability will be tempted to seek risk minimising and strategic (i.e. usually central) positions in a multinodal network.

Moreover, corporate organisations and multiplant firms are of course facing a situation of information management among different branches, and here also the principle of centrality and multinodality applies. Despite the technical possibility for decentralisation of firms, we still observe a strong centrality of multinodality tendency, especially at the levels of management and decision making.

The polyvalence of information flows also evokes the problem of a structured access to telecommunications systems and a systematic use of such information. In this framework, decision support systems (DSS) and artificial intelligence (AI) may set the stage for new interactive forms of decision making, in which centralised and decentralised information is linked in a coherent manner.

REFERENCES

Bakis, H., Elements for a Geography of Telecommunications, Geographical Research Forum, Vol. 4, 1981, pp. 31-45.

Baumol, W.J. and E.N. Wolff, Feedback Models: R&D, Information, and Productivity Growth, in: M. Jussawalla and H. Ebenfield, eds., Communication and Information Economics, North-Holland Publishing Company, Amsterdam, 1984, pp. 73-92.

Brotchie, J., Technological Change and Urban Form, Environment and Planning A, 1984, Vol. 16, pp.583-596.

Charles, J., Approaches to Teleconference Justification, Telecommunications Policy 5, 1981, pp. 296-303.

Davis, S., The Diffusion of Process Innovations, Cambridge University Press, Cambridge, 1979.

Dosi, J., Technical Change and Industrial Transformation, MacMillan, London, 1984.

Ergas, H. and J. Okayama (eds), Changing Market Structures in Telecommunications, North-Holland Publishing Company, Amsterdam, 1984.

Fritsch, M., and H.-J. Ewers, Telematik und Raumentwicklung, Selbstverslag Gesellschaft Regionale Strukturentwicklung, Bonn, 1985.

Goddard, J.B., Technology Forecasting in a Spatial Context, Futures, April 1980, pp. 90-105.

Goddard, J.B., and D. Morris, The Communications Factor in Office Location, Progress in Planning 6, Vol. 1, 1976, 80 pp.

Gold, E.M., Attitude to Intercity Travel Substitution, Telecommunications Policy 1, 1979, pp. 88-104.

Goldhar, J.D. and M. Jelenek, Plan for Economies of Scope, Hardvard Business Review, November-December 1983, pp,. 141-148.

Goldhar, J.D. and M. Jelenek, Computer Integrated Flexible Manufacturing, Interfaces, Vol. 15, No. 3, 1985, pp. 94-105.

Gottmann, J., Urban Settlements and Telecommunications, Ekistics, 302, 1983, pp. 411-416.

Hagerstrand, T., Innovation Diffusion as a Spatial Process, University of Chicago Press, Chicago, 1967.

Hills, J., Information Technology and Industrial Policy, Croom Helm, London, 1984.

Holland, J., Capital versus the Regions, MacMillan, London, 1976.

Jimenez Montano, M.A. and W. Ebeling, A Stochastic Evolutionary Model of Technological Change, Collective Phenomena, Vol. 3, 1980, pp. 107-114.

Jonscher, Ch., Information Resources and Economic Productivity, in: M. Jussawalla and H. Ebenfield (eds), Communication and Information Economics, North-Holland Publishing Company, Amsterdam, 1984, pp. 94-103.

Kamien, M. and N. Schwarz, Market Structure and Innovations, Cambridge University Press, Cambridge, 1982.

Kellerman, A., Telecommunications and the Geography of Metropolitan Areas, Progress in Human Geography 8, Vol. 2, 1984, pp. 222-246.

Korzenny, F., A Theory of Electronic Propinquity, Communications Research 5, 1978, pp. j3-24.

Malecki, E.J., Corporate Organization of R&D and the Location of Technological Activities, Regional Studies 14, 1982, pp. 92-110.

Mandeville, T., The Spatial Effects of Information Technology, Futures 15, Vol. 1, 1983, pp. 65-72.

Manski, C. and I. Salomon, Information Acquisition and the Demand for Telecommunications, presented at the International Conference on Telecommunications Demand Modeling, New Orleans, 1985.

Meyrowitz, J., No Sense of Place , Oxford University Press, New York, 1985.

Moss, M.L., The Urban Telecommunications Infrastructure, Paper presented at the Landtronics Conference, The Lincoln Land Institute and the University of Southern California, Los Angeles, Ca., 1985.

Naisbitt, J., Megatrends Warner Books, New York, 1982.

Nelson, R. and S. Winter, An Evolutionary Theory of Economic Change, Harvard University Press, Cambridge, 1982.

Nijkamp, P., New Technology and Regional Development, Research Memorandum, Department of Economics, Free University, Amsterdam, 1985.

Nijkamp, P. and P. Rietveld (eds), Information Systems for Integrated Regional Planning, North-Holland Publishing Company, Amsterdam, 1984.

Nijkamp, P. (ed), Technological Change, Employment and Spatial Dynamics, Springer Verlag, Berlin, 1986.

Nijkamp, P., Informatics and Oracles in Regional Planning, in: M. Giaoutzi and P. Nijkamp (eds), Informatics and Regional Development Planning, Gower Publishing Company, Aldershot, 1987

Nijkamp, P. and I. Salomon, Future Spatial Impacts of Telecommunications, Research Memorandum, Free University, Amsterdam 1986.

Olson, M.H., Remote Office Work: Changing Work Patterns in Space and Time, Communications of the ACM 26(3), 1983, pp. 182-187.

Pred, A., City Systems in Advanced Economies, Hutchinson, London 1977.

Prigogine, I., Order Through Fluctuations: Self-Organisational and Social System, in: E. Jantsch and C.H. Woddington (eds), Evolution and Consciousness, Addison-Wesley, Reading, 1976, pp. 93-133.

Pye, R., Office Location and the Cost of Maintaining Contact, Environment and Planning A, Vol. 9, 1977, pp. 149-168.

Rogers, E.M., Diffusion of Innovations, Free Press, New York, 1983.

Salomon, I. and M. Salomon, Telecommuting: The Employee's Perspective, Technological Forecasting and Social Change, Vol. 25, 1984, pp. 14-28.

Salomon, I., Telecommunication and Travel Relationships: A Review, Transportation Research, 20A, 1986, pp. 223-238.

Shamir, B. and I. Salomon, Working-at-Home and the Quality of Working Life, Academy of Management Review, Vol. 10, 1985.

Stoneman, P., The Economic Analysis of Technological Change, Oxford University Press, Oxford, 1983.

Terleckyj, N.E., A Growth Model of the US Communication Industry 1948-1980, in: M. Jussawalla and H. Ebenfield (eds), Communications and Information Economics, North-Holland Publishing Company, Amsterdam, 1984, pp. 119-145.

Webber, M., Order and Diversity: Community without Propinquity, in: L. Wingo (ed), Cities and Space. The Future Use of Urban Land, RFF, Baltimore, 1963.

Wegener, M., Spatial Planning in the Information Age, Paper Workshop on Innovation, Technological Change and Spatial Impacts, CSIRO, Melbourne, August, 1985.

THE LONG-TERM IMPACTS OF THE TELECOMMUNICATION INDUSTRY AND INFORMATION TECHNOLOGY

Lay Gibson

1. PROLOGUE

Telecommunications has become a major topic in both the scholarly literature and the popular literature. Early forms of telecommunications, e.g., the telephone and telegraph have had a substantial impact on the 'way business is done'. More advanced forms of telecommunication will produce additional impacts. Restructuring related to telecommunications can be expected but it is likely to be 'marginal', not 'absolute', i.e., it is more likely that existing patterns and trends will be reinforced than it is that totally new patterns will be created.

The term teleconferencing (a generic term for a whole range of electronic meeting aids) is a favoured term for describing telecommunication applications. Six basic forms can be identified: audio, telewriting or drawing, telecopying or fax, computer conferencing or electronic mail, still video and motion video. Business and governmental activities well suited to teleconferencing include general staff management, project management, crisis management, intergroup coordination, training/information dissemination, problem solving, fact finding, negotiations, and conflict resolution.

Although enthusiasm for these new technologies runs high, there seems to be a widespread belief that traditional practices, e.g., face-to-face meetings will persist. For teleconferencing in general, and for particular types of teleconferencing (voice telecommunications, print telecommunications, and video telecommunications) a variety of potential pros and cons can be articulated. Over-time, it is virtually certain that telecommunications will become more influential but a variety of factors, including cost of adoption, will certainly act to slow the process of transferring these technologies to a variety of users in a variety of locales.

Restructuring has both spatial and aspatial dimensions. The aspatial cases consider the various costs of institutionalising telecommunications: cost of purchasing, sending and receiving equipment, cost of maintenance, access to maintenance services, space requirements of new equipment, cost of training operators, and cost of training users.

Spatial restructuring must consider a) potential impacts on the way that business is done and b) existing anticipated patterns of telecommunications equipment manufacture and service. The former question requires consideration of blending of communication resources within an organisation - to what extent will telecommunications replace another form? Several authorities suggest that face-to-face interaction will always be essential although it might be enhanced by telecommunication. Further, over time more sophisticated forms of telecommunication will replace existing forms but adoption will be slowed by cost, technical shortcomings of advanced systems, and by slower than expected learning curves of potential users.

Substitution potentials are substantial but limited by the aforementioned considerations. Journey to work patterns, for example, might eventually be marginally modified by home based work or adoption of the neighbourhood work centre concept. However, it is likely that such changes will more likely influence an individual's day-to-day interaction patterns than an industry's overall pattern of flows and linkages.

External economies, both urbanisation economies and localisation economies, tend to favour maintenance of existing spatial structures. Considerations such as high levels of aggregate demand (for telecommunications services, maintenance and training) together with more general urbanisation amenities such as infrastructure, size of market, depth of labour pool, etc., all point to large, established centres. Telecommunications has the potential to be a deconcentrating force but there is little evidence to suggest that this has, to any significant extent, actually been the case.

Localisation economies become significant when telecommunications are viewed as an industry rather than as an ancillary activity supporting other activities. Given the fact that telecommunications is an activity where product life cycle is short and innovation is rapid, localisation economies can be critical. Proximity of a skilled labour force, to universities and research centres, to services and to suppliers of parts and components are all potentially critical considerations.

As a high-tech industry, telecommunications might be expected to follow patterns of computer software and other similar activities. High-tech's tendency to agglomerate seems to be related to a) early links between these sectors and earlier sectors, b) a common need for access to pools of highly skilled professionals and technical workers and a good university, and c) a high-quality lifestyle. Decentralising forces include a) job creation in regional centres, b) a spatially dispersed and heterogeneous list of potential clients, and c) high-cost of living in established centres. However, on balance, these decentralising forces will likely be largely offset by centre-reinforcing forces. Teleconferencing makes it easier to meet the needs of a dispersed clientele and agglomeration economies (as discussed above), and 'reputation' of existing centres are likely to persist as powerful centre-reinforcing considerations.

Implications for public policy are numerous. Government adoption of products and regulatory policy and direct subventions to support research and systems development are all important considerations. A critical question which was the focus of recent debate in Japan was whether telecommunications should be viewed as an ancillary activity serving national needs or should it be viewed as an industry in its own right, competing in the national and international market places. One might also look at the potential role of telecommunications in government policy aimed at either encouraging concentration or deconcentration of industry. The production of telecommunications equipment itself seems to have, at most, limited potential as an employer in underdeveloped areas. But as a service industry it appears to have potential for increasing efficiency of activities placed in remote locations.

2. TELECOMMUNICATIONS: AN INTRODUCTION

The literature on telecommunications is abundant and growing rapidly. Some of it is, essentially, promotional in nature whereas increasingly large portions could be considered critical. This is not to say that those concerned with telecommunications are becoming negative - they are simply becoming more thoughtful and realistic. After reviewing the evidence available one might guess that increased utilisation of telecommunications will lead to substantial restructuring, but that restructuring will be 'marginal', not 'absolute'.

This paper first focusses on the multiple dimensions of telecommunications as an activity and then moves on to restructuring as a spatial and aspatial/technical problem. Included in the later sections are discussions of telecommunications and its effect on communication patterns, of this industry as an element of the space economy, i.e., on the prospects for the geographic distribution of telecommunications goods and services, and discussions of the anticipated adoption patterns through the world's regional economies.

The telecommunications area is now viewed as a cutting edge topic. It is both frequently discussed in the general literature on the 'information society', or 'information revolution', and it is the primary focus of a more narrowly defined literature of its own. Perhaps not surprising is the fact that the private research sector gives us a convenient definition of 'telecommunication':

> "Telecommunication encompasses all transfers of information, both internally and externally, to organizations by electromagnetic means, including telephone, data, telegraphic and 'picture' transfer facilities and services" (Booz, Allen and Hamilton 1974)

The Booz, Allen and Hamilton definition describes the technology but not its utility - the term 'telecommunications' seems to be the common term used to describe the several forms and functions. The utility of telecommunications is commonly described by the term 'teleconferencing'. Robert Johansen (1984) says that "teleconferencing is a generic term for the whole range of electronic meeting aids". He goes on to identify and describe five teleconferencing components (Table 1).

A wide variety of business and governmental activities are especially well suited to teleconferencing. Maher and Fischell (1985) list nine areas where one or more teleconferencing forms might find application.

1. General Staff Management

The decentralisation of many organisations brings with it the requirement to meet regularly to coordinate routine ongoing staff operations.

TABLE 1
Basic Teleconferencing Components

Function	Teleconferencing Form	Description
Voice	Audio	Voice-only communication, using various equipment options for voice amplification and transmission, so as to allow multipoint communications among individuals and groups. A conference telephone call is the simplest form of audio teleconferencing.
Drawing	Telewriting or drawing	Electronic transmission of writing or drawing over an electronic circuit.
Page	Telecopying or facsimile (fax)	A device for sending page-size photocopies over a normal telephone line or special transmission circuit.
Typing	Coputer conferencing or electronic mail	A text-based group communications medium, in which all exchanges are accomplished through a computer with a typewriter-like keyboard.
Video	Still video (slow-scan; freeze-frame)	A snap shot picture that is updated periodically and displayed on a television monitor.
	Motion video	Full-motion television linking individuals or groups at two or more locations. Transmission is via microwave, coaxial cable, cable television systems, or satellites or other means.

Source: Johansen, 1984.

2. Project Management

Regular meetings are usually scheduled throughout the course of the life cycle of a major corporate project, especially in those projects which require coordination
Regular meetings are usually scheduled throughout the course of the life cycle of a major corporate project, especially in those projects which require coordination
with several different functional organisations.

3. Crisis Management

Crisis management often involves the coordination of efforts of experts in a number of different areas. While advanced planning generally provides procedures to be followed in many crisis situations, there is a need to manage and coordinate the execution of emergency plan implementation.

4. Intergroup Coordination

Coordination of the efforts of different functions or departments is frequently
4. Intergroup Coordination

Coordination of the efforts of different functions or departments is frequently necessary to fulfil corporate commitments including coordination of Production and Operations with Marketing and Sales with regard to timely delivery of a

5. Training/Information Dissemination

In most companies there is a frequent need to provide training and to disseminate information to groups within the organisation, as well as to customers, suppliers and co-contractors. This includes policy announcements, new product information, lectures, demonstrations, and training.

6. Problem Solving

There is frequently a need to bring together technical experts from both within and outside the company to discuss solutions to specific problems in areas such as management/administration, corporate finance, sales/marketing, engineering, data processing, manufacturing/production, public relations, and personnel, and training and development.

7. Fact Finding

Fact finding frequently requires discussions with corporate managers to ascertain, for example, the current status of a major corporate project, or to ascertain the reasons for a delay fo such a project.

8. Negotiations

Negotiations frequently involve discussions between different entities within and outside the company. Meetings of this type include negotiations with vendors regarding job specifications, budgets, and bid procedures; discussions with labour relations and plant managers with regard to preparation for labour negotiation meetings and/or the formulation of plans for resolving collective bargaining issues.

9. Conflict Resolution

In some instances one would prefer to resolve conflicts via a face-to-face meeting. However, time constraints and geographical dispersion of the organisations involved frequently make a simple teleconference meeting the most efficient and effective way of resolving a conflict.

The potentials for telecommunications/teleconferencing are tremendous but those promoting these approaches may tend to overstate both the ease of adoption of new technologies and the 'completeness' of the adoption. In their paper "Video Teleconferencing and Performance", Rosetti and Surynt (1985) take a more cautious view - they feel that even those who adopt advanced forms such as video teleconferencing are likely to continue with traditional practices such as face-to-face meetings. Overtime, they predict that distinctions between non-electronic and electronic meetings will diminish but that the two approaches will still persist even in the distant future.

3. COSTS AND BENEFITS/PROS AND CONS OF TELECONFERENCING

The pros and cons of teleconferencing are numerous. In his book on teleconferencing, Johansen (1984) lists a large number of potential positive impacts of this technology and a smaller number of potential negative impacts (Table 2).

One of the most comprehensive discussions of telecommunications is provided by Penrose (1984). He notes that the pros and cons of teleconferencing vary from category to category; the three major categories are Voice Telecommunications, Print Telecommunications, and Video Telecommunications.

Voice telecommunications is the oldest of these categories, the most widely spread, and the least expensive to utilise. It is not glamorous, but it is here to stay. In fact, its utility has been increased by the development of equipment for conference calls where more than two parties can interact and telelecture. Disadvantages include:

1. the fact that it is difficult to 'get to know someone'
2. extra effort may be required for planning and encouraging conversion
3. attention spans for listening tend to be short
4. speakers do not have the benefit of non-verbal cues
5. for data transmission, the telephone has a narrow bandwidth, hence a 'low data rate'.

On the positive side:

1. cost is low
2. access to most geographic locations is easy

3. telephones are widespread
4. the speed of information transmission is substantial.

Print telecommunications, after the telephone, is the most widely used telecommunications device. Print telecommunications may or may not be fully interactive and there may be voice and facsimile links. Penrose identifies ten advantages of 'electronic mail' and one half as many disadvantages. Advantages included the fact that it can

1. be sent certified with receipt acknowledgement
2. provide guaranteed next day service
3. go directly to Western Union
4. save phone and word processing charges
5. save paper and duplication costs
6. be connected to modems at small additional cost
7. free the user from time and location constraints such as having to work at the office
8. providing uninterrupted operation
9. allow speed of moving information
10. facilitate typing an electronic document to something else.

On the other hand, there are potentially several disadvantages:

1. the user sometimes (there are exceptions) needs a computer
2. it may cost money to check for electronic mail
3. photos take a long time to transmit by facsimile
4. commercial networks may have a minimum usage requirement
5. there is a strong potential for encouraging junk mail.

Finally, the most complex, expensive, and probably exciting form in the Penrose trinity is video telecommunications. Two-way conferencing is possible. Video conferencing seems to be especially appropriate for:

1. meetings that involve people who know each other and who are low in conflict
2. meetings of people with poor verbal skills
3. meetings which emphasise cooperative problem solving and information transmittal.

Still, there are numerous disadvantages:

1. transmission costs can be huge
2. technical equipment is expensive and there is high potential for technical and logistic problems
3. participants may find it impersonal
4. users often complain about poor quality graphics and lack of eye contact
5. some participants claim that it robs them of the status of travel.

Video conferencing may be the current fad but its adoption has been slowed by cost considerations and by misguided marketing which has stressed technology,

TABLE 2

Positive Impacts

Cost Reduction

- Reduces net travel expenses
- Reduces nonproductive time while travelling, as well as travel fatigue
- Reduces mistakes made because the 'right person' was not present at meeting
- Allows less nonproductive duplication of effort by people at sites separated geographically
- Shortens time necessary for some business cycles to be completed or for key decisions to be made
- Reduces the need to update people who could not travel to a face-to-face meeting, as well as reduces the possibility of summarising information inaccurately
- Reduces equipment downtime required if the repair person is needed at another site
- Reduces the possibility of business being affected by disruptions, such as fuel availability or political unrest

Straightforward Value-Added Benefits

- Allows new communication that was impractical before teleconferencing
- Improves opportunities to prepare for, and follow up on, face-to-face meetings
- Provides faster and better responses to emergencies when key people are separated geographically
- Increases degree of managerial choice regarding frequency and timing of communication
- Improves managerial control over field sites and decentralised offices
- Improves ability to share 'people resources' when people needed are geographically separated
- Provides an alternative way of maintaining good personnel relations
- Allows additional people to attend a meeting, even without advance notice
- Increases employee's sense of interpersonal contact, morale

Unconventional Approaches

- Makes job assignments less dependent on where a given employee happens to live
- Allows new opportunities for change meetings among people who could benefit from working together
- Encourages consideration of alternative solutions to given problems
- Allows new potential for intelligent computer programmes to contribute to the work of teleconference participants
- Alters how employees think about themselves and organisations

Negative Impacts

- Increases nonproductive time spent in meetings, because teleconferencing meetings are easier to arrange and useless meetings may be called
- Decreases freedom of operation for remote field sites, resulting in too much control by management
- Encourages overspecialisation and narrowness
- Decreases sense of interpersonal contact, morale
- Allows too much dependence on technology to develop, creating a potential for breakdowns, or even sabotage

Source: Johansen 1984

TABLE 3

	Face-to-Face	Video	Audio	Computer Conferencing
Geographic coincidence?	Yes	No	No	No
Time coincidence?	Yes	Yes	Yes	No
Group size Limits	Tens to hundreds	Few tens	Few tens	Hundreds
Speed	Talking Rate	Talking Rate	Talking Rate	Reading Rate
Nonverbal cues	All	Most	Audio only	None
Memory	Recordings	Record-ings	Record-ings	Unlimited retrieval and modification

Source: Hilts, Starr Rozanne, The Computer Conference, Journal of Communications, 28, Summer 1978, p. 159.

not user need (Kastle 1986). Still, within the general area of telecommunications, video conferencing is clearly the current growth industry. US firms have assumed an aggressive position here as have Japanese firms, e.g. Ricoh.

The full capabilities of video teleconferencing have not really been tested although a number of corporations have systems in place. A recent article based on the experience of Southern California Edison provides an interesting case study (Hausel, Shornstein and Donovan 1986). The case study points to both technical problems and user problems. Several potentially valuable observations can be drawn from Southern California Edison's experience. First, video conferencing's cost is high; such a system may reduce travel cost but savings are far too small to justify the system. Simple payback, i.e., payback without considering the time value of money, is estimated to be nine years. The System is best justified in terms of communication timeliness, efficiency, and plant safety - not travel cost tradeoff. Second, for the system to be a success, usage will need to be encouraged. Third, a user training programme will need to be established. And fourth, technical problems of transmission will need to be solved. In short, the system has potential but substantial additional investment will be required to realise its full potentials, and indeed, to keep it in place. Penrose borrows from Hiltz to summarise the capabilities of face-to-face conferencing with methods of teleconferencing (Table 3).

4. RESTRUCTURING AND TELECOMMUNICATIONS

Restructuring has both spatial and aspatial dimensions, although the latter case may ultimately have consequences for the former. The aspatial case considers the various costs associated with adapting the various technologies of telecommunications. Even a well capitalised firm in an industrialised nation is faced with a series of fundamental issues; it must rationalise:

a. the cost of purchasing sending and receiving equipment
b. the cost of maintenance
c. access to maintenance services
d. space requirements of new equipment and the cost of retrofitting office space
e. the cost of training operators
f. the cost of training users.

All of these are factors which may retard adoption of telecommunications technologies.

Spatial restructuring can be discussed in two ways. First, one can look at the potential impacts of telecommunications on the way business is done. Second, one can look at the existing and anticipated patterns of telecommunications equipment manufacture and telecommunications services and speculate about the significance of these industries as a component of regional economic structure.

5. POTENTIAL IMPACTS ON GOVERNMENT AND INDUSTRY

Rosetti and Surynt 1985 refer to 'blending' of communication resources when they discuss adoption of various technologies. The term is a useful one because the question is not so much 'what forms of communication will be abandoned' as it is 'what will the mix of forms be in the future?' Put another way - a) to what extent will telecommunications replace face-to-face interaction? and b) to what extent will one form of telecommunication be replaced by some other, perhaps more sophisticated form? In short, what opportunities exist to increase efficiency through straight substitution. In addition, one can speculate that telecommunications may actually promote additional interaction. The champion of telecommunications might point to telecommunication's potential to enhance the effectiveness of face-to-face meetings by encouraging electronic premeeting sessions that allow face-to-face meetings to be more efficient and bottom-line oriented or post meeting sessions which facilitate follow-through on face-to-face meeting agenda items. The cynic, however, might suggest that copy machines have encouraged waste by making copying 'too easy' and similarly, telecommunications will encourage useless meetings and electronic junk mail.

In his widely discussed, and perhaps controversial book ***Megatrends***, Naisbitt (1984) examines the information based society from the perspective of reducing the 'information float' among networks. He insists that there will continue to be a tradeoff between high technology and high touch (human contact) within the telecommunications industry. Naisbitt argues that the need for human interaction and face-to-face contact has an extremely high threshold which may never be broken down by technological advancements housing sterile time-space convergence/savings. People will simply choose to interact with other people on a more personal basis - face-to-face.

6. SUBSTITUTION POTENTIALS

The potentials for substitution are enormous and widely discussed in the literature. The literal implications for localised spatial restructuring are reviewed in some detail by Claisse (1983). First, he notes that there is some potential for substitution for urban travel - both journey to work trips and urban business trips and non-business trips such as shopping or social trips. Claisse reviews several studies which suggest that the number and/or duration of journey to work and business trips might be reduced by 15-30% if telecommunications were to be used to allow people to work at home or in neighbourhood work centres. His brief discussion on non-business trips suggests that urban trips might be reduced by 15-20% or they might, in fact, be increased over present levels by an inducement effect. Second, he suggests that studies dealing with urban travel indicate that perhaps two-thirds of all intercity trips might be replaced by telecommunications. Given data limitations and the narrow scope of the studies which have been completed, substitution estimates must be considered highly tentative. Nevertheless, the potentials for substitution appear to be considerable and the possibilities for energy savings and reductions in congestion that might come from increased use of telecommunications could be substantial.

Claisse also reviews the abundant opportunities for substitution of telecommunications for mail. Various studies indicate that telecommunication might, with relative ease carry 13% to 31% of all mail. Facsimile transmission and telex services especially have enhanced opportunities for substitution.

In short, existing firms can expect to see some changes in the years ahead. Similarly, firms, especially those in the finance, insurance, and real estate (FIRE) and service sectors might take advantage of new telecommunications technologies when selecting sites for new operations. But it remains to be seen if any spatial restructuring that does occur is done on a large scale basis and in association with new telecommunication technologies or if it simply represents modest fine-tuning of established patterns of change.

7. AGGLOMERATIONS AND OTHER CONSIDERATIONS PROMOTING THE STATUS QUO

Some items have already been discussed - the cost of adapting new telecommunications technologies can be substantial, preferences for face-to-face meetings apparently remain strong, and in some cases, simple resistance to change will certainly slow adoption. In addition, traditional concepts of agglomeration may continue to be valid in accounting for the maintenance of established spatial structures. External economies and especially urbanisation economies, in combination with other location factors, can be expected to continue to hold even 'telecommunication sensitive' sectors such as FIRE and services in cities. Urbanisation economies which are telecommunications specific, e.g., firms selling telecommunications services, those offering equipment maintenance, and those training operators are likely to be best developed and most competitive in places with substantial aggregate demand. Firms using telecommunications are also likely to find even more generic types of urbanisation economies attractive - infrastructure, size of market, deep labour pool, abundant suppliers of goods and services, urbanisation amenities, etc. are examples. One could easily envision a scenario where individual daily work patterns were modified by telecommunications but where the location of firms remained essentially unchanged because telecommunications was simply too small a part of the total mix of location factors to force basic restructuring. On the other hand, it is equally easy to imagine telecommunications supporting (but not driving) various existing patterns of decentralisation by facilitating communications between, say, a downtown bank and a suburban cheque clearing operation, or between a high tech firm in California's Silicon Valley and its assembly plant in Arizona. Both service based and commodity based multinationals have already benefitted from improved telecommunications. Whereas one might claim that the relatively basic forms of telecommunications that have been available for years were, in fact, responsible for much of the deconcentration of activity that has been experienced, Nicol (1985) and others (correctly) assert that there is scant proof that recent improvements have actually promoted deconcentration. Further, one might question whether the dramatic advances in telecommunications will produce new patterns or simply reinforce current trends.

Another perspective on the role of agglomeration is to focus on telecommunications as an industry rather than as an ancillary activity supporting other activities. Such a view is supported by Nicol, who points out that communications budgets of large corporations is 5-10% of total revenues and growing. Further, and more important, he sees information services evolving from ancillary to commodity status. Given the fact that telecommunications is seen as being a rapidly evolving industry where innovation is common and product life cycle is relatively short, it would appear that traditional localisation economies would be critical. Concentration of telecommunications manufacturers and those providing telecommunications services should benefit from proximity to a labour force with particular skills; to universities and private research centres geared to this industry; services; and suppliers of parts and components.

As an industry, telecommunications equipment may follow the pattern of computer software and other high tech industries. Ironically, telecommunication applications seem to play a significant role in determining the spatial patterns of these high tech industries. Markusen (1985) notes that high tech's tendency to agglomerate seems to be related to three sets of factors. First, early links between these sectors and earlier sectors. Second, a common need for access to pools of highly skilled professionals and technical workers and the presence of a good university to both produce these workers and to provide R&D support; and third, lifestyle, including urban, cultural, (natural) environmental, and recreational amenities.

Actually, future patterns of high tech activity are likely to be the product of both centre-reinforcing and decentralising forces (Hall et al. 1985). Decentralising forces include a) job creation in regional centres as firms work to reach national and even international markets; b) a spatially dispersed and heterogeneous list of potential clients; and c) high cost of living in established high tech centres. This third item could produce a spatially bifurcated industry with routine activities deconcentrating to low wage areas and administrative and R&D type activities staying in the major centres. Ironically, telecommunications itself is centre-reinforcing. Teleconferencing and other forms of telecommunications make it easier to meet the needs of a dispersed clientele. In addition, the aforementioned agglomeration economies, and 'reputation; of existing centres will also be centre-reinforcing.

8. IMPLICATIONS FOR PUBLIC POLICY

The implications for public policy are both fascinating and numerous, and they include both equity and efficiency considerations. Governments can influence telecommunications both by encouraging the development of the industry and by adopting its products. The US Department of Defense alone, through its procurement procedures, could very likely support the development of a sizeable telecommunications industry.

Similarly, telecommunications regulatory policy and direct subventions to support research and systems development are very influential. For example, the passage of three laws by the Japanese national Diet in December of 1984 has important implications both for the Japanese telecommunications industry and for the development of this industry elsewhere in the world (Ito 1986). Ito suggests that interagency conflicts can have critical long run implications for policy development. He notes that in Japan MPT (Ministry of Posts and Telecommunications) and MITI (Ministry of International Trade and Industry) were both 'interested parties' in the development of the Telecommunications Business Law which abolishes the monopoly enjoyed for over 30 years by NTT (Nippon Telegraph and Telephone). MPT considers the communication and information services industry as part of telecommunications policy whereas MITI sees them as an essential, and increasingly important part of the larger area of industrial policy. Ito's model (Figure 1) introduces a critical variable, supply. He refers to increased supply with the phrase "Relaxation of the limitation or scarcity of the resource by technological development". Essentially, his argument is that supply increases demand. An aggressive player, e.g., MITI, recognises opportunities and through pressure frees the resource (telecommunications) for widespread use through privatisation. Another dimension of this agreement is prescribed in Figure 2. Supply both drives demand and the privatisation of technology. In some respects, Ito's Figure 2 may raise more questions than it answers. It is interesting, for example to note that the two oldest forms of telecommunication, telephone and telegraph, are still largely regulated whereas, data communication is already in the free competition phase.

Virtually every industrialised nation has, or will, experience battles over agency 'turf'. The winners of these battles will be in a position to develop policy in a variety of areas. But most important, perhaps, are the implications for telecommunications itself - will it be viewed as an ancillary activity serving national needs, or will it be viewed and encouraged to develop as an industry in its own right, competing in the national and international market place?

Another policy dimension concerns the role that governments might play in encouraging concentration or deconcentration of industry. The production of telecommunications equipment itself seems to have, at most, limited potential as an employer in underdeveloped areas. But as a service industry it appears to have potential for increasing efficiency of activities placed in remote locations. Whereas telecommunications availability may not cause deconcentration, it might make remote locations in depressed areas marginally more attractive. Government support of telecommunications can, obviously, influence both the rate of adoption and the mix of telecommunication forms available. The role of telecommunications as an element of national development policy is not well understood. As various forms of telecommunications become more widespread it is likely that this technology will figure more prominently into the thinking of those charged with articulating regional development policy.

Finally, in the US (and elsewhere) there are numerous policy type questions which concern the transfer of technology from the US government or universities to private industry. A recent *Wall Street Journal* article (Smith 1986) called attention to this as a general problem. Those associated with US universities know that 'commercialisation of research' is an important topic with ethical overtones. Public universities especially, are torn between the goals of openly sharing knowledge and those of seeing a dollar return on their investments in research.

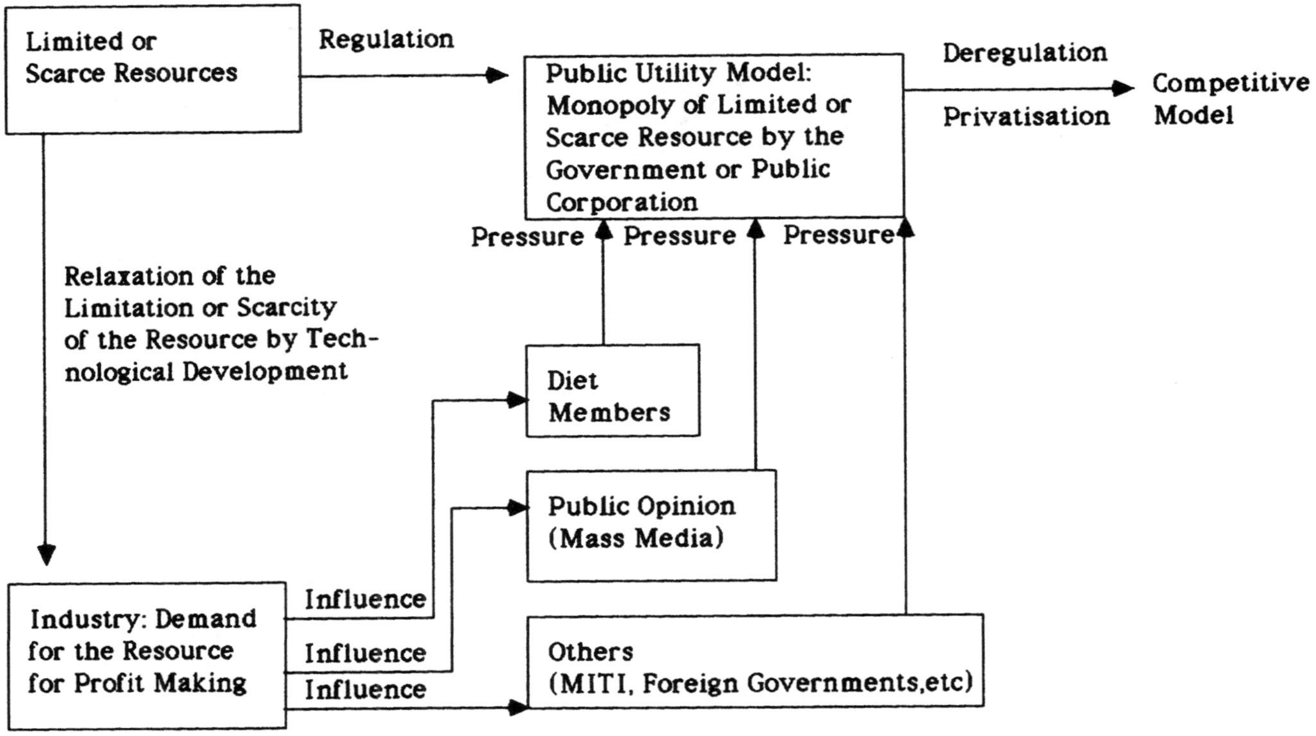

FIGURE 1 Policy developments in telecommunications

Source: Ito 1986

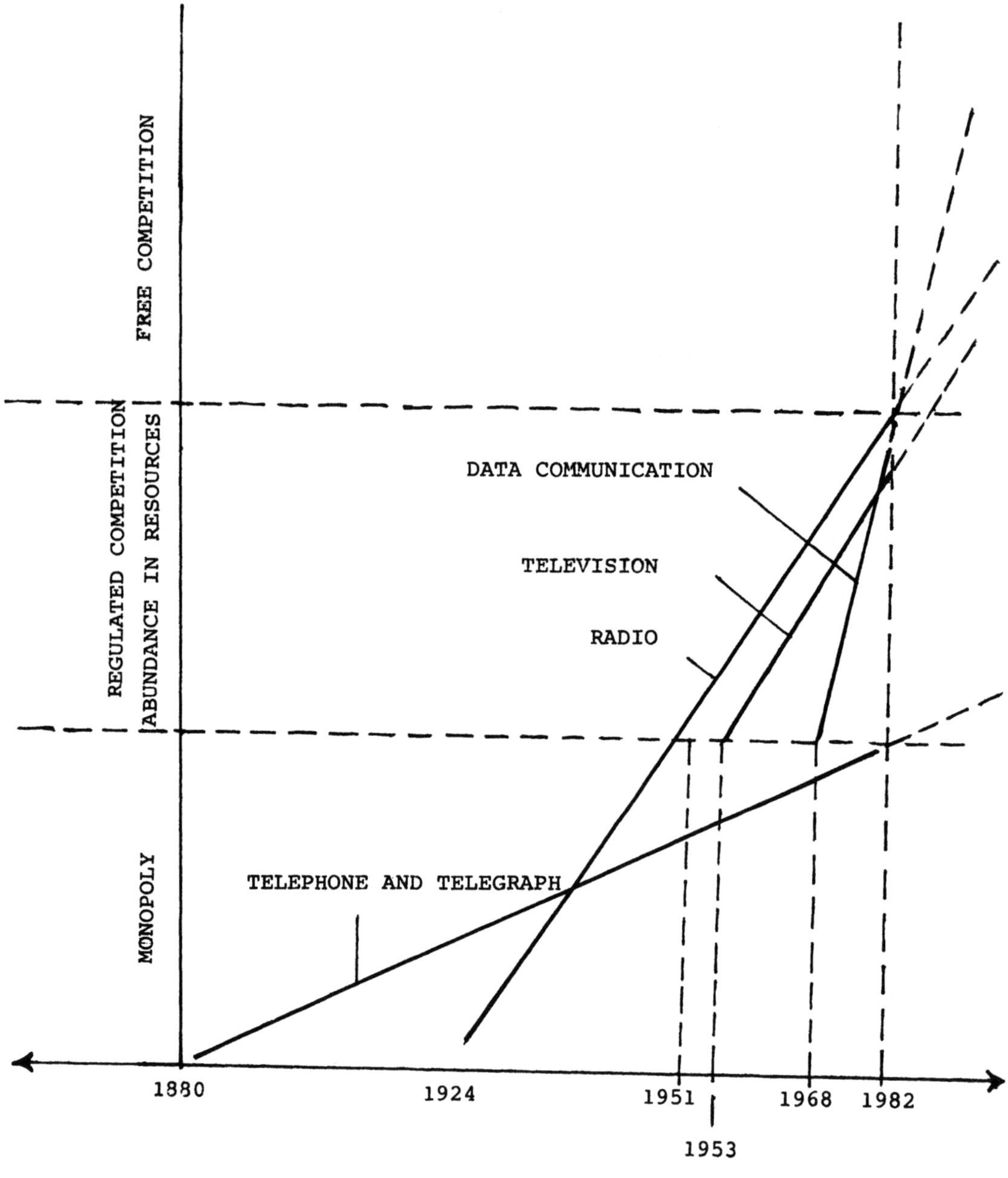

Figure 2 Time (technological development)

Source: ITO, 1986

ACKNOWLEDGEMENT

The author would like to thank Timothy Fik, Department of Geography and Regional Development, University of Arizona for his many useful comments and suggestions.

REFERENCES

Booz, Allen and Hamilton, Are You Ready for the Telecommunications Revolution? Industry Week, Vol. 182, No. 2, July 8, 1974, p. 42.

Claisse, G., Transport and Telecommunications, Report of the Fifty-Ninth Round Table on Transport Economics, European Conference of Ministers of Transport, OECD Publications Department, 2, rue Andre Pascal, Paris, France, 1983, 94 pages.

Cowan, R., Teleconferencing - Maximizing the Human Potential, Reston Publishing Company, Reston, Virginia, 1984, 288 pages.

Hall, P., A.R. Markusen, R. Osborn and B. Wachsman, The American Computer Software Industry: Economic Development Prospects, in: P. Hall and A. Markusen, (eds), Silicon Landscapes, Allen and Unwin, Boston, 1985, pp. 49-64.

Hausel, T.J., H. Shornstein and P. Donovan, Video Conferencing at Southern California Edison: A Case Study, Public Utilities Fortnightly, May 15, 1986, pp. 3-7.

Ito, Y., Telecommunications and Industrial Policies in Japan: Recent Developments, in: M.S. Snow, (ed), Marketplace for Telecommunications, Regulation and Deregulation in Industrial Democracies, Longman, New York, 1986, pp. 201-230.

Johansen, R., Teleconferencing and Beyond, Communications in the Office of the Future, McGraw-Hill, New York, 1984.

Kastie, D., Video Conferencing Vendors Tout New Solutions-Orientation, Business Marketing, June 1986, pp. 84,86,99-100,102,104.

Kelleher, K. and T.B. Cross, Teleconferencing: Linking People Together Electronically, Prentice-Hall, Inc., Englewood Cliffs, New Jersey, 1985, 303 pages.

Maher, J.A. and D.R. Fischell, Performance Considerations for Audio Teleconferencing Systems, Network Performance Center, ATT&T Bell Laboratories, Holmdel, New Jersey, Paper presented at the 9th Annual Conference on Teleconferencing and Interactive Media, Madison, Wisconsin, May 1985.

Markusen. A.R.. High-Tech Jobs. Markets and Economic Development Prospects: Evidence from California, in: P. Hall and A. Markusen (eds), Silicon Landscapes, Allen and Unwin, Boston, 1985, pp. 35-48.

Markusen, A.R. and R. Bloch, Defense Cities: Military Spending, High Technology, and Human Settlements, High Technology, Space, and Society, in: M. Castells, (ed), Urban Affairs Annual Reviews, Vol. 28, Sage Publications, Beverly Hills, California, 1985, pp. 106-120.

Naisbitt, J., Megatrends, Warner Books, New York, 1984, 333 pages.

Nicol, L., Communications Technology: Economic and Spatial Impacts, in: M. Castells, (ed)_High Technology, Space and Society, Urban Affairs Annual Reviews, Vol. 28, Sage Publications, Beverly Hills California, 1985, pp. 191-209.

Penrose J., Telecommunications, Teleconferencing, and Business Communications, The Journal of Communications, Vol. 21, No. 1, Winter 1984, pp. 93-111.

Rosetti, K. and T.J. Surynt, Video Teleconferencing and Performance, The Journal of Business Communications, Vol. 22, No. 4, Fall 1985, pp. 25-31.

Smith, T.K., Bill Aims to Ease Transfer of Technology from Federal Laboratories to Business, Wall Street Journal, October 1, 1986, p. 37.

INFORMATION TECHNOLOGY, THE URBAN SYSTEM AND URBAN POLICY CONSEQUENCES

Rolf Funck, Reiner Koblo, Jan Kowalski

1. INTRODUCTION

As with many other mature economies in recent years, the economy of the Federal Republic of Germany has - among other factors like the population decline - experienced serious structural changes connected with the rapid development and spread of new technologies leading to the creation of new economic activities, reshaping the character of the old ones and influencing the structure of the labour force. In this chapter, various aspects of the relationships between new technologies on the one hand, and the regional structure and the development of the urban system in West Germany on the other are analysed. Among the influences of the cluster of new technologies (Lakshmanan and Chatterjee 1986, p.15) which cause these cumulative effects, information technologies play an important role. A continuing structural change in the sectoral composition of the economy, leading to a growing dominance of the service sector and to changes within this sector itself (see Table 1), indicates the extent of these influences.

TABLE 1

Structural change in the West German Economy

Employment by sectors in %	1950	1960	1970	1983	1984	1985
Agriculture Forestry and Mining	28.2	16.5	10.6	7.5	7.4	7.4
Manufacturing and Construction	39.1	45.1	46.8	39.7	39.4	39.1
Services	32.7	38.4	42.6	52.8	53.2	53.5

Source: Institut der Deutschen Wirtschaft, Zahlen zur Wirtschaftlichen Entwicklung, 1986, p.6

Development and diffusion of new information technologies are determined by various factors which are regionally unequally distributed. Some of these factors are (Funck 1986):

- the regional and urban economic structure as described by sectoral relationships, the size and control structure of the regional economy,
- the quality of the regional and urban transportation and communication infrastructure,
- the quality and diversity or regional and urban labour markets,
- the existence of dynamic, risk-accepting entrepreneurs in the Schumpeterian sense,
- the availability of technological information,
- the accessibility of technological information,
- the presence and the level of activity of innovation-supporting institutions in the public and private sectors.

In general, it can be stated that the regional and urban deficits in the supply of relevant information and of other factors as enumerated above constitute spatial barriers for the development of new technologies.

2. SPATIAL ASPECTS OF NEW INFORMATION TECHNOLOGIES

A distinct shift of viewpoints in considering the role of technological information in urban and regional development has occurred in recent years. While, during the seventies, the economic-technological content of information, the degree of access to it and the spatial patterns of information flow have been predominant as objects of research, in the early eighties, the advent of new communication technologies has moved to the centre of analytical interest (Funck and Kowalski 1984, 1986a).

In the first approach, spatial access to innovation has been recognised as the most important factor for enabling or facilitating technology-based activities as a prerequisite for regional development especially in backward, lagging regions. The peak of this type of approach to the role of information in regional development has been epitomised by the formulation of the "innovation-oriented regional policy" and related proposals (Ewers and Wettmann 1980, Kowalski 1982).

In contrast to this concept of indirect effects of information - through innovation in production techniques - on regional development, the second approach visualises a more direct impact of new communication technologies on locational requirements of production and on mobility.patterns. At the same time, fears and anxieties concerning the negative impacts of these technologies come to the fore. The ease with which the 'friction of distance' may be overcome with the help of these technologies, is held to constitute danger for jobs and for the traditional role of cities, without leading by itself to a diminishing of the differences in the development levels between core and peripheral areas. At present, a real danger exists that the spread of new information technologies will be directed predominantly to already developed areas whereas the peripheral regions will remain largely devoid of information transfer networks (see Hoberg 1983, Schulz-Trieglaff 1982).

Referring to the long term effects of these technologies on employment as a whole, no consensus has so far been achieved in the literature. Some studies maintain that the overall impact will be neutral or negligible, since the disappearance of workplaces will be compensated by the creation of others (see Dostal 1982). Other authors are more pessimistic in predicting considerable loss in the employment level (e.g. Henckel et al. 1984), still other reports recognise that the results of forecasts are extremely sensitive to the underlying assumptions so that very little in the way of hard facts can be achieved (OECD 1981). Generally, the overall effects of new technologies on society and its functioning can be estimated only in a value-loaded way.

It seems obvious that the advent of new communication technologies will lead at least to serious structural changes in the labour market. Many routine jobs will vanish and certainly others will be created. But with respect to the possible overall decrease of the number of workplaces some fears seem exaggerated, at least in long term perspective, considering the present demographic tendencies in industrialised societies (Funck and Kowalski 1986b).

The conclusion can be stated that the new information technologies will exert diverse effects on spatial structure and development. They may have *deconcentrating* or *concentrating* impacts with respect to physical distribution of activities in space, with the deconcentration tendency prevailing in all probability. On the other hand, they may lead to *decentralisation* or *centralisation* of power and control throughout space with the probability of centralisation higher than vice versa (see Funck 1986, and Spehl 1985). If no specific measures are employed to achieve a contrary effect, the new technologies will most probably reinforce existing trends in spatial development, i.e. lead to an increased disparity between the strong and weak regions.

What their effects will be in future reality will largely depend on the distribution of new communication infrastructure in space. It must be considered that the explosive spread of these technologies, while in principle making it easier to provide information facilities and to enable the processing and transfer of information in practically every location in peripheral areas, will also lead to tensions concerning the viability of the centres of large cities and increase the relative backwardness of the periphery (Castells 1985).

Thus, the introduction of new communication media does not diminish the relevance of regional policy measures including activities to provide innovation-relevant information and conditions. On the contrary, the growing importance of information technologies in the reshaping of the society will enhance the potential role of regional policy in the future.

3. EMPIRICAL INVESTIGATION

Since the development of new information technologies and their spread into commercial applications depends on the innovative behaviour of entrepreneurs and other economic agents an attempt has been made to empirically analyse the differences in the 'propensity to innovate' in various urban and non-urban areas in the Federal Republic of Germany. We assume that this 'innovative propensity' will be responsible, among other factors, for the future development of new technologies, and consequently for the spatial impacts of these technologies. Our interests focus on the question whether visible differences in innovative behaviour exist between cities and rural counties, between cities of various sizes and between cities and rural counties located in economically fast growing Southern Germany (the States of Bavaria and Baden-Württemberg) and Northern Germany, which is often considered to lag behind. We also wanted to gain insight into the particular situation of selected Old Industrial Regions, which face almost insurmountable problems due mainly to the structure of their economies (see Funck 1985, Funck and Kowalski 1986b).

Even a very tentative answer to these questions can provide valuable information on the possible future fate of various urban centres and regions in the high technology era.

3.1 Data Base

In our investigation we relied on the data for 1980 and 1981 taken from a study of innovation density performed at the Institute of Systems Technology and Research on Innovation in Karlsruhe (ISI 1984), which were recomputed, extended, and adapted to more spatially desaggregated units by Blum (1985) and Blum and Koblo (1986).

Innovation density in a given region is defined as a ratio of the number of enterprises which applied for grants for employment of R&D personnel in the framework of regional innovation support programmes in the Federal Republic of Germany to the total number of enterprises in this region [1]. It may be argued, of course, that this ratio is at best a very rough indicator of the innovation activities in the region, expressing to some extent the bureaucratic skills of management rather than their innovativeness. But at present this is the only indicator available for all regions in the Federal Republic of Germany. This is why we decided to use it, being aware of its weaknesses.

We investigated 326 counties (Kreise) in Germany, of which 91 are so called city-counties (kreisfreie Städte), meaning a city constituting a county in the administrative sense. In some cases we additionally subdivided the group of city-counties into large (over 200 thousand inhabitants), medium sized (100 thousand to 200 thousand) and small cities (less than 100 thousand).

3.2 Methodology

First of all we estimated the impacts of various regional variables on innovation density for the whole of the Federal Republic of Germany by means of cross-regional regression analysis in order to gain insights into the general determinants of innovation activities in Germany. Then we investigated in greater detail spatial differences in innovation density for various types of regions.

Regressions for the whole of the Federal Republic of Germany have been conducted by employing the L-1.1 Programme (Liem et al. 1985). In comparison with other methods, which assume a linear or logarithmic functional form to be present in the data, L-1.1 has the advantage of allowing a determination of the functional form in the data based computation. It also considers statistical irregularities in the data like heteroscedasticity, interdependencies in the data or autocorrelation.

In order to determine the best fitting functional form for the underlying data several functions are estimated with the programme. In every iterative estimation one or several parameters are excluded. At first a very restricted linear or loglinear function is estimated, then a more flexible functional form is developed. The estimations are compared with each other through a likelihood value which is computed by the programme. The difference in the likelihood value of the two estimations provides a measure of improvement in the functional form from one estimation to the next. Finally a best fitting functional form for the data is derived.

3.3 Results and Interpretation

The effects of the exogenous variables on the endogenous ones are measured by the elasticities of the exogenous variables. In nonlinear functions the often used regression coefficient is not an appropriate parameter for this purpose.

We call the effect of an exogenous variable 'stable' if the elasticity has the same sign in every estimation. If the sign of the elasticity changes in some estimations or if the value of the t-statistics is very low, we call it 'unstable'. The results are given in Table 2. In this table, we do not provide absolute values for the elasticities because in the nonlinear transformations which have been used in the L-1.1 programme the absolute values cannot be used to quantify the effects. For this reason the table contains only '+' and '-' signs to indicate the direction of the influence.

It should be noticed that the 'best', i.e. the strongest impacts are obtained for variables which may be labelled 'classical', e.g. population, fixed assets, income and unemployment. The results for infrastructure variables and variables expressing the administrative status of a region do not provide any clear indication of the direction or strength of their influence.

Among the 'classical' variables one can observe the positive impact of population density (which may be interpreted as an agglomeration factor). Interestingly the impact of fixed assets per capita is strongly positive in the non-city counties and negative in the city counties. Possibly, this could be explained by the high levels of fixed assets values in the heavy industry and mining, which are not as innovative as other sectors and which are concentrated in the cities, especially in the northern part of the Federal Republic of Germany. The fact that income per capita levels in counties adjacent to cities exert a positive influence seems plausible.

TABLE 2

Influence of determinants of Innovations Density in West Germany

	Overall	Non-city counties	Cities
Population density[1]		++	+
Fixed assets per head		++	-
Income of adjacent[2] counties or cities per capita	+	++	+
Income per capita[2]	-	--	+
Unemployment[3]		++	-
Interstate highway density[4]		-	+
State highway density[4]		-	-
Other roads density[4]	-		
Density of road networks nodes[5]		+	-
Number of beds in hotels per 1,000 inhabitants		+	
High level centre[6]			
Site of regional authorities[7]	-		-
Capital of State or of the Republic	+	-	+

Legend:

++ (--) high and stable positive (negative) effect

+ (-) low positive (negative) effect

1) Number of inhabitants per km^2

2) In thousand DM per capita

3) Number of unemployed persons per thousand inhabitants

4) Length in km per km^2

5) Number of nodes per km^2

6) Oberzentrum

7) Bezirksregierung

TABLE 3

Innovation Densities in the Federal Republic of Germany (in per cent)

Federal Republic of Germany average	16,627
small cities	11,331
medium sized cities	15,143
large cities	17,124
all cities	15,870
non-city counties	16,627
North Germany	15,961
Southern Germany	17,718

TABLE 4

Innovation Densities in the Federal States for Various Types of Areas

	Large cities	Hinter-land of large cities	Medium sized cities	Hinter-land of medium sized cities	Small cities	Rural counties
Schleswig-Holstein	8.20	9.60	10.38	6.67	7.55	7.14
Hamburg	16.51	0.00	0.00	0.00	0.00	0.00
Niedersachsen	18.90	15.14	11.60	17.84	14.71	15.37
Bremen	24.46	0.00	0.00	0.00	0.00	0.00
Nordrhein-Westfalen	17.99	10.15	24.56	21.98	0.00	18.50
Hessen	15.79	16.03	13.68	15.93	0.00	12.44
Rheinland-Pfalz	0.00	16.28	8.52	17.74	8.21	14.83
Baden-Württemberg	16.02	25.52	14.75	18.70	8.93	17.11
Bayern	17.35	20.65	9.00	22.07	12.41	12.91
Saarland	16.59	17.65	0.00	0.00	0.00	0.00
Berlin	15.12	0.00	0.00	0.00	0.00	0.00
North	16.90	17.18	16.18	18.61	9.29	15.03
South	16.81	24.56	12.99	18.35	12.25	14.85

It seems somewhat difficult to try and explain the impacts of income per head and unemployment levels on the innovation density. In the case of non-city counties, it seems that low incomes coincide with less innovativeness, but where unemployment is high, it leads to more innovative efforts. In cities, on the other hand, higher income levels go hand in hand with increased innovation density, but higher unemployment levels coincide with decreased innovation. It would be necessary to study in depth the economic structure and organisational features of firms in particular cities in order to be able to provide definitive interpretations of those results. This was outside the scope of this introductory paper.

Let us now proceed to a spatially differentiated analysis of innovation density levels in the Federal Republic of Germany. Table 3 summarises the results, Figures 1 and 2 show the densities graphically. From Figure 1 it can be seen that no clearcut statement considering innovation densities in the 11 West German states considering their location and levels of economic prosperity is possible. High densities are recorded in Baden-Württemberg as expected, but also in Bremen, with its stagnating ship building industry and high unemployment. As can be seen in Table 3 and Figure 2, small cities as a group record the lowest density levels as compared with medium and large cities, but also with non-city counties.

The advantageous position of the large cities should be noted. On the other hand, as can be seem from Table 3 if Northern Germany is compared with Southern Germany as a whole, the advantage of the South becomes visible. This advantage is, however, not equally pronounced if we consider various types of areas (see Table 4 and Figure 3).

As separate categories, we have distinguished the hinterlands of large and medium cities, meaning counties adjacent to those cities, and as rural areas all non-city counties which are not hinterlands in the described sense. It can be seen that especially the hinterlands of large cities enjoy extremely high innovation densities in the southern part of the country (see the results for Baden-Württemberg and Bavaria). In contrast, medium sized cities in the South lag behind their northern counterparts, due mainly to very low values for cities in this category in Bavaria.

It should be noted that rural areas are performing better than small cities, both in the South and North of the country. With respect to the large cities which, on the whole, record high innovation densities, it seems that their location does not influence their performance. Two federal states which are in the North and record above average innovation density levels (Nordrhein-Westfalen and Bremen) probably owe their high performance to the fact that their urban structures are dominated by large cities (in the case of the former) or that they consist of just one large city (in the case of the latter).

Taken together, our results indicate that large cities and hinterlands of large and medium cities coincide especially with strong innovation activities. Being in the non-city region is therefore no disadvantage in comparison with small and medium cities, especially if the non-city region in question happens to lie in the vicinity of large cities, preferably in the South.

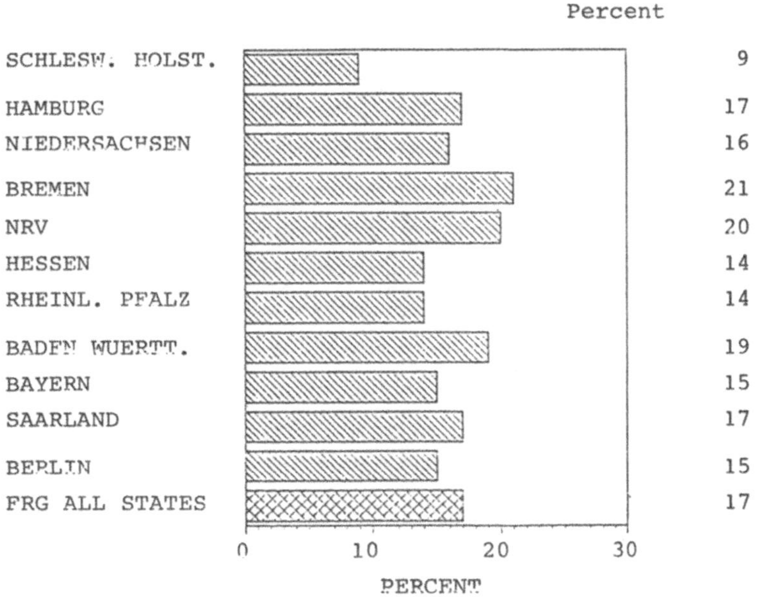

Figure 1: Innovation density in 11 states and the Federal Republic of Germany

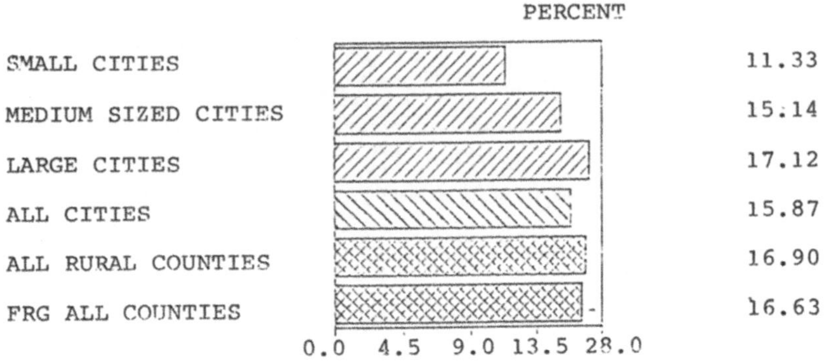

Figure 2: Innovation density in different sized cities, rural counties, and the Federal Republic of Germany

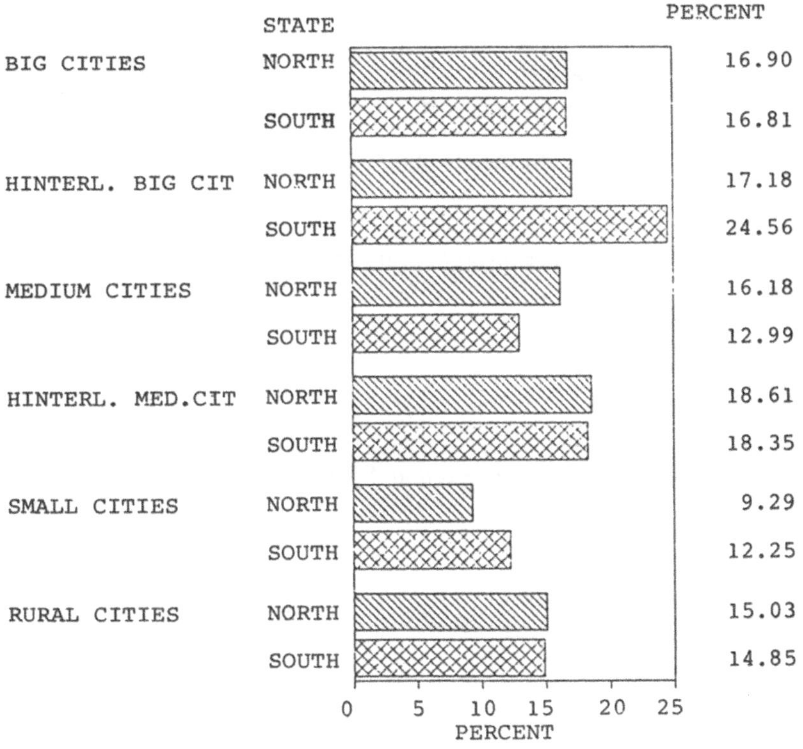

Figure 3: Innovation density in north and south Germany in different areas

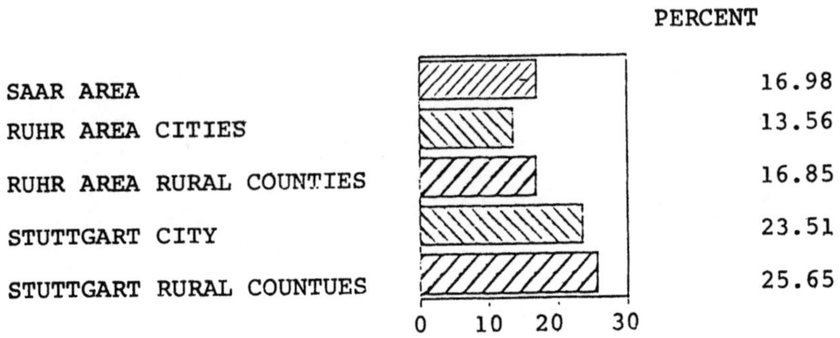

Figure 4: Innovation density in old and new industrial areas

TABLE 5
Innovation densities in selected old and new industrial areas

Saarland	16,984
Ruhrgebiet, cities	13,557
Ruhrgebiet, other counties	16,847
Stuttgart, city	23,515
Stuttgart, hinterland	

This last statement is also supported by the evidence given in Table 5 and Figure 4 where we provide innovation densities for a selected new industrial region and its hinterland (Stuttgart) and for two Old Industrial Regions (Ruhr and Saarland).

Stuttgart shows a very high value but its hinterland boasts an even higher level. The Ruhr area as expected, records a low density, but its non-city counties do not deviate from the Federal Republic of Germany average. The same is true in the case of Saarland.

3.4 Concluding Remarks

On the whole, the empirical evidence presented indicates that the distribution of innovation activities which are, as a rule, connected with the information based new technologies seems to favour the economically stronger highly developed areas of large cities and their hinterlands as opposed to the lagging peripheral regions and old areas. The long term spatial effects of new information technologies are not certain: to a large extent, they will depend on the efficiency of future regional and urban policies and on technology policies as pursued by the federal and state governments. Left to itself, the development of new technologies will reinforce rather than cure, various regional 'diseases' of which the North-South disparity and the problems of Old Industrial Regions are the prime examples.

4. POLICY RECOMMENDATIONS

In the short run no policy is possible which would improve the disadvantageous positions of regions which do not participate in the technological revolution at an equal rate with the rest of the country. Only a well conceived, concerted and persistent application of a package of measures, aimed at an improvement in the locational attractiveness of these areas, mainly by an improvement of the quality and supply levels of a specialised labour force, provision of research and education centres and specialised financial and other services can help to avoid the growing polarisation between the strong and weak regions as a consequence of the development of new information technologies.

Based on these considerations as well as on the results of interviews with more than thirty enterprises and more than thirty research institutions, financial institutions, public and semipublic institutions engaged in technology oriented research and development, technology transfer and innovation related activities in the Karlsruhe region (see Auctor-IWW 1987), the following policy claims may be stated (see also Funck and Kowalski 1986a):

- Elaboration and extension of services of innovation-advisory units, provision of access to technical data banks and other sources of innovation-relevant information is necessary.

- Expansion of technology-oriented institutions of higher learning and research (universities, institutes of technology) in non-centre areas, particularly in medium sized cities performing central place roles in the periphery is basic.

Although the establishment of such an institution will not necessarily lead to development through an expansion of information dependent innovative activities, it will in the long run change the intellectual milieu and the level of technological knowhow in the social environment, thus gradually creating important preconditions for development.

- Relocation from core to periphery of adequate units of public administration, particularly directed towards distribution of technological information (e.g. Patentinformationsstellen) will be helpful.

- Supply and support of technology centres (technology parks) can considerably improve the local starting conditions for technology-oriented production.

Similar recommendations can be made with respect to Old Industrial Areas. They can usually offer

- good existing connections in the traffic and communications networks,

- ample supply of land and building structures for redevelopment towards a use as technology centres,

- good provision with institutions of higher learning and research,

but suffer from

- unattractive residential environments and low quality consumer-oriented infrastructure,

- surplus supply of labour inadequately skilled for high technology employment.

Thus, under the requirements of technological change, an adequate restructuring is advisable regarding

- industrial (sectoral) structure,

- size-structure of enterprises (to medium and small-sized),

- urban structure: better infrastructure supply in old centres and medium/small-sized centres,

- provision of tie-in with high quality transport and communications networks.

Finally, it should be stressed that the advent of new communication technology will very probably lead to a shift in the emphasis of regional policy and planning. New technology means, in its locational essence, a reduction of the importance of physical accessibility as a location variable. The specific characteristics of a given geographical site as a location for a particular activity become more and more decisive in locational choice for investment. The role of regional planning will increasingly move toward political action intended to help create these specific site characteristics.

In conclusion we claim that the role of regional and urban planning will not diminish but gain in importance in the high technology future.

NOTES

[1] Enterprises of up to 1,000 employees or less than 200 Million DM in sales.

REFERENCES

Auctor, Institut für Wirtschaftspolitik und Wirtschaftsforschung (IWWI, Innovationspotential des Wirtschaftsraumes Karlsruhe, Lörrach, 1987.

Blum, U., Karlsruher Regionaldatenbank, Institut für Wirtschaftspolitik und Wirtschaftsforschung, Universität Karlsruhe, 1985.

Blum, U. and R. Koblo, Regionale Determinanten des Innovationsprozesses, Institut für Wirtschaftspolitik und Wirtschaftsforschung, Universität Karlsruhe, Discussion Paper 8/1986.

Castells, M. (ed), High Technology, Space and Society, Urban Affairs Annual Review, Vol. 28, Sage Publications, Beverly Hills, London, New Delhi, 1985.

Dostal, W., Fünf Jahre Mikroelektronik - Diskussion, Mitteilungen aus Arbeitsmarkt- und Berufsforschung, H.2, 1982.

Ewers, H.-J. and R.W. Wettmann, Innovation Oriented Regional Policies, Regional Studies, Vol. 14, 1980.

Funck, R.H., Die Obersteiermark hat eine gute Chance - vergleichbare Regionen in der Bundesrepublik Deutschland, Paper presented at a conference 'Neue Kraft für traditionelle Industrieregionen', Graz, 2nd October, 1985, mimeo, Karlsruhe.

Funck, R.H., Technologiepolitik und Regionalentwicklung, Paper presented at August Lösch Tage, Heidenheim, Federal Republic of Germany, 11-13 September 1986.

Funck, R.H. and J.S. Kowalski, The Role of Information in Regional and Urban Development, in: IARUS (International Association for Urban and Regional Statistics), 11th Meeting, Copenhagen, 1984.

Funck, R.H. and J.S. Kowalski, Innovation and Urban Change, in: J. Brotchie, P. Hall and P. Newton (eds), The Spatial Impact of Technological Change, Croom Helm, London, 1986a, pp.229ff.

Funck, R.H. and J.S. Kowalski, Possible Employment Effects of New Technologies in Old Industrial Regions, Paper presented at the conference of the French Section of the Regional Science Association, Paris, 1-3 September 1986, mimeo,

Karlsruhe.

Henckel, D., E. Nopper and N. Rauch, Informationstechnologie und Stadtentwicklung, Kohlhammer, Stuttgart, Berlin, Koln, Mainz, 1984.

Hoberg, R., Raumwirksamkeit neuer Kommunikationstechniken - innovations - und diffusionsorientierte Untersuchungen am Beispiel des Landes Baden-Württemberg, Raumforschung und Raumordnung, November/December 1983.

ISI (Fraunhofer-Gesellschaft), Institut für Systemtechnik und Innovationsforschung), Erfassung regionaler Innovationsdefizite, in: Schriftenreihe des Bundesministers für Raumordnung, Bauwesen und Städtebau, Heft Nr. 06.054, 1984.

Kowalski, J.S., Information Development Poles: the West German Context, Research Memorandum No. 8219. Department of Economics, University of Amsterdam, The Netherlands, 1982.

Lakshmanan, T.R. and L. Chatterjee, Technical Change and Metropolitan Adjustments, Regional Science and Urban Economics, 16, 1986, p. 7-30.

Liem, T.C., M. Dagenais, M.J.I. Gaudry and R. Koblo, L-1.1: Ein Programm fur Box-Cox-Transformationen in Regressionsmodellen mit heteroskedastischen und autoregressiven Residuen, Institut für Wirtschaftspolitik und Wirtschaftsforschung, Universität Karlsruhe, Discussion Paper 4/1986.

OECD, Microelectronics, Productivity and Employment, Paris, 1981.

Schulz-Trieglaff, M., Können neue Medien einen Beitrag zum Ausgleich von Entwicklungsunterschieden einzelner Regionen leisten?, Informationen zur Raumentwicklung, H.3, 1982.

Spehl, H., Raumliche Wirkungen der Telematik. Stand der Diskussion und Programm des Arbeitskreises der Akademie für Raumforschung und Landesplanung, Raumforschung und Raumordnung, November/December 1985, pp.254-270.

COMBINING COMMUNICATION AND TRANSPORT TECHNOLOGY TO IMPROVE URBAN TRAVEL CHOICES

David E. Boyce

1. INTRODUCTION

Throughout the history of urban settlements, the phenomenon of traffic congestion seems to have been as pervasive as it is today. The late twentieth century version of traffic congestion may be generally described as the absence of smoothly flowing automobiles, trucks and buses on urban streets and expressways. In some cases, the flow of vehicles is impeded only by the excess of demand as compared with roadway capacity. In others, it is compounded by the presence of pedestrians, bicycles, motorcycles and in some cases, carts and wagons moved by both animals and men. In earlier times, motorised vehicles were absent, but vehicles drawn by animals were much more prevalent, evidently with similar results in terms of loss of time, excessive operating costs and environment degradation.

A concerted effort to improve urban traffic conditions has been made in large urban centres of both developed and developing regions of the world during the past forty years. Massive expenditures on freeways and public transit lines have transformed street and streetcar systems into modern high speed expressway and rapid transit networks. Automobiles have been greatly improved with regard to safety, operating efficiency and atmospheric emissions, while maintaining the high level of performance and comfort desired by consumers. Traffic signal systems have also been improved in terms of their level of automation and response to traffic conditions; a detailed survey of advanced traffic control systems and recent experience with their application is given by Strobel (1982). The design of roadways, parking garages and other facilities has been upgraded in terms of performance, cost and aesthetic attributes. Finally, the capability to predict future use of proposed facilities has advanced to the point that it may truly be regarded as a science.

Despite these advances, urban traffic congestion remains a pervasive, negative feature of the urban condition, especially in areas undergoing rapid development. Newspapers of major cities frequently editorialise about the need for relief. Opinion surveys indicate a general dissatisfaction with traffic conditions, and often compare them unfavourably with the problems of crime, access to health care, housing conditions as so forth. A recent report of the (US) Engineering Research Board (1987, P.282) cites urban traffic congestion as one of the most important transportation problems requiring research.

Urban transportation planners and researchers generally agree that the phenomenon of traffic congestion is reasonably well understood and that the present programmes of road improvement and operation are cost effective and appropriate. Few would argue for a major programme of new urban expressway construction since the social and environmental consequences appear to be far more severe that the modest benefits to motorists; however, some suburban areas do appear to be seriously deficient in both arterial street and expressway capacity. Likewise, there is a general reluctance to recommend construction of major rapid transit systems, except in very large cities, since their cost seems highly excessive as compared with the expected level of use. Recently, I advocated that a moderate level of traffic congestion is not only a characteristic of a viable urban city, but is even beneficial in terms of reducing excessive trip length, encouraging the use of alternate modes, and emphasising the importance of urban travel in housing and job location choices (see Boyce and Kim 1987).

Still one wonders whether our perception of these issues and their present solutions is correct. Why is it that other fields such as telephone communication, television, computers and even electric power generation and transmission have made major technological advances during the past forty years, whereas urban transportation technology has remained basically static? Is it simply that urban transportation technology has fully matured with little possibility for further advancement? Clearly, the advances which were cited earlier are limited to levels of components or subcomponents, as described by Garrison (1984). Is there no system level innovation or technological development that could raise the productivity of the entire urban transportation system to a new, previously unimaginable level of efficiency?

The invitation to prepare this chapter, which in fact coincided with two other similar requests, has offered a stimulating challenge to reconsider this issue. In doing so, I have examined a recent technological innovation, being marketed as a rather simple navigational aid to drivers, in a new light by drawing on a workshop discussion chaired by Hearn (1985). Suppose this navigational aid was combined with current communication and traffic monitoring technology and with present and prospective analytical capability to identify network routings which are best from either an individual user's or society's point of view? Could this system, once implemented, achieve the increase in productivity and relief from inefficiency which is so frequently requested? What increase in traffic operations efficiency might be expected from the full implementation of such a system? How would these changes, and the improved level of travel information that might accompany them, influence travel choices beyond route choice, such as choice of departure time, trip frequency and even the choice of alternative modes? How might this system change the choice of housing and job location choices, or the choice of shopping and recreational travel? What would be the benefits to users of a partial implementation?

These seem to me to be the questions that require examination concerning such a system. In this paper, I attempt an initial exploration of these issues. Because fully answering these questions requires an in-depth analysis, the principal contribution of this paper is to suggest an analytical framework. Nevertheless, some hints at the results may emerge.

The remainder of this chapter is organised as follows. First, a brief, relatively nontechnical description of the navigational aid is offered, together with some necessary assumptions concerning other technology needed to use this aid in a new way. Then, travel behaviour of urban commuters is examined to determine how this assumed technology would affect their travel and location choices, and what differences it could make. The assumptions and limitations of this current analytical framework are also examined to determine whether it is suitable for answering the questions. Finally, a refined set of questions stated in the terminology of this framework is offered.

2. DESCRIPTION OF THE TECHNOLOGY

The technological innovation that makes it possible to imagine an urban automobile guidance system is a navigational aid for automobiles utilising dead reckoning or inertial navigation technology described by Zygmont (1986). The navigational aid consists of an onboard location monitoring system, a network database of digitised road maps and a dashboard mounted video display terminal. Distance travelled by the vehicle is measured by sensors in the wheels of the vehicle's nonpowered axle; direction changes are read by an electronic compass. These raw data are augmented by the system's network database; a microprocessor correlates the vehicle's motion with the network data, yielding an estimate of the vehicle's location relative to its starting point. The vehicle's location and network in its vicinity are displayed on the terminal screen. This display is updated every second, causing the network to scroll over the screen. In addition, the driver's destination may be entered into the system and displayed on the screen.

The only dead reckoning system now commercially available is the Navigator from Etak of Menlo Park, California. This system, which has the computational capacity of an IBM PC, sells for less that $2,000. Etak also plans to introduce its Fleet Vehicle Locator, which consists of a dead reckoning location finder with a modem for transmitting location information over the vehicle's two way radio to a base station, where it is decoded and displayed on a computer terminal together with the location of other vehicles in a fleet. A fleet dispatcher can transmit messages which are displayed on the receiving vehicle's screen. Another Etak product under development is a computerised workstation which would allow dispatchers to specify individual vehicle routes; from the material available, it is unclear whether these would be transmitted or displayed, or recorded for later use, such as to specify the daily itinerary for a delivery vehicle.

General Motors Corporation recently acquired exclusive right to the Etak system among North American automakers. In addition, Etak is selling the Navigator as an add-on component, and may license its technology overseas. General Motors plans a limited introduction of the system in 1990.

A navigator system developed by Blaupunkt-Werke of Stuttgart, West Germany, actually guides drivers to their destinations. For a driver-entered destination, the Electric Traffic Pilot directs the driver with arrows on the system's liquid crystal display and with audio prompts from a voice synthesiser. If a turn is missed, directions are recalculated automatically. Like Etak's Navigator, the Electronic Traffic Pilot correlates vehicle motion with digital maps; however, unlike Etak, it does not provide a map display. Simpler dead reckoning devices are available from Plessey Radio Systems of England for about $700 and VDO Adolf Schindling of Schwalback, West Germany, for about $400, suggesting that a large market is possible for such technology. Frost and Sullivan, a New York market research firm, predicted that the automotive market for navigators could reach $100 million by 1990.

What additional technology would be necessary to extend these navigational aids into an ***automotive guidance system***? First, a communication system is needed. A radio receiver would enable the navigator to receive digital information on the best available routes from a specific origin to a specific destination, as well as current and future travel time estimates. For the purposes of this chapter, it is assumed that this information could be provided for sufficiently small origin and destination areas so as to yield meaningful routings. Adding a radio transmitter could enable a central controller to receive information on a vehicle's origin-destination and departure time. Moreover, from reports of the vehicle's location en route, additional data on vehicle demand could be obtained. Alternately, origin-destination and departure time information could be transmitted by telephone prior to departure.

Second, a comprehensive sensing system is required. Elements of this system are already in place in the form of expressway flow monitoring systems and traffic signal sensors. Data from these sensors would be transmitted to a central analysis unit for the purpose of estimating travel times on all network links. Historical data could also be utilised. Travel times over alternative routes between hundreds of thousands of origin-destination pairs could be evaluated, and best route information transmitted to the vehicle-based navigators. This information would need to be updated very frequently, perhaps as often as every five minutes.

The third component of the system is the central analysis unit itself. This unit would consist of one or more large computers, probably of the supercomputer, multiprocessor type. Travel time information from sensors would be used to calculate shortest time routes, or to determine the travel time over precalculated alternative routes, whichever proved to be more efficient. (Average vehicle operating cost could also be included in determining best routes, but for simplicity I shall describe these in terms of time.) If origin-destination data for current and prospective trips were available, together with recent historical data, expected shortest routes for several time intervals of perhaps 15 minutes could also be calculated. These estimates could be used by drivers to decide their best departure times, or to avoid unusual conditions caused by accidents or other traffic flow interruptions.

These three subsystems (communications, flow sensing and computation) together with the navigator location sensing and display subsystem constitute a proposed ***automobile guidance system***. An analysis of the technological feasibility and design of this system is well beyond the scope of this chapter. However, a similar but more comprehensive technological system concept, Automobile Road Information System Evolution (ARISE), has been described by a group of Swedish experts. A feasibility study made by ConNova (1985) concluded that such a system could be cost effective, especially if an integrated system for route guidance and dynamic system management could be achieved. The following sections examine the implications of such systems for urban travel and location behaviour and for reducing traffic congestion.

3. A FRAMEWORK FOR ANALYSING THE IMPACTS OF THE AUTOMOBILE GUIDANCE SYSTEM

How would the system described above change the use of the urban transportation system by commuters? Is it possible to predict in advance of the partial or full deployment of such a system whether it would reduce travel time and congestion? These are questions for which transportation network modellers should be able to offer some insights, if not complete answers. In this section, an initial framework for addressing these issues is described.

Perfect Information versus Uncertainty

The classic transportation network equilibrium model of Beckmann, McGuire and Winsten (1956) relates flow dependent travel costs to route choices and travel demands on a highway network. In its simplest form, the model states for a fixed rate of trips per time period from each origin to each destination, that the travel times on routes which are used are equal and that no unused route has a lower travel time. Thus, each driver is on a minimum travel time route. In this model the route travel times are determined as increasing functions of the flows on the links comprising each route. Thus, traffic congestion is endogenous to the model.

The model is based on two important assumptions. First, it is a static, rate of flow model. All variables are expressed in trips per time period, and the implied duration of the flows is sufficiently long that the flow of trips from each origin to destination occurs on each link of each used route. In other words, there is no concept of a vehicle moving through the network in this model; rather there are vehicle flows per time period on routes and links.

The issue of the static or rate of flow formulation of the model is quite perplexing. If such models are to be used to predict route conditions over a dynamically changing commuting period, clearly a static model is unacceptable. Current research to develop dynamic models, however, suggests these models are presently intractable for networks of even modest size (see Ben-Akiva et al. 1986). A solution to this issue may lie in a quasi-dynamic approach. One example of a quasi-dynamic model is given by van Vliet (1982, p.580); however, my idea is somewhat different.

Suppose the commuting period was divided into relatively short time periods of perhaps 15 minutes, If an origin-destination (O-D) table of vehicle flow appropriate to this time period was available, the solution of the model would correspond to travel conditions during this short time interval. Clearly, this O-D table could not contain trips longer than 15 minutes in duration; therefore, it must contain segments of longer trips which would occur during the short period under consideration. How these trip segments should be extracted from an O-D table of all trips occurring during a week day is an unanswered question. However, it is also an approach that seems to have been overlooked in efforts to formulate dynamic network models, and one that may be susceptible to analysis.

A second major assumption of the network equilibrium model is that drivers have perfect information; that is, somehow they 'know; which routes to use. Horowitz (1984) has investigated a model in which drivers are assumed to acquire this information through their prior commuting experience; even assuming this information, he finds it cannot be shown that the flows will converge to a stable equilibrium. The proposed auto guidance system would have the capability of providing much better information than is presently available, and thus may be a way to assure that equilibrium solutions can be achieved. The imperfect information presently available, therefore, results in longer trips than a system with perfect information, which might be termed *user-optimal* in that each driver is on his shortest route. In a system with less than perfect information, some drivers are bound to take longer routes, thereby not only increasing their travel time, but also the travel time of others through the congestion they add to the system.

The classic user-optimal network equilibrium model, in fact, may be generalised to include the dispersion in choices to longer routes resulting from imperfect information. This model is generally not solved because there exists no efficient way of fully or even partially enumerating the set of candidate routes between each origin-destination pair; however, Dial (1971) did propose an implicit enumeration method which might be used in this context. Moreover, since no data exists on actual route choices for urban networks, and little data for total travel time, even for samples of links, there is presently no good basis for implementing such a *dispersed* network equilibrium model. Nevertheless, in the context of the questions raised in this chapter, some estimates of the savings in travel time from improved route information could be made using these models.

One functional form for the dispersed network equilibrium model is the following:

$$h_{ijr} = \frac{T_{ij} \exp(-\theta c_{ijr})}{\sum_{r \epsilon R_{ij}} \exp(-\theta c_{ijr})} \tag{3.1}$$

where h_{ijr} is the number of trips/hour from origin zone i to destination zone j by route r, one route in a set of feasible routes, R_{ij}; T_{ij} is the given number of trips/hour from origin i to destination j, c_{ijr} is the flow-dependent travel time from origin i to destination j by route r; and q is a dispersion parameter. If q is zero, the trips are equally dispersed across the routes in R_{ij}. As q becomes large, the solution tends to the user-optimal solution.

The total travel time of a trip pattern may be calculated as:

$$C_\theta = \sum_i \sum_j \sum_{r \epsilon R_{ij}} h_{ijr}\, c_{ijr} \tag{3.2}$$

The relationship between C_q and q is shown in Figure 1, where C^* indicates the user-optimal solution and C_0 the fully dispersed solution. Although user-optimal solutions have been computed for large urban networks (see Eash et al. 1983) there is very little experience in solving the dispersed model. Hence, the possible savings that might be achieved by improved route information is unknown. In large congested urban networks, however, it seems reasonable to assume that the ratio of the total time of the dispersed network flows to the total time of the user-optimal flows is in the order of 1.2 to 1.5.

One further point should be made with regard to the user-optimal equilibrium. It is a property of the solution of the model that the number of used routes for most O-D pairs is greater than one. This multiple route property may be expected to hold for user-optimal flows in the real world as it presently does for dispersed flows. Thus, a guidance system instructing all drivers from each origin to each destination to follow *one route* would actually increase congestion, even if the origins and destinations were quite small areas. ,another operational question requiring investigation concerns how to allocate drivers to multiple, equal time routes. But before this question is addressed, it should be analysed to

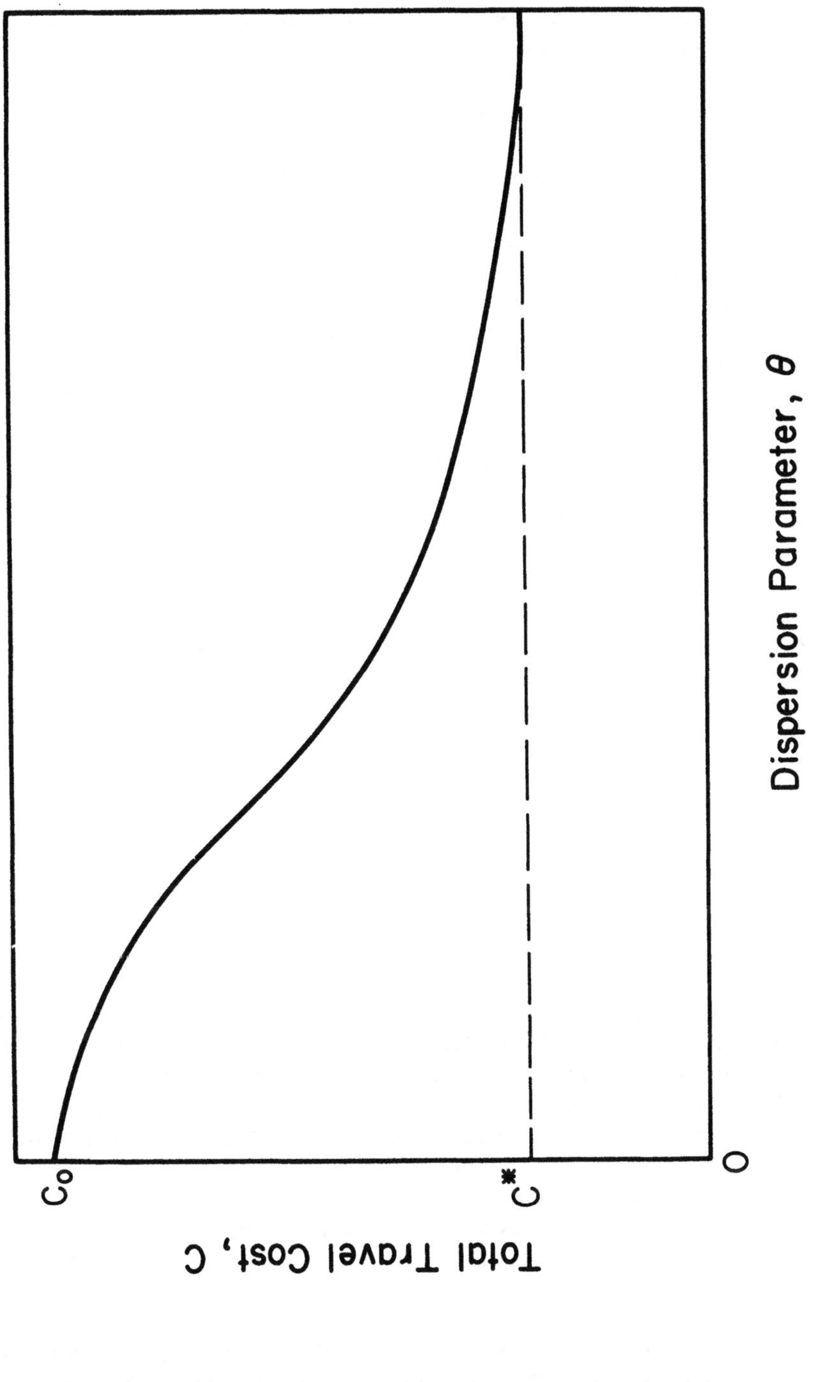

FIGURE 1: Total travel cost versus dispersion parameter θ.

what extent multiple routes are used in the solution of the user-optimal model and how the number of routes depends on zone size and the level of congestion.

System-Optimal Network Equilibrium

The user-optimal network equilibrium for a congested urban network has the property that each driver follows a shortest route. However, this solution does not minimise the total travel time of all drivers except in the uninteresting case that link travel times are fixed. The model in which the total travel time is minimised results in a *system-optimal* network equilibrium. In this solution each driver follows a minimum marginal travel time route, that is, a route in which the driver's travel time plus the additional time he/she imposes on other drivers is minimised. The system-optimal solution may result in drivers between some O-D pairs following longer routes in order that total travel time is reduced. With the automobile guidance system, these drivers could be advised to follow these longer routes in order to reduce total congestion.

What is not known about the system-optimal equilibrium is how much it reduces total travel time. Clearly, the extent of the reduction depends on the level of congestion. In a very congested network, the savings may be sufficiently large that the 'longer' marginal time routes of the system-optimal solution may be shorter than the user-optimal routes for every O-D pair. If this were true and the difference were even as large as 10-20%, there would be a very strong incentive for drivers to cooperate to achieve a system-optimal solution. Without the route advice from the auto guidance system, however, they would be unable to do so. The time incentive could be strengthened by a system of user tolls dependent on the time loss each driver imposes on the other drivers (see Vickery 1965). Investigating the magnitude of the time difference between system and user-optimal solutions is clearly a researchable question. Until now, however, it has been a question of only hypothetical interest.

4. IMPLICATIONS FOR CHOICE OF DEPARTURE TIME, MODE AND LOCATION

The auto guidance system also has profound implications for travel choices other than simply the route of travel. Improved travel time information would tend to improve other travel choices as well. Most important among these is the time of departure. In some cases it may be possible for a driver to delay his/her departure time and actually arrive earlier or at least avoid unpleasant driving conditions. An ability to predict route travel times to a destination for a fixed arrival time would permit a driver to optimise the time of departure and also to help to reduce the level of congestion. This feature of the system implies a prediction capability as well as a real time monitoring capability. Using historical data from recent days or similar conditions, such a capability would appear feasible to develop.

Commuters consider many factors in choosing between the use of their private automobile versus public transit modes. One of these factors is the travel time of the journey which they may tend to underestimate for auto and overestimate for transit. By improving the quality of travel time information for both auto and transit, the automobile guidance system would allow commuters to improve their choices so as to raise their overall utility. For highly congested routes, this information might result in more use of public transit. The information from the system might also enable transit operations planners to make transit services more competitive.

Choice of residential and job location is also partially influenced by commuting time and cost. While the true extent of the effect of commuting time on these locational choices is unknown, it is widely believed to be important in determining the general area in which to conduct a detailed housing or job search. Although public transit timetables provide information on commuting times, travel times by automobile to alternative locations may be unknown and seem likely to be underestimated. The availability of information on auto commuting times to alternative locations might well result in households choosing residences with lower travel times than would otherwise be the case. The same remark would apply to choice of job location for persons with multiple employment opportunities with similar requirements such as salespersons, office workers and factory workers.

5. IMPACTS ON THE OPERATION OF THE HIGHWAY SYSTEM

It was suggested above that the auto travel time information would be useful to transit planners in offering more competitive services. The estimates of route and link flows would be useful to traffic engineers in optimising the timing of the traffic signal system and in the overall design of the traffic control system. The state-of-the-art of traffic signal system timing is that signals are optimised for fixed traffic flows. The problem of optimal settings when the flows are user-optimal, for example, is unsolved and extremely difficult in a mathematical sense. The opportunity to draw on route choice information, either in a historical or real time sense, could dramatically improve the traffic engineer's capability to optimise the signal system. The travel time savings from this effort are also unknown but could equal or exceed those of improved route information.

6. BENEFITS FROM A PARTIALLY IMPLEMENTED SYSTEM

One attractive feature of the system described is that a partial implementation of the system would yield substantial benefits concurrently with research and development of the full system. A first generation system might consist of a) calculation of shortest routes using sensor-collected and historical data and b) transmission and display of this information on vehicle navigator systems. The same information would be available on especially equipped television receivers in homes and offices. This partial system would provide travel time and route information for a specified origin and destination on request.

An enhancement of this system would be to use historical data to provide short run forecasts of shortest routes and travel times. This enhanced system might display likely shortest routes and times at 15 minute intervals through the peak commuting period. Both of the systems described so far would utilise only digital radio receivers in the vehicles, a requirement that seems both feasible and cost effective.

A second generation automobile guidance system, in contrast to the first generation system described above, would utilise data transmitted from the vehicles. Initially, only a small fraction of vehicles would be equipped to transmit their origins, destinations, and locations en route. These data would be used to enhance the historical data for forecasting travel demand in the next time interval and to obtain route travel time information from actual vehicles moving through the street network. If the technology for receiving transmissions from many vehicles were feasible to implement, then the number of vehicles with transmitters would gradually expand. At this stage a capability to allocate vehicles to multiple routes between specific origins and destinations might be necessary in order to achieve a user-optimal equilibrium.

The third generation system would implement the potentially more efficient system-optimal equilibrium. This system would require that most vehicles be able to transmit and receive information. It might also require implementation of a toll system to provide incentives for use of the system-optimal routes.

Secondary benefits of all three generation systems would be enhanced information on origin-destination travel times by automobile. These times could be displayed on a cable television channel or obtained from a dial-up service, and used to improve travellers' decisions regarding departure time, mode and location of residence and workplace, as discussed above.

7. FUTURE PROSPECTS

The design, testing and implementation of the automobile guidance system described in this chapter seems unlikely to progress beyond the simple navigator systems now available unless a compelling case can be made in terms of the system's benefit and feasibility. A number of basic questions concerning the system have been identified in the paper including the following:

1. What are the likely savings in travel time from user-optimal route choices as compared with existing dispersed route choices?

2. What additional savings would result from the introduction of system-optimal route choices and the timing of traffic signal systems with much better historical and real time information?

3. How would improved highway travel time information change the behaviour of commuters with regard to departure time, choice of mode and choice of residential or job location? What would be the benefits or costs of these changes?

In addition, a number of more technical questions need to be addressed, including the following:

1. Can the existing static network equilibrium models be adapted to a quasi-dynamic format suitable for analysing shorter time periods?

2. Can the communications problems inherent in the system described be solved in a cost effective manner? What would be an optimal communication system design?

3. Is the traffic flow information obtained from sensor equipment adequate for determining route travel times? If not, what improvements would be necessary to make it adequate?

The implementation of an urban automobile guidance system would likely be the most important advance in urban transportation since the construction of urban freeway systems in many developed countries in the 1950-1980 period. It would combine major technological advances in communication, computers and transportation to produce a truly high technology urban transportation system which could substantially enhance the quality of life of the working population in large urban centres throughout developed countries of the world. While it may not address more fundamental problems of health, education and the general welfare of the population, this system could release other resources including time, the scarcest resource of all, to improve these conditions as well.

REFERENCES

Beckmann, M., C.B. McGuire and C.B. Winsten, Studies in the Economics of Transportation, Yale University Press, New Haven, 1956.

Ben-Akiva, M., A. de Palma and P. Karanoglou, Dynamic Model of Peak Period Traffic Congestion with Elastic Arrival Rates, Transportation Science, 20, 1986, pp. 164-181.

Boyce, D.E. and T.J. Kim, The Role of Congestion of Transportation Networks in Urban Location and Travel Choices of Households and Firms, Transportation, 16, 1987, pp. 53-62.

ConNova Research and Innovation, Automobile Road Information System Evolution, Stockholm, 1985, 13 pages.

Dial, R.B., Probabilistic Multipath Traffic Assignment Model Which Obviates Path Enumeration, Transportation Research, 7, 1971, pp. 39-61.

Eash, R.W., K.S. Chon, Y.J. Lee and D.E. Boyce, Equilibrium Traffic Assignment on an Aggregated Highway Network for Sketch Planning, Transportation Record 944, 1983, pp.30-37.

Engineering Research Board, Directions in Engineering Research, Chapter 8, Transportation Systems Research in the United States: An Overview, National Academy Press, Washington D.C., 1987, pp. 281-320.

Garrison, W.L., Introduction to Special Issue on Technology Development, Transportation Research, 18A, 1984, pp. 267-276.

Hearn, D.W., Fundamental Research on Transportation Networks: Workshop Report, in Boyce, D.E. (ed), Transportation Research: The State of the Art and Research Opportunities, Special Issue, Transportation Research, 19A, 1985, pp. 411-412.

Horowitz, J.L., The Stability of Stochastic Equilibrium in a Two-Link Transportation Network, Transportation Research, 18B, 1984, 13-28.

Strobel, H., Computer Controlled Urban Transportation, John Wiley and Sons, Chichester, UK, 1982.

Vliet, D. van, SATURN - A Modern Assignment Model, Traffic Engineering and Control, 23, 1982, pp. 587-581.

Vickery, M., Pricing as a Tool in the Coordination of Local Transportation, in J.R. Meyer (ed), Transportation Economics, National Bureau of Economic Research, New York, 1965.

Zygmont, J., Keeping Tabs on Cars and Trucks, High Technology, 6(9), 1986, pp. 18-23 and 69.

INFORMATION TECHNOLOGY AND LOCATION

Martin J. Beckmann

1. INTRODUCTION

In understanding the present and future impacts of information technology on urban and environmental systems the key theoretical issue would seem to be predicting the effects that changes in information technology are having and will have on the spatial structure of the economy, viz. the location of economic activities.

For what it is worth we must apply location theory to this question. Now location theory makes no direct reference to information technology (Lösch 1940, Isard 1950, Beckmann 1968, Beckmann and Puu 1985). We must first establish a connection between developments in information technology and the parameters that enter location theory. These are in fact the parameters of demand and cost functions, for location theory is still largely based on these and not on the more basic utility functions and production sets (cf. however Beckmann and Puu 1985, Orishimo 1988).

We shall not consider the location of the information technological industries themselves. Their share of GNP is too small in order that any locational changes in this group of industries could generate such far reaching and pervasive changes that would result in a spatial restructuring of the entire economy. Moreover their location has been touched upon already in several other contributions to this volume. The same goes for demand shifts due to this industry or to income changes in households generated by this industry. We are left with the effects that information technology can exercise on the spatial structure of the economy through general changes in costs. To be considered are two types of costs: transportation costs k and production cost, the latter being usually considered as linear with a fixed cost F and a unit cost c.

It is to be expected that location patterns are particularly sensitive to transportation costs. We shall begin with an examination of how information technology affects the cost of overcoming distance for persons, goods and information. This will be followed by studying the impact of transportation cost changes on market areas in both the short and long run.

2. INFORMATION TECHNOLOGY AND TRANSPORTATION COST

2.1 Communication and Transportation

One question already raised in various contributions to this volume is whether communication and transportation are substitutes or complements. Conceivably the message can save a trip, and on this could be based an argument that communication and transportation are substitutes, at least in the short run.

In the long run the following scenario is typical. Due to decreased communication cost the establishment of a branch plant (or outlet) becomes feasible. This then generates business travel between headquarters and branch plant managers. A decrease in communication cost thus increases the quantity of travel demanded - a classical definition of complementarity between communication and transportation.

For purposes of location theory it is not communication cost and transportation cost alone but their aggregate that is relevant. When buyer and seller are spatially separated, a business transaction requires both communication and transportation cost and their sum constitutes the cost of overcoming distance.

For convenience this will still be labelled transportation cost although it always contains a communication cost component. By decreasing communication cost, the development of information technology has also decreased this aggregate transportation cost.

2.2 Cases

We shall argue that in certain cases information technology has also decreased the transportation component proper of aggregate transportation cost. Here it will be necessary to make no distinction between computer technology and communication technology, for both would seem to operate in similar ways in regard to transportation costs.

The first case concerns materials management. Through Operations Research utilising computer technology, scientific inventory control has greatly reduced the combined costs of storage and transportation. In fact, in all applications storage costs appears in combination with transportation cost, sometimes hidden under the label of 'ordering cost'. Thus information technology has helped to reduce both transportation and storage cost and thereby the combined cost per unit sold.

That transportation and inventory costs are both incurred in trading between spatially separated buyers and sellers is apparent also in the case of household shopping. As the distance to stores increases, shopping trips are made less frequently, and in consequence more storage becomes necessary.

Deregulation of air transportation is another illustration of information technology leading to savings in transportation cost. A deregulated market for air transportation can function only when the vast schedules and tariffs on the variety of routes can be effectively compared in order to determine the cheapest applicable fare for a trip. The saving in air travel cost to users could not have been achieved without information technology.

Here we should note the uneven structure of the resulting fare reductions. They have decreased transportation costs between major centres but increased, often sharply, transportation costs from medium size cities to these centres when these cities are away from principal air traffic hubs, and these hubs are always in major cities occupying the higher ranks in a central place hierarchy. (Noted hubs in US: Chicago, Atlanta, Detroit, St. Louis.)

An interesting further case is yet to be developed: reducing travel costs in congested road networks through the allocation of particular road users or classes of road users to particular routes (cf. Boyce 1988). This calls for both sophisticated traffic flow analysis by means of computers and the signalling of routing orders through suitable communication equipment. Since solutions by means of efficiency tolls for road use appear to have failed (for political rather than technical reasons), this is the only hope right now to escape from ever increasing traffic problems in our urban networks. Here information technology has an immediate challenge to improve the quality of life in the urban world we live in.

To summarise, information technology has decreased the costs of overcoming distance - transportation costs for short - both by decreasing its communication cost component, and sometimes by reducing the transportation cost component as well. The implications of this will now be considered.

3. TRANSPORTATION COST AND MARKET AREAS

It is true that any fall in transportation cost serves to loosen the ties that bind any particular economic activity to any particular location. it would be hasty, however, to conclude from this that economic activities thereby become footloose and thereafter will spread themselves more evenly over the two dimensional region of any economy.

To study the true implications of a fall in transportation cost it is convenient to employ the classical notion of ***market area***

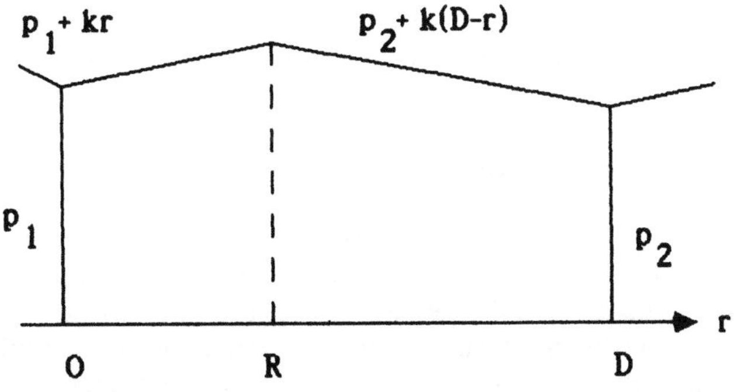

Figure 1: Market area

In a one-dimensional diagram (Figure 1) two producers offer the same good quoting mill prices p_i at their respective locations. The diagram shows the prices paid by buyers and the distance R within which firm one is the cheaper supplier. This distance is in fact given by

$$R = \frac{D}{2} + \frac{P_2 - P_1}{k} \tag{2.1}$$

where
D distance between two firms
k transportation cost.

When prices P_i are equal, the radius R of firm one's market area does not change - but total sales increase - when k falls. When prices are different it is the firm with the lower price that expands its market radius at the expense of the higher priced firm. When prices reflect production cost, the decrease in k results in both cheaper production (on average) and cheaper transportation. As Launhardt (1885) has remarked (and Hotelling later in 1929) higher transportation cost acts like a protective tariff: it protects the less efficient firm by securing for it a local market of some size.

When transportation costs fall sufficiently, the cheaper firm can undersell the dearer one at its own location and thereby wipe out its market area entirely. This short run effect of falling k was first demonstrated when transportation technology was revolutionised in the railroad and steamship era. In many branches less efficient producers for local markets were wiped out by more efficient producers for larger regional or national markets based at locations offering better access to inputs (material and/or labour) or reaping economies of scale through larger output - and better management.

Industries for which each location has the same production cost and optimal sized plants are small relative to aggregate demand in the economy, are naturally dispersed. Here presumably all firms can offer the good at the same price, so that any fall in transportation cost will not adversely affect the market area of any firm. None has need for the protection of high transportation cost.

4. LONG RUN: THE LÖSCH MODEL

Even in the last mentioned case there will be long run changes in the spatial configuration of an industry. The classical analysis of this is given by the Lösch model (Lösch 1940). Losch considers an industry in spatial monopolistic competition. Firms use profit maximising mill pricing. Alternatively, we may consider this as an oligopoly in which each firm seeks to protect its own market area - successfully as long as the number of firms does not change - and assumes that other firms do the same.

Mathematically this may be formulated as follows. (Unlike Lösch we assume that the density of customers is not uniform in the 2-dimensional plane but may be any given function of distance from the supplier.)

For a given market radius R and a mill price p profits are

$$(p - c) \int_0^R (a - p - kr)\, \rho(r)\, dr - F \qquad (4.1)$$

where

p	mill price
c	constant marginal cost
F	fixed cost
a	demand intercept
q = a-p	demand function
k	rate of transportation cost
r	distance from plant
r(r)	density of customers
R	market radius

Maximisation of (4.1) with respect to mill price p yields maximal profits in the given market of radius R

$$G(R) = \frac{1}{4} M(R)(a - c - k\bar{r}(R)) - F \qquad (4.2)$$

Here

$$M(R) = \int_0^R \rho(r)dr \qquad (4.3)$$

is the mass of customers and

$$\bar{r}(R) = \frac{\int_0^R r\rho(r)dr}{\int_0^k \rho(r)dr} \qquad (4.4)$$

is the average distance of customers.

The profit maximising mill price is

$$P_M = \frac{1}{2}\{a + c - \bar{r}(R)\} \qquad (4.5)$$

and the optimal uniform price is easily shown to be

$$P_u = \frac{1}{2}\{a + c + \bar{r}(R)\} \qquad (4.6)$$

This uniform price is also the average price paid by customers under mill pricing (Beckmann 1976). Notice that prices and profits are closed form expressions in terms of the mass M(R) and average distance r(R).

For our purposes, formula (4.4) is the important one. Setting profits equal to zero determines the radius R of a market area that can support a plant of this industry. In the Löschian theory, customer density is uniform so that

$$r(r) = 2p$$
$$M(R) = aR^2$$
$$r(R) = bR\,.$$

Here a and b are constant coefficients derived from the hexagonal shape of market areas.

In a more general and more realistic approach, population density is not constant and the shape of market areas need not be hexagonal. In the framework of a Central Place System (4.2) determines the lowest rank of a Central Place that can support production of this product or service by allowing profits to be nonnegative. The higher the rank of a Central Place the greater is the mass M(R) that can be reached with an average distance of r(R). For Central Places of higher rank the market may suffice to permit more than one plant.

The question is how a fall in k will change equilibrium in such a Central Place System. Clearly any fall in k increases profits. This is true under both mill and uniform pricing, in fact both pricing systems are equally profitable (Beckmann 1976). Small changes in k will neither increase the number of plants that can live in a Central Place of higher rank, nor lower the critical rank that just permits this activity. When k falls enough, however, the critical rank will be lowered and/or plants will be added in places of higher rank. This means that changes in information technology will encourage the dispersal of economic activities of the Löschian type. This is an important long run effect resulting from the fall in transportation cost.

These conclusions were derived on the assumption of linear demand and cost functions. It is not difficult to extend the argument to arbitrary (downward sloping) demand functions and to arbitrary convex cost functions, using implicit differentiation. This may be left as an exercise to the reader.

5. COMPETITIVE PRICING AND CONCLUSION

The Löschian model of monopolistic competition represents on extreme form of oligopolistic pricing available to firms with adjacent market areas. The other extreme is competitive behaviour. We shall examine this in the case of uniform pricing and interpret competitive behaviour as marginal cost pricing.

A firm selling its product in a market of radius R must charge a uniform price:

$$P_U = c + kR \tag{5.1}$$

to cover the marginal cost of supplying the most distant customer. Demand per customer is then:

$$a - P_u = a - c - kR \tag{5.2}$$

and quantity sold equals this times M(R). To calculate profits observe that the profit margin on a sale to customers at distance r equals

$$P_U - c - kr = k.(R - r)\,. \tag{5.3}$$

Profits are then:

$$\begin{aligned} G_U &= (a - c - kR)k \int_0^R (R - r)p\,dr - F \\ &= k(a - c - kR).M(R)\,.\,\{R - \bar{r}(R)\} - F \end{aligned} \tag{5.4}$$

This is a concave quadratic function in k. It follows that profits increase with k for small R and decrease for large R. Thus, when fixed costs are high and market areas must be large, any decrease in k reduces profits and requires an even larger market area to support a plant. The opposite is true when fixed costs and hence market areas are small.

In conclusion, it is seen that the effects of changes in information technology on the location of economic activities are complex and conflicting. Forces operate in the direction of a greater dispersal of industries, but other forces tend towards greater concentration. In the short run and when production costs are unequal, any reduction in transportation costs serves to favour the low cost producers, expanding their market areas and reducing or even eliminating market areas of high cost local producers.

Since the low cost producers tend to be operating on a larger scale and supplying the larger markets to begin with, this is a force operating in the direction of greater spatial concentration. When production costs are homogeneous, neither a concentrating nor a decentralising effect occurs in the short run. In the long run under monopolistic pricing, the saving in transportation costs enables additional firms to exist and thus a greater degree of dispersion. Under competitive pricing and related oligopolistic strategies, however, a fall in transportation costs will reduce profits in firms with large fixed costs and increase profits in firms with low fixed costs. If both coexist in the same industry we have once more an expansion of the firms with lower costs and hence an increase in spatial concentration.

That a fall in transportation cost is beneficial to consumers in the economy is axiomatic. It is true even when the result is a higher degree of spatial concentration.

There is no reason to believe that changes in information technology will upset the fundamental structure of the spatial economy. Any changes will be changes of degree. In particular, the spatial organisation of an economy as a Central Place System will continue even though the distribution of economic activities within such a Central Place system will change. These changes may even go so far as to eliminate the lowest layer in a Central Place hierarchy, a process that was initiated by the motorisation of customers since World War II. So far these effects have been most prominent in the rural areas of the United States and Canada. Whether there is a world wide tendency in this direction remains an open question.

REFERENCES

Beckmann, M., Location Theory, New York, 1968.

Beckmann, M., Spatial Price Policies Revisited, The Bell Journal of Economics, 1976, pp. 19-30.

Beckmann, M. and T. Puu, Spatial Economics: Density, Potential and Flow, North-Holland Publishing Company, 1985.

Boyce, D., Combining Communication and Transportation Technology, (this volume).

Isard, W., Location and the Space Economy, New York, 1956.

Hotelling, H., Stability in Competition, Economic Journal, 1929, pp. 41-57.

Launhardt, W., Mathematische Begrundung der Volkswirtschaftslehre, Leipzig, 1885.

Lösch, A., The Economics of Location., Yale University Press, 1954, (German edition, 1940).

Orishimo, I., Development of Informatics and Possible Changes in Urbanization Processes, (this volume).

PART C: Impact Models of New Technologies

TECHNICAL INNOVATION AND INPUT-OUTPUT ANALYSIS

Geoffrey J.D. Hewings, Michael Sonis and Rodney C. Jensen

1. INTRODUCTION

In the last two decades, research in regional input-output analysis has focussed almost exclusively on the problems of estimation of coefficients, updating the coefficients and using the input-output model for impact analysis and forecasting. In this chapter, we begin to devote attention to some rather non-traditional uses of input-output analysis, namely the issues of regional economic structure and structural change over time and space. In essence, the questions we seek to answer focus on our ability to identify regularity in the structure of regional economic systems and also on our ability to be able to suggest ways in which this structure might change over time in response to internal and external growth impulses. One of the major impulses will be the role of technical change and the way that this is manifested in changes in structure. However, the format and approaches which we have developed may be used in the context of a variety of responses to change.

The inspiration for our research was provided by Simpson and Tsukui's (1965) work in comparing the economic structure of Japan and the United States using input-output models which had been developed for both countries. In the course of their work, they attempted to compare the structures using a variety of techniques; in particular, they triangulised both input-output tables and, from this 'reduced form',they proposed the notion of a common fundamental structure of production. We have modified this term and in the process generalised the notion of **fundamental economic structure (FES)** since the structure of regional economics involves more than just the production accounts.

In this chapter, we provide a sample of some of the results of this application to a number of different input-output systems. In essence, we attempt to provide three dimensions of regional economic structure: (i) stability, (ii) predictability and (iii) importance. These categories are not mutually exclusive; for example, individual coefficients, sectors or blocks of a regional economic structure may be simultaneously stable and important. Several methods are used to identify these dimensions which then provide us with the basis for identifying the FES of a region.

The following section of the chapter explores the ways in which the identification of the FES can be of use in the context of structural change induced by innovation. Furthermore, we believe that this approach to the identification of FES will be of value in comparative analysis of the structure of regional economic systems - a task which has been largely ignored in the literature. In this context, we note in the final section that some modifications may have to be made in our accounting frameworks to accommodate the new perspectives which are sought on the various aspects of technical change in general.

2. THE NOTION OF FUNDAMENTAL ECONOMIC STRUCTURE (FES)

In his *Preface to Urban Economics*, Wilbur Thompson (1965) characterised the growth and development process of an urban region in the context of an expansion and deepening of a set of linkages between activities (see Diagram 1). Conceptualised within the economic base framework initially, Thompson was able to trace the possible path of a 'generic' region from early dependence on agricultural exports to eventual growth of an industrial core and the concomitant export of manufactured goods and services.[1] While many other authors, such as Kuznets (1971), have described the evolution of national economies in some sequential manner, there has been little attempt to focus on this evolution in the context of the structure of production and its changes.

If we consider a continuum from small rural, sparsely populated regions to large, metropolitan complexes of the size of Tokyo, how would we expect the structure of production and the interdependence of industries to change as we moved across this set of *regional* economies? Similarly, as we move across a continuum from the least developed to the most developed *national* economies, would we find some pattern of change which could be described and interpreted using prevailing theories of growth and development? We are not arguing for a deterministic path of growth and development but the degree to which certain facets of an economy at a given stage in space and time might be in some sense 'predictable'. In Diagram 2, we provide this space-time continuum and some indications about aspects of the structure which we feel we can suggest on the basis of a great deal of causal empiricism.

However, we wish to go further and surmise that the change in structure over time and space may be related to some common thread or skeletal form which we refer to as the **fundamental economic structure (FES)** (see Jensen, West and Hewings 1988) for further elaboration). At the outset, it should be stated that this FES may not be common to all economies - regional or national, developed or undeveloped; our empirical base is too small for us to be able to offer a conclusive statement at this point. What we suggest, however, is that the FES may be characterised in three important ways:

1. stability - the degree to which certain elements are present across substantial samples (i.e., all regions or all nations).

2. predictability - the degree to which some elements are present in varying amounts, the size of which may be predictable using some aggregate measures of an economy (e.g., gross regional or national product, the degree of industrial concentration by sector) and

3. importance - the degree to which the elements of the FES are part of a set of components of the economic structure which may be regarded as analytically important in the sense that change in these elements would likely create the most potential for system-wide change.

These conceptual ideas have been developed in an attempt to focus attention on the need to utilise the substantial set of empirical data which is currently available in more creative ways and to promote some discussion about the ways in which structural change, broadly defined, might be measured, interpreted and evaluated. Hence we may consider the fundamental economic structure to be a subset of the relationships between industries (or between factors, institutions and industries in a social accounting framework) which may

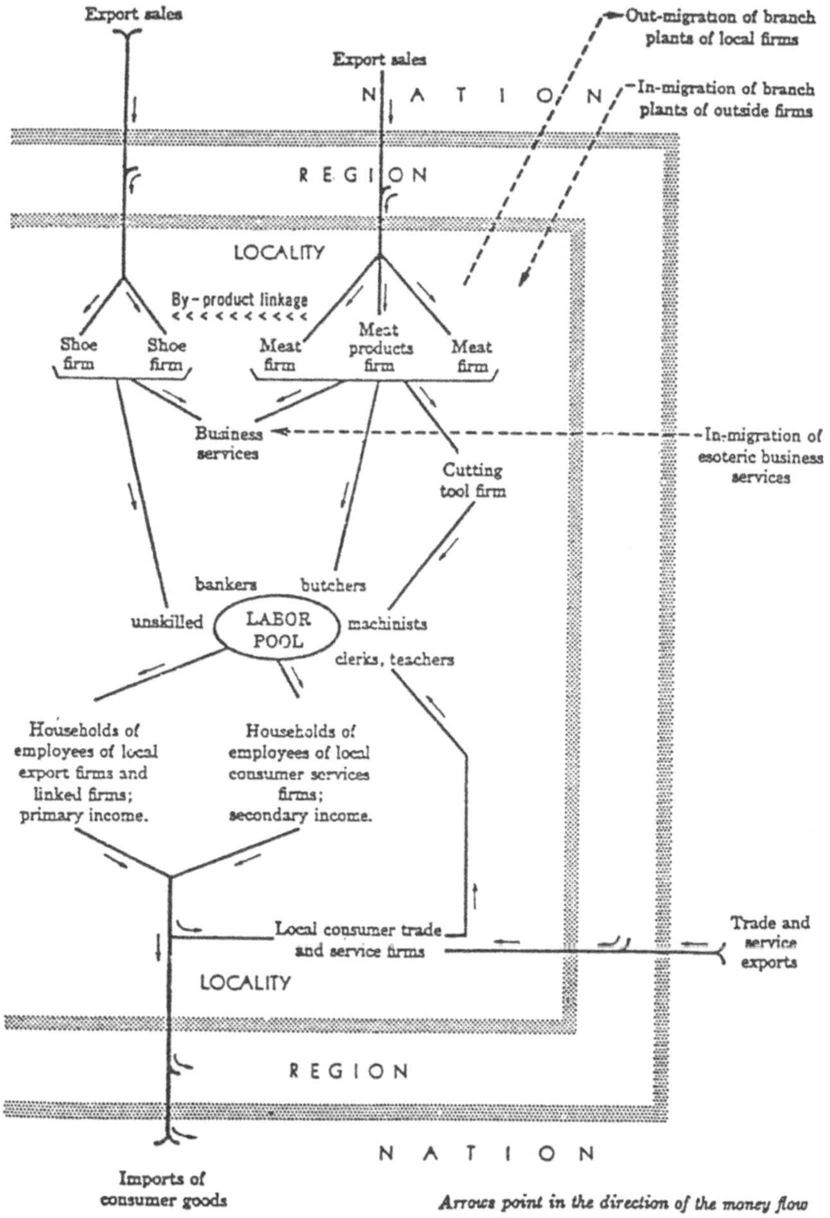

Diagram 1 The Urban Growth Complex

Diagram 2
Space-Time Representation of Regional Ecomomic Structures

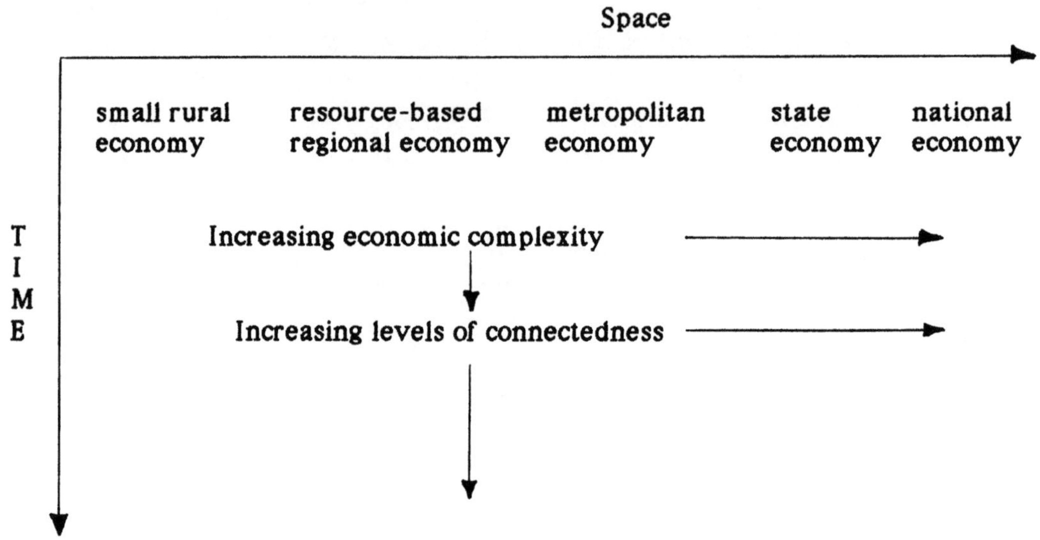

be considered to have some or all of the characteristics of stability, predictability and importance. In the next section, we will briefly review some of the methods which have been proposed for the purposes of identification of FES; thereafter, some sampling of the empirical applications to date will be reviewed. In conducting this review, we will consider the role in which this whole process might play in handling innovation diffusion.

3. TECHNICAL INNOVATION AND DIFFUSION

From the literature on innovation diffusion and the process of technical change as it is manifested in production, we may be able to suggest two dominant relationships which assume the form of logistic curves; these are shown in Diagram 3. Essentially, we postulate that a new innovation evolves through three major phases - (i) research and development, (ii) growth and (iii) mass production and/or consumption. In terms of the effect on production technology or the process used to produce the new product (or modify an existing one), we may hypothesise that the number of adopters rises from close to zero to almost one hundred per cent of any fixed set of actors in the system (i.e., firms in an industry, consumers in a given market). What is not made clear on these diagrams is the way adoption of new techniques may result in rather radical reorganisation of production; the three-part division shown in Diagram 3 may be overly simplistic but it does allow us to focus on the fact that at different stages in the life cycle of a product, we may find not only differences in productive process but differences in the location of production. This presents a multidimensional challenge to input-output analysts who must now grapple with a non-Leontief production function and, at the regional level, the possibility for rather unstable trading patterns as production is shifted according to the level of demand. Furthermore, as new innovations enter the system, the problem of replication of the life cycle process - in terms of the organisation and location of production - would need to be examined. An additional complication arises from the fact that the market in which intermediate goods are traded, as well as the final markets, may themselves change as a result of innovation. For example, we may see a tendency towards oligopoly or oligopsony as a small number of firms are able to adapt their production structure or adopt a new technique more rapidly than others within the same industry. The increasing concentration of control of production in multiregional and multinational corporations adds a further complicating dimension. Thus, we find our static input-output model in need of adjustment to capture (1) differences in productive process within the same industry (this is different from the aggregation problem, although the effects may be similar), (2) changes in location of production, (3) differences in organisational/ownership structure and (4) the degree to which the onset of new innovations may be considered to follow paths of earlier innovations. The needs created here are somewhat daunting. A concern of the present authors has been that far too much attention in input-output modelling has been focussed on data collection to ensure accuracy of the individual cells of the input-output matrix. We would like to initiate a new approach which would focus basic data collection of the more traditional kind on a smaller subset, and thus provide the opportunity for us to begin to consider ways in which the input-output accounting framework could be modified to address the issues raised in this section. We proceed to examine the possibilities for the identification of what we might refer to as the *basic* data in the next section prior to examining some possible changes to our framework and thinking about input-output modelling.

Diagram 3
Innovation Diffusion

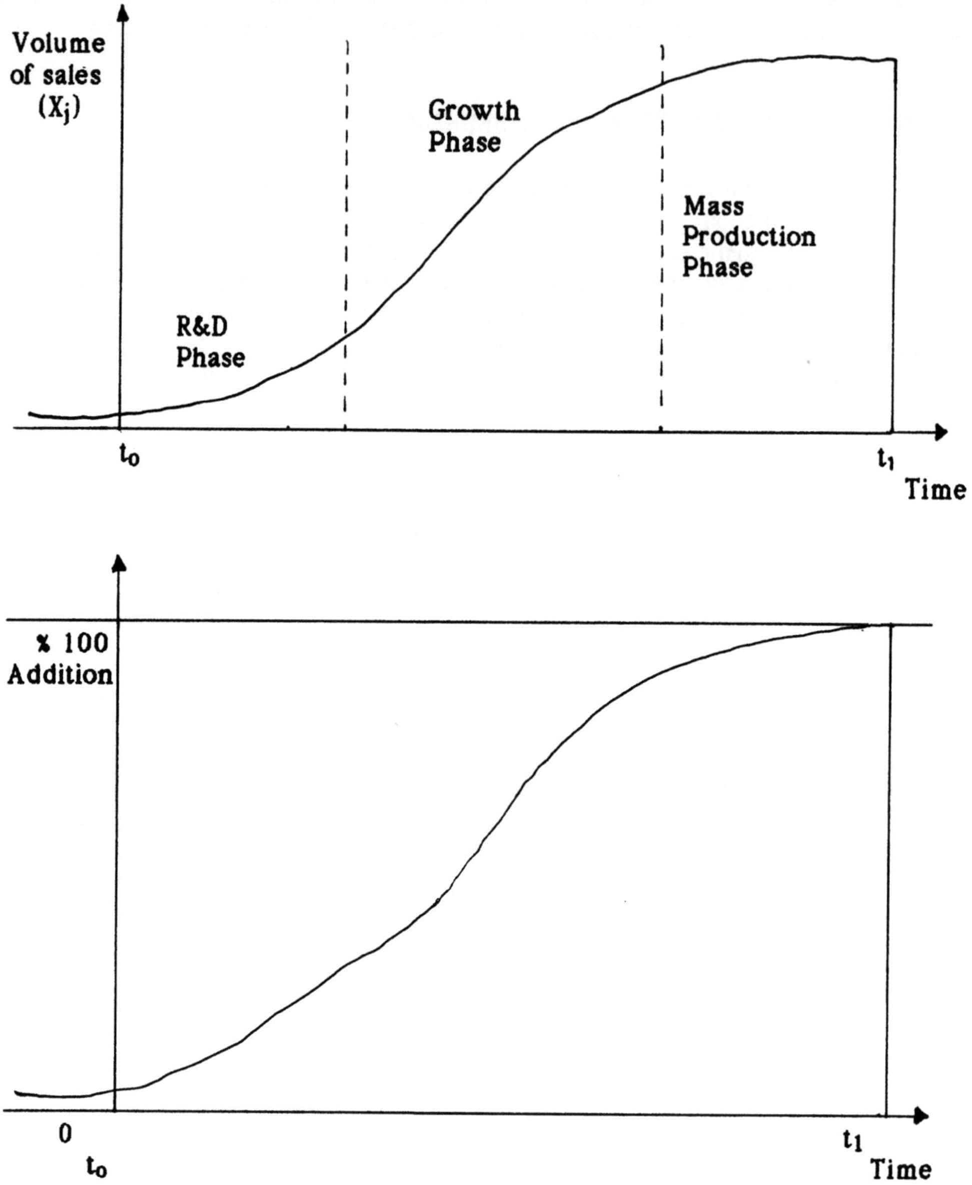

Diagram 4 Decomposition of an Input-Output Model Applied to Washington State (1963)

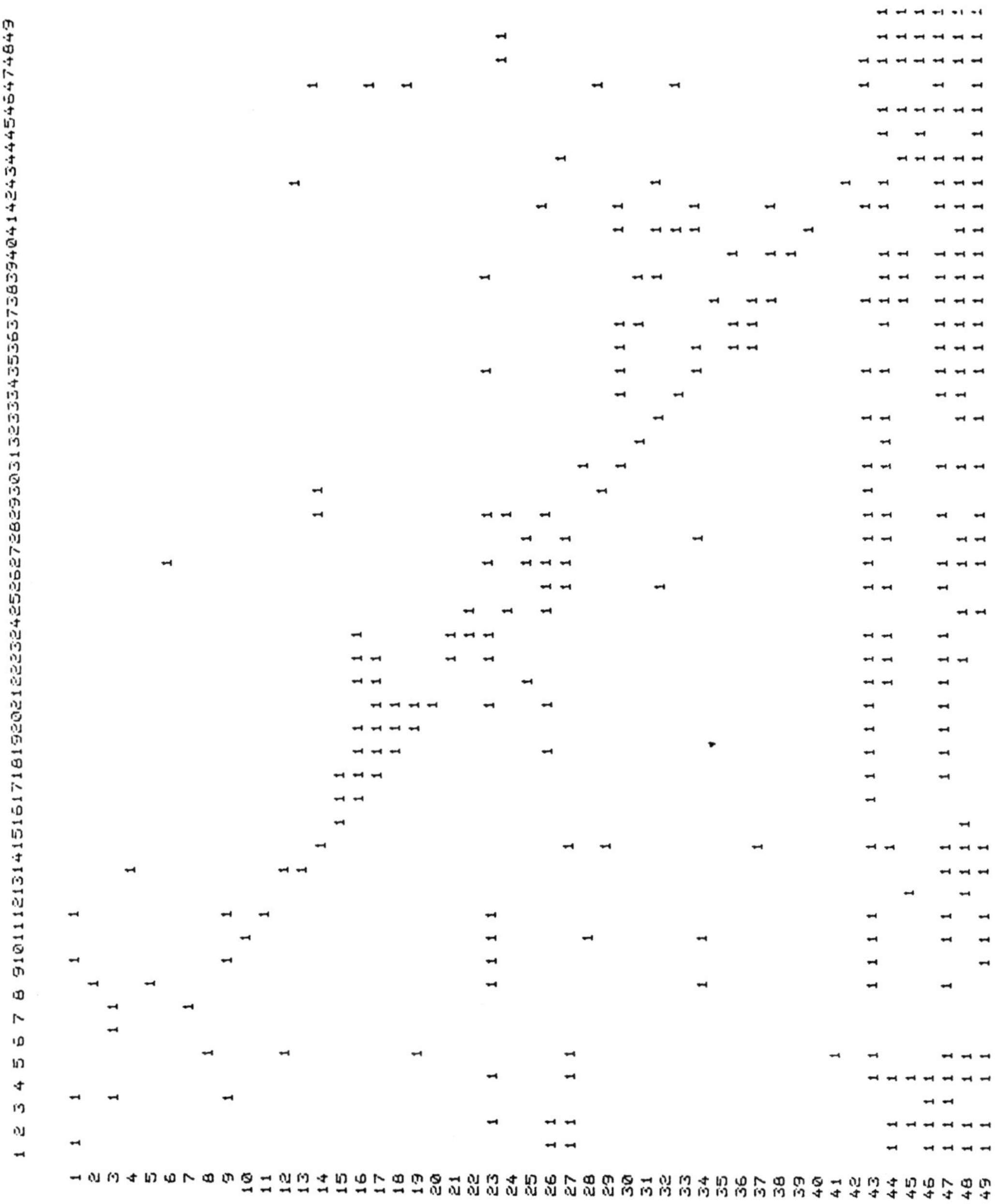

Diagram 3 Decomposition of an Input-Output Model Applied to Washington State (1967)

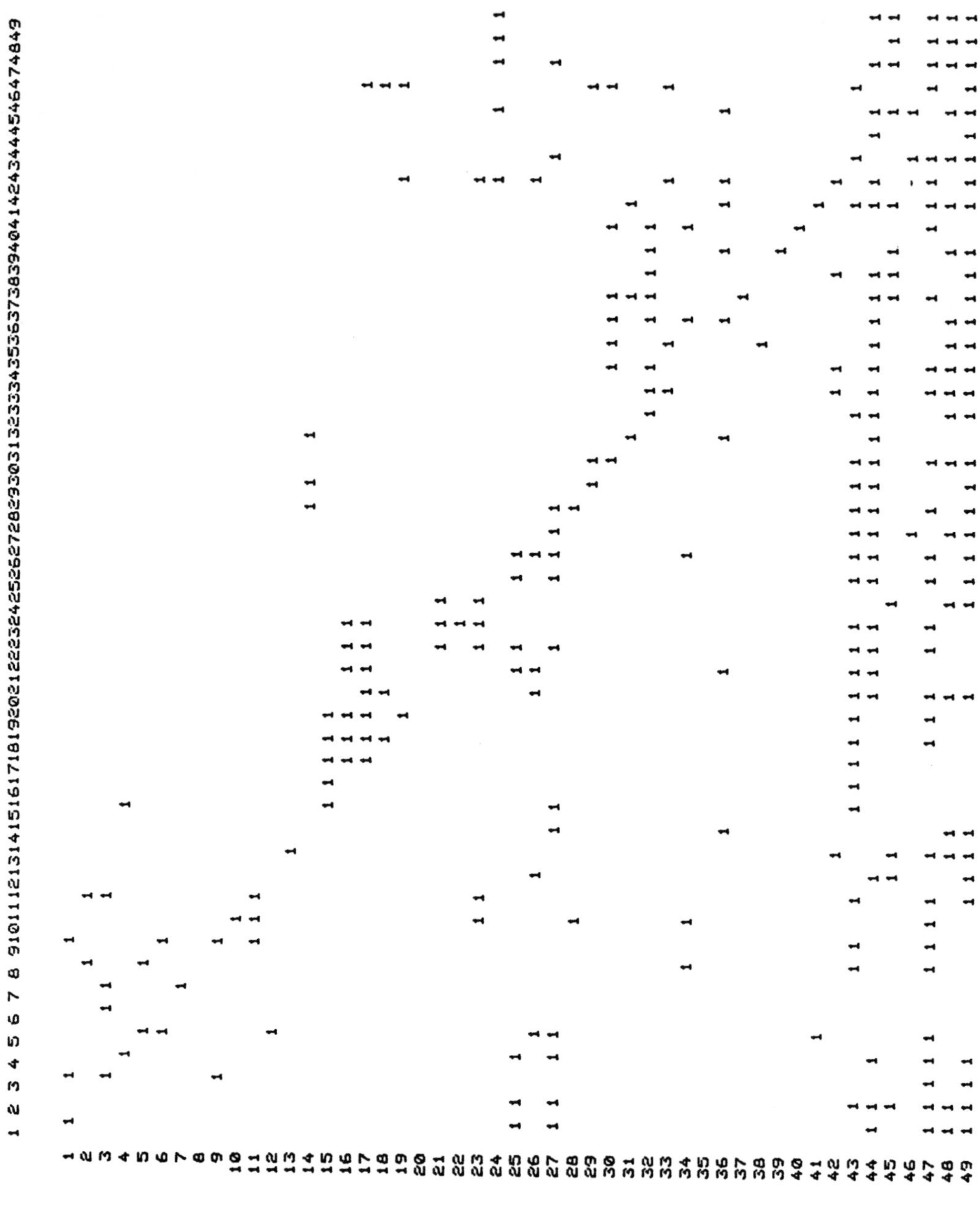

Diagram 6 Decomposition of an Input-Output Model Applied to Washington State (1972)

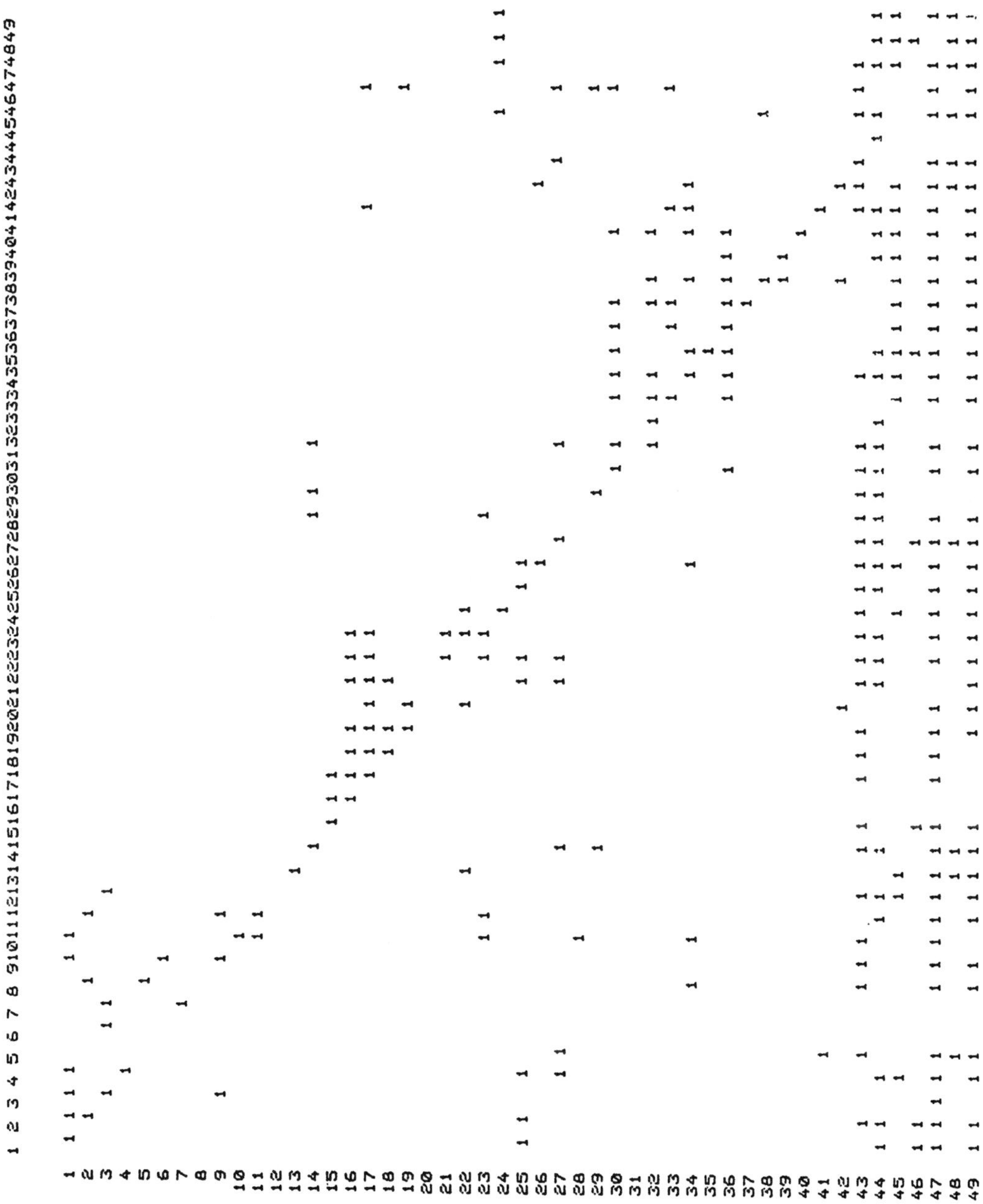

Diagram 7 Decomposition of an Input-Output Model Applied to Brazil (1959)

	1	2	3	4	5	6	7	8	9	10	11	12	13	14	15	16	17	18	19	20	21	22	23	24	25	26	27
1	1							1			1	1	1		1		1		1	1	1						
2		1	1	1									1														
3			1																				1		1		
4	1			1	1	1	1		1														1	1	1	1	
5						1																					
6					1	1																					
7							1																			1	
8								1	1														1		1		
9																											
10										1						1					1	1	1	1		1	
11							1				1							1								1	
12												1						1									
13	1	1	1	1		1		1	1	1	1	1	1	1	1	1	1			1		1	1	1		1	1
14																											1
15																											
16									1							1											
17									1		1					1	1	1					1			1	
18																											
19																			1	1							
20																				1							
21																					1						
22																											1
23																											1
24				1						1	1												1	1			
25																											1
26	1	1	1	1	1	1		1	1	1	1	1	1	1	1	1	1	1	1	1	1	1	1		1	1	1
27	1	1	1	1	1	1	1	1	1	1	1	1		1	1	1	1	1	1	1	1	1	1	1	1	1	1

Diagram 8 Decomposition of an Input-Output Model Applied to Brazil (1970)

	1	2	3	4	5	6	7	8	9	10	11	12	13	14	15	16	17	18	19	20	21	22	23	24	25	26	27
1	1							1	1	1	1	1	1				1		1	1	1						1
2		1	1										1														
3			1											1	1					1			1		1		
4		1	1	1	1	1	1		1					1	1					1			1		1	1	
5		1			1	1	1							1									1	1			
6					1	1	1																1	1	1		
7					1		1																			1	
8								1	1																1		
9																											
10			1							1				1	1	1					1	1				1	
11							1				1												1			1	
12												1						1									
13	1	1	1	1	1	1			1	1	1	1	1	1	1	1	1			1	1	1	1	1	1	1	
14	1													1													
15																											
16						1			1							1											
17									1		1		1	1		1	1	1					1				
18																											
19	1											1	1	1	1				1	1							1
20																				1							
21																					1						
22																						1					1
23		1	1																					1			1
24		1	1							1														1		1	1
25																										1	
26	1	1	1	1	1	1	1	1	1	1	1	1	1	1	1	1	1	1	1	1	1	1	1	1	1	1	1
27																										1	1

Diagram 9 Decomposition of an Input-Output Model Applied to Brazil (1975)

	1	2	3	4	5	6	7	8	9	10	11	12	13	14	15	16	17	18	19	20	21	22	23	24	25	26	27
1	1							1					1				1		1	1	1						
2		1	1										1														
3			1											1	1					1					1		
4				1	1	1	1		1											1			1		1		
5		1	1	1	1	1	1																1	1			
6					1	1																	1	1	1		
7							1																			1	
8								1	1	1															1		
9																											
10										1				1	1						1	1					
11											1												1			1	
12												1						1									
13	1	1	1	1					1	1	1	1	1	1	1	1	1		1	1		1	1	1	1	1	
14														1													1
15																											
16									1					1	1	1							1				
17									1		1					1	1	1					1				
18																											
19	1											1		1	1				1	1							1
20																				1							1
21																					1						
22																						1					1
23		1																						1			
24		1	1																					1		1	1
25																											
26	1	1	1	1	1	1	1	1	1	1	1	1	1	1	1	1	1	1	1	1	1	1	1	1	1	1	1
27																										1	1

4. THE MEASUREMENT OF FUNDAMENTAL ECONOMIC STRUCTURE

In Hewings, Jensen and West (1987), an extensive review of approaches to the measurement of structure was conducted. The methods varied from simple calculations of the percentage of flows on intermediate account to more complex calculations involving entropy decomposition techniques; a summary of the methods is provided in Table 1. While Hamilton and Jensen (1983), Szyrmer (1985, 1986), Hewings (1983) and Jackson and Hewings (1984) have provided some empirical testing of some of these techniques, an extensive comparative analysis has yet to be undertaken.

In this section of the chapter, we will introduce two new approaches which we believe have the potential for addressing some of the issues of change which might be associated with the adoption of new technology. These approaches may be characterised as (1) the bottleneck decomposition and (2) the field of influence methods. While further information on them may be found in Hewings and Sonis (1986) and Sonis and Hewings (1988), a brief review will be provided here.

4.1 The Bottleneck Decomposition

Consider a standard interindustry accounting system:

$$AX + f + X \qquad (4.1)$$

where A is an n x n matrix of technical coefficients and f and X 1 x n vectors of final demand and total output respectively. The issue to be addressed here is the degree to which the interindustry flows might be represented in some reduced form structure of the following kind:

$$AX - p_1x' + p_2x'' + p_3x''' ...... p_kX^k \qquad (4.2)$$

where p_1......p_k represent coefficients such that $\sum_k Pk = 1$ and X' ... X^k represent various decompositions of the gross flows matrix AX. Essentially, p_1 represents the minimum value of a vector of coefficients representing the bottleneck allocation of flows in the interindustry table. In other words, we try to allocate as much of the total flow in a column to just one element of that column. In the succeeding rounds, the residual not allocated in the first round in then allocated to a single element in each column and so forth until all the interindustry flows are accommodated. The coefficients p_k thus provide information on the degree to which the interindustry transactions might be represented by a significantly reduced set of flows; thus if we consider the first 10 values of p, the maximum number of flows[2] represented would be 10n. Diagrams 4, 5 and 6 show a decomposition applied to the Washington State (US) economy for the years 1963, 1967 and 1972 while Diagrams 7, 8 and 9 reveal a similar decomposition for the Brazilian economy in 1959, 1970 and 1975. In the case of Washington, other work has indicated that the state's economy underwent some rather important structural changes during the period 1963 to 1972 yet the Diagrams reveal a great deal of stability in the degree to which interindustry transactions were dominated by a small set of flows. Tables 2 and 3 show the percentage of the transactions accounting for by these ten extreme tendencies. Note that stability of these extreme tendencies over this time period for the state of Washington; in Brazil, the value of the first ten extreme tendencies declined over the three tables (reflecting a

TABLE 1

Summary Measures of Economic Structure

1. Measures of Connectedness
   - percentage of nonzero coefficients
   - percentage of intermediate transactions
   - average output multipliers
   - determinants
   - interrelatedness functions

2. Measures of Dispersion
   - ecological measures of total flow
   - entropy decomposition

3. Ordering of Input-Output Tables
   - triangulation
   - band matrices
   - LDU decomposition
   - graph theoretic measures
   - clustering

4. Pattern Analysis

5. Table Comparisons

TABLE 2
Extreme Tendency Percentages 1959

Decomposition Number	Percentage Explained	Cumulative Percentage
1	.196671	.196671
2	.135975	.332646
3	.112351	.444997
4	.103798	.548796
5	.067429	.617225
6	.062948	.680173
7	.049771	.729945
8	.038165	.768109
9	.036224	.804333
10	.026959	.831292

Exteme Tendency Percentages 1970

Decomposition Number	Percentage Explained	Cumulative Percentage
1	.182602	.182602
2	.134588	.317190
3	.118426	.435615
4	.064920	.500535
5	.063759	.564294
6	.056321	.620615
7	.041804	.662419
8	.040128	.702548
9	.031589	.734136
..10	.025485	.759621

Extreme Tendency Percentages 1975

Decomposition Number	Percentage Explained	Cumulative Percentage
1	.179321	.179321
2	.150092	.329414
3	.084577	.412991
4	.083382	.496373
5	.067069	.563442
6	.053536	.616978
7	.044845	.661823
8	.040991	.702814
9	.036493	.729306
10	.026438	.765745

TABLE 3

Extreme Tendency Percentages 1963

Decomposition Number	Percentage Explained	Cumulative Percentage
1	.142857	.142857
2	.117274	.260131
3	.089701	.349823
4	.070175	.420008
5	.052623	.472639
6	.043860	.516499
7	.043860	.560359
8	.038462	.598820
9	.035088	.633908
10	.033333	.667241

Extreme Tendency Percentages 1972

Decomposition Number	Percentage Explained	Cumulative Percentage
1	.145833	.145833
2	.128049	.273882
3	.094595	.368477
4	.081567	.450044
5	.055882	.505926
6	.052941	.558867
7	.038235	.597103
8	.029412	.626514
9	.029412	.655926
10	.029412	.685338

Extreme Tendency Percentages 1967

Decomposition Number	Percentage Explained	Cumulative Percentage
1	.170940	.170940
2	.084112	.255052
3	.084112	.339164
4	.074766	.413931
5	.065421	.479351
6	.054421	.544772
7	.056818	.601590
8	.037383	.638973
9	.029979	.668952
10	.029979	.698930

Diagram 10 1959 Brazil Input-Output Table (27x27): Top 20 inverse important elements

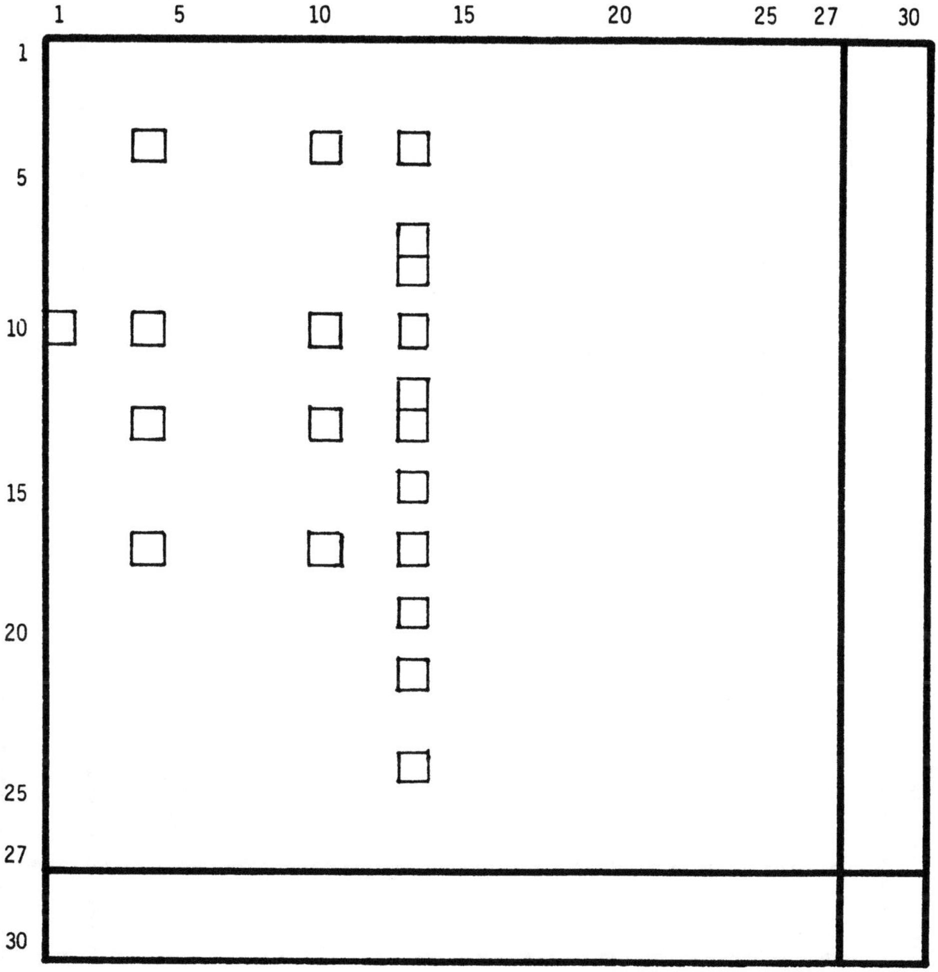

Diagram 11 1970 Brazil Input-Output Table (27x27): Top 20 inverse important elements

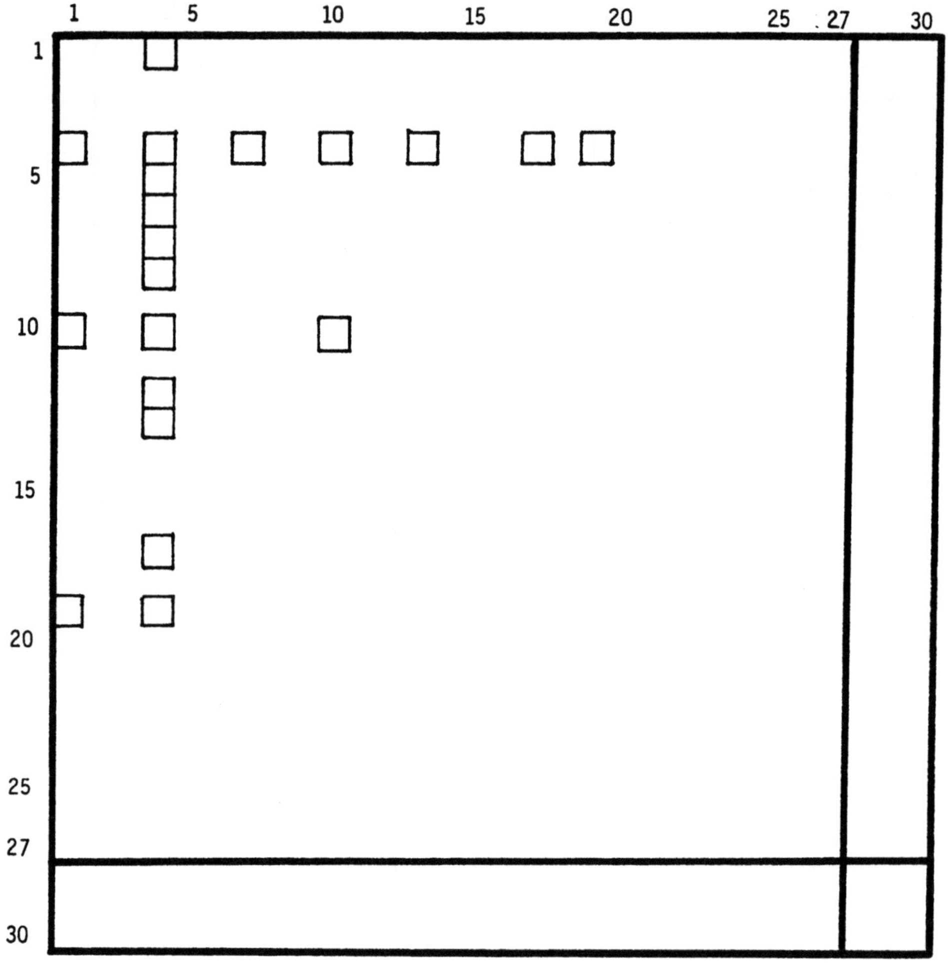

Diagram 12 1975 Brazil Input-Output Table (27x27): Top 20 inverse important elements

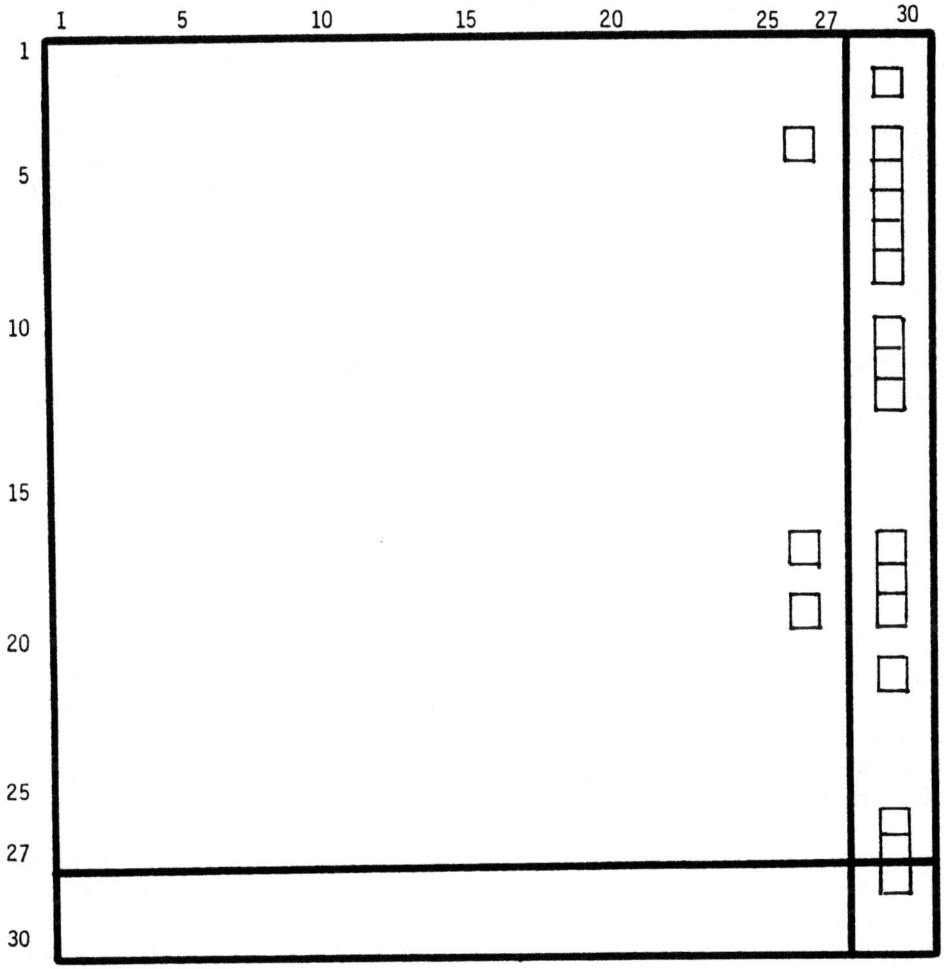

greater dispersion of flows, something which one would expect with increasing development) although the dominance of the first two tendencies hardly changed at all. In a sense, we might wish to characterise these tendencies as a way of measuring an underlying structure - perhaps a fundamental economic structure? Note that even though the number of sectors was not the same, the sector classifications proceeded from primary to tertiary, and the overall patterns were not dissimilar. This interpretation is casual rather than scientifically determined but does provide some suggestive possibilities of a general pattern to the dominant elements in production across a variety of economies.

4.2 The Field of Influence Approach

Some earlier work By Bullard and Sebald (1977) at the national level and by Hewings (1984) at the regional level has revealed that the number of elements in an input-output model which might be considered important in an analytical sense was very small. Sonis and Hewings (1986) have now been able to generalise these approaches into what may be referred to as a field of influence approach. In summary form, it may be presented as follows:

$$B(\varepsilon_{ij}) \cong B + F(j) \tag{4.3}$$

where $B(\varepsilon_{ij})$ is the $[I-A]^{-1}$ matrix with one element A, a_{ij}, = $a_{ij} + \varepsilon_{ij}$ where ε_{ij} is a small perturbation. B is the $[I-A]^{-1}$ matrix and F is the field of influence. F is a function of the signed minor of the matrix derived from A with the row and column in which i and j are located eliminated. The method can be generalised to include changes in two or more coefficients (to capture the synergistic effect of change), to consider changes in all coefficients in a column or row and to consider changes which operate simultaneously on a row and a column (the biproportional or RAS problem is thus a specific form of a field of influence).

Diagrams 10, 11 and 12 illustrate the location of the top 20 important parameters in the Brazilian economy; these were the parameters whose change created the most extensive 'disruption' in the rest of the economy. In other words, they had the largest field of influence. Note how the top twenty parameters were not defined consistently over the three time periods. The reasons for this need to be explored in the context of the changes which the economy experienced during these two decades.

When attention is focussed on the synergistic effects, the results (Diagrams 13, 14 and 15) reveal some important relationships. The lines do not indicate the direction of influence which the change in one parameter would have on another coefficient One can see, by comparison with Diagrams 10, 11 and 12 that the most important coefficients dominate the synergistic changes.

Thus, in examining these results, we may be able to provide some insights into the possible direction and magnitude of technological change within an input-output framework. Of course, these relationships are based on 'old technology', and thus reflect linkages which may or may not be important as the process of technological change diffuses through an industry.

Diagram 13 1970 Brazil Inout-Output Table (27x27): Top 20 pairs of elements with strongest synergetic effects (elements are not in same row/column)

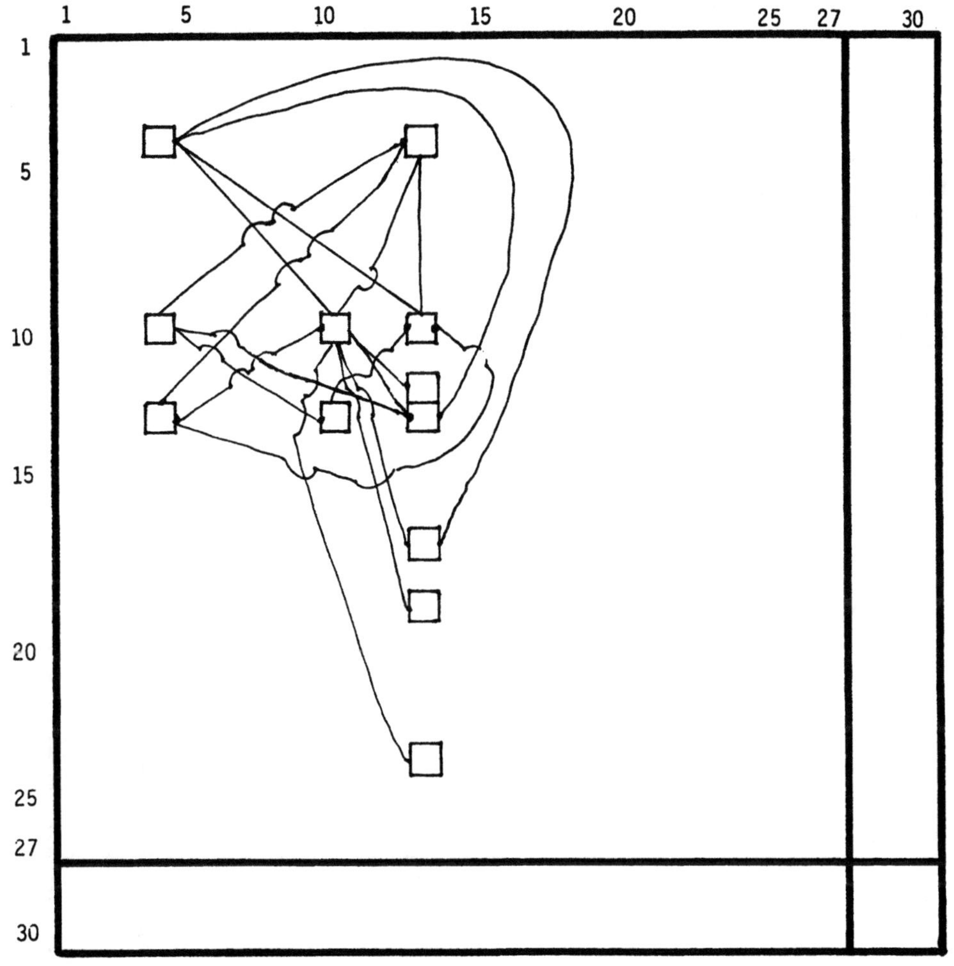

Diagram 14 1959 Brazil Inout-Output Table (27x27): Top 20 pairs of elements with strongest synergetic effects (elements are not in same row/column)

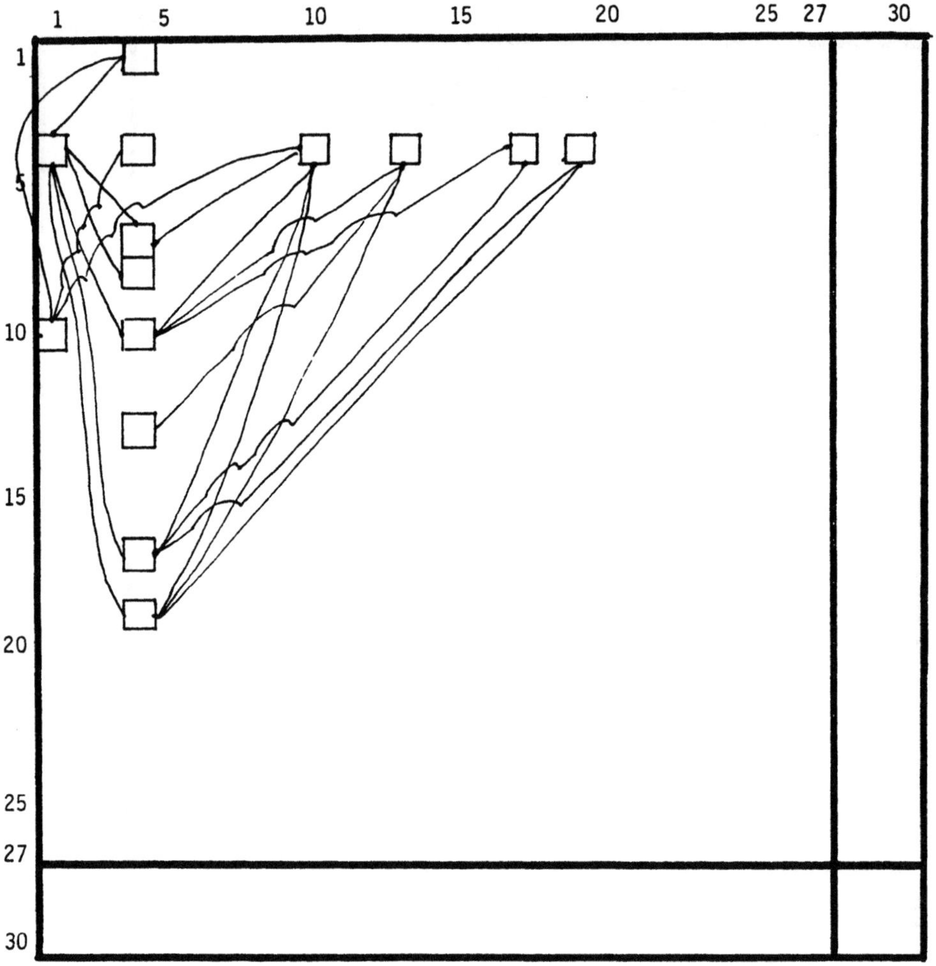

Diagram 15 1975 Brazil Input-Output Table (27x27): Top 20 pairs of of elements with strongest synergetic effects (elements are not in same row/column)

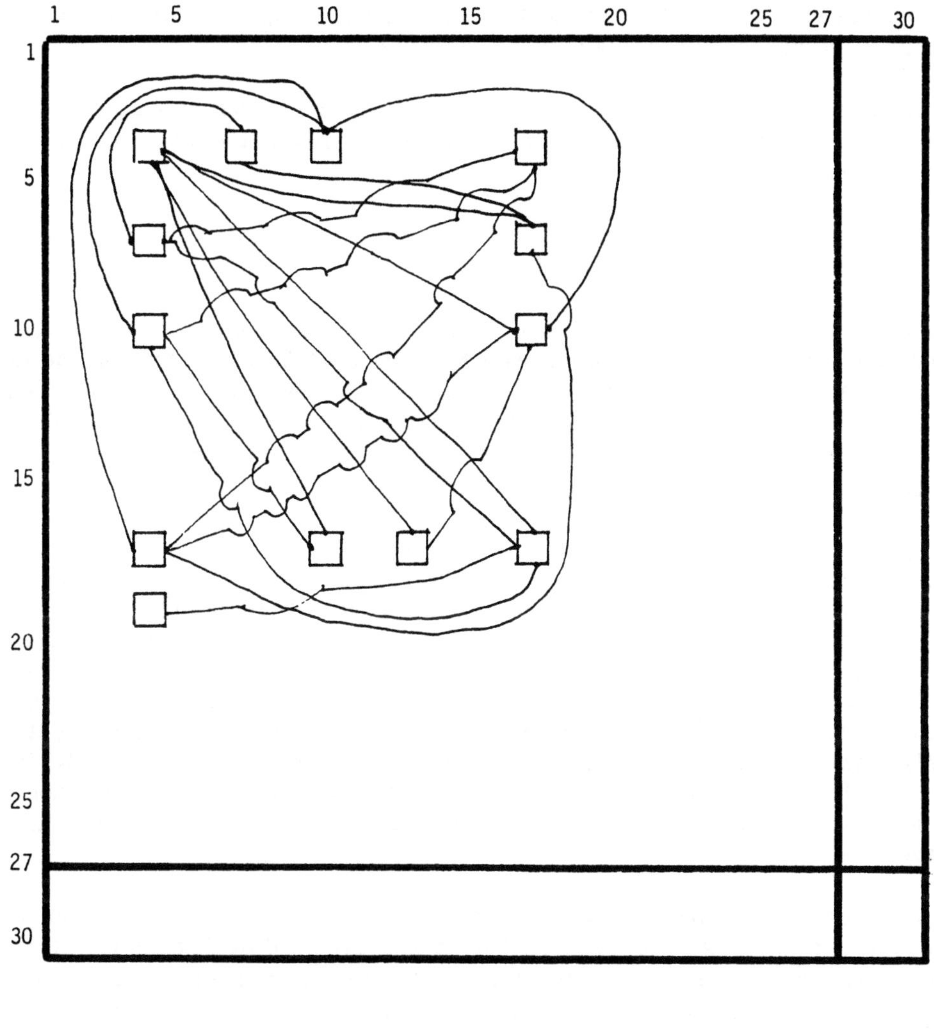

Diagram 16 suggests some possible patterns of diffusion of change which might occur within an economy; these changes would need to be related to specific processes, something which would have to be accomplished outside the context of the input-output model. For example, the degree to which technical change might signal predatory pricing policy in an attempt to 'eliminate' competition or the degree to which technical change and its diffusion through an industry is accommodated by reorganisation of the way in which production occurs (see below). The changes suggested in this Diagram might be considered to represent some of several 'characteristic' changes; they might include a clustering effect (technical innovation might be restricted to small subsets of the economy) or a spiralling effect (inward or outward) in which successive sectors might be influenced by the change. As our empirical work begins to yield a large enough sample, we may be in a better position to provide a better set of potential classifications.

While the methods discussed here and the array of other approaches suggest many valuable possibilities, several problems remain. These will provide the focus for the final section of the chapter.

5. NEW ACCOUNTING FRAMEWORKS

The input-output framework was designed many years ago when the process of change in economies moved at a much more modest pace than that which has characterised the last several years and which is likely to be a feature of the next several decades. Thus, we need to consider some modifications to this framework into which the attractive feature of the input-output model could be blended with new concerns about the process of technical change.

Three suggestions are provided here. The first recognises that production may be organised differently in firms which are larger or part of a multinational/large corporate structure; a very simply extension to the input-output model is shown in Diagram 17. A second extension, shown in Diagram 18, builds on the product cycle notion introduced in Diagram 3 and suggests that production might bye organised not only according to size of the firm but the stage of the product cycle. Thus, with different stages would come a different production process. Lahiri (1976) suggested a procedure whereby the choice of input coefficients might be a function of demand; Diagram 18 suggests a way of formally dividing structure. In addition, there is some suggestion that choice of process and location might be linked with mass production activities situated in locations far away from the R&D phase.

The final suggestion involves a way in which micro and macro level elements can be combined into one model. Drawing on some of the work developed by Eliasson (1978) in Sweden, the suggestion here is to identify the set of firms which might be regarded as key initiators of technological change to model their behaviour outside the context of the traditional macro model (Diagram 19). Thus, the techniques described in the earlier sections might be useful in separating out these industries/firms. Thus, the diffusion process might be characterised at the micro level and which eventually proceeds 'upwards' into the macro system. Anne Carter (1970) once described the process of change as a moving average one, in which old technologies are gradually replaced by new ones - but the rate of change may concentrate as firms become more flexible and adaptable.

Diagram 16 Types of Diffusion in an Input-Output Framework
Summary... Manufacturing... Tertiary

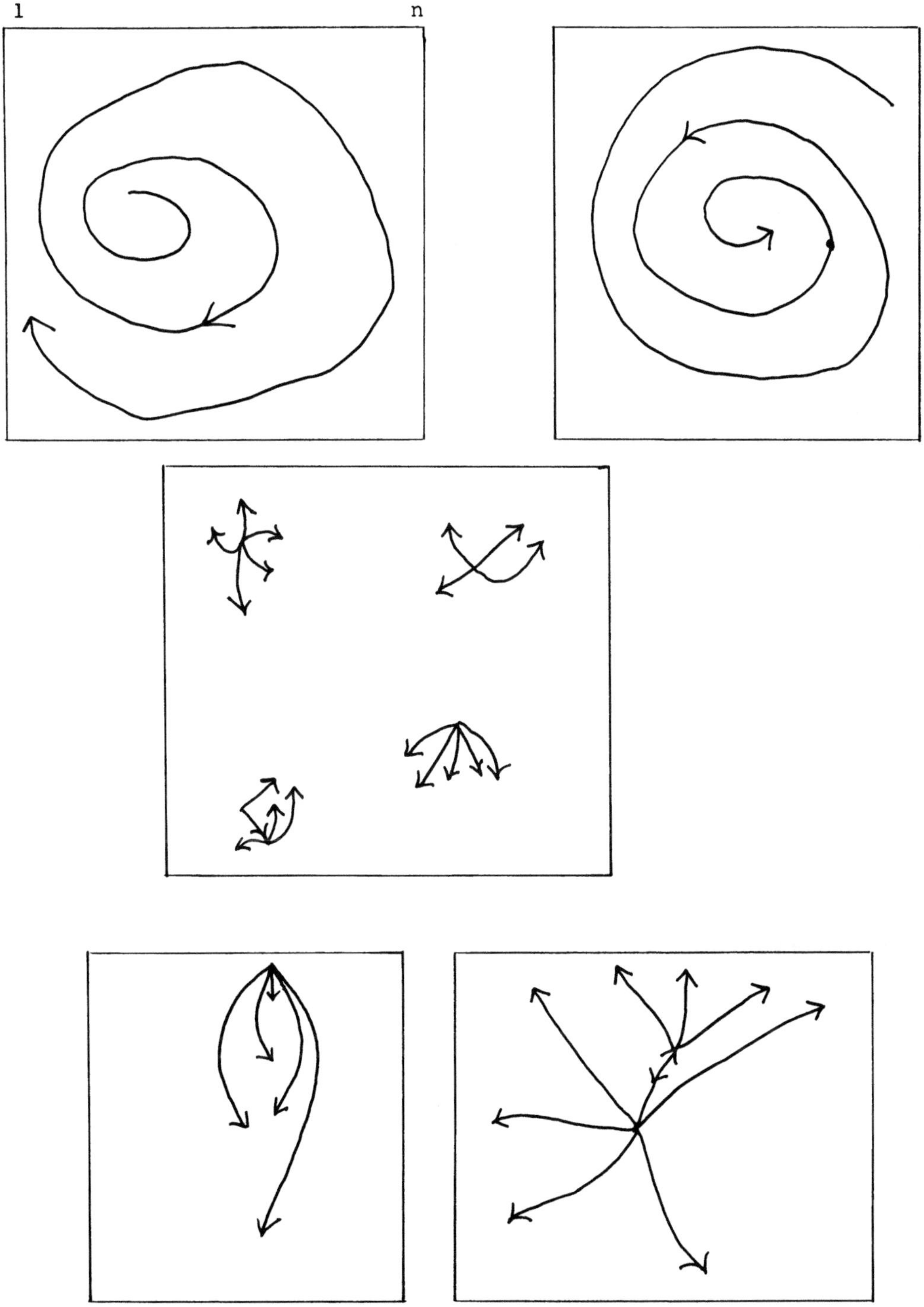

Diagram 17 **A multiregional firm-to-firm accounting model for a national economy**

From		To: firms in region 1 1 2 3 4 ...	To: firms in region 2 1 2 3 4 ...	To: firms in region 3 1 2 3 4 ...	...
firms in region 1	1 2 3 4 ...	A-A	A-B	A-C	
firms in region 2	1 2 3 4 ...	B-A	B-B	B-C	
firms in region 3	1 2 3 4 ...	C-A	C-B	C-C	
...					

[a] The firms could be, for example, 1--Exxon; 2--General Motors; 3--AT & T; 4--Texaco; etc.

Source: Beyers 1980b

Diagram 18 Standard I.O Model

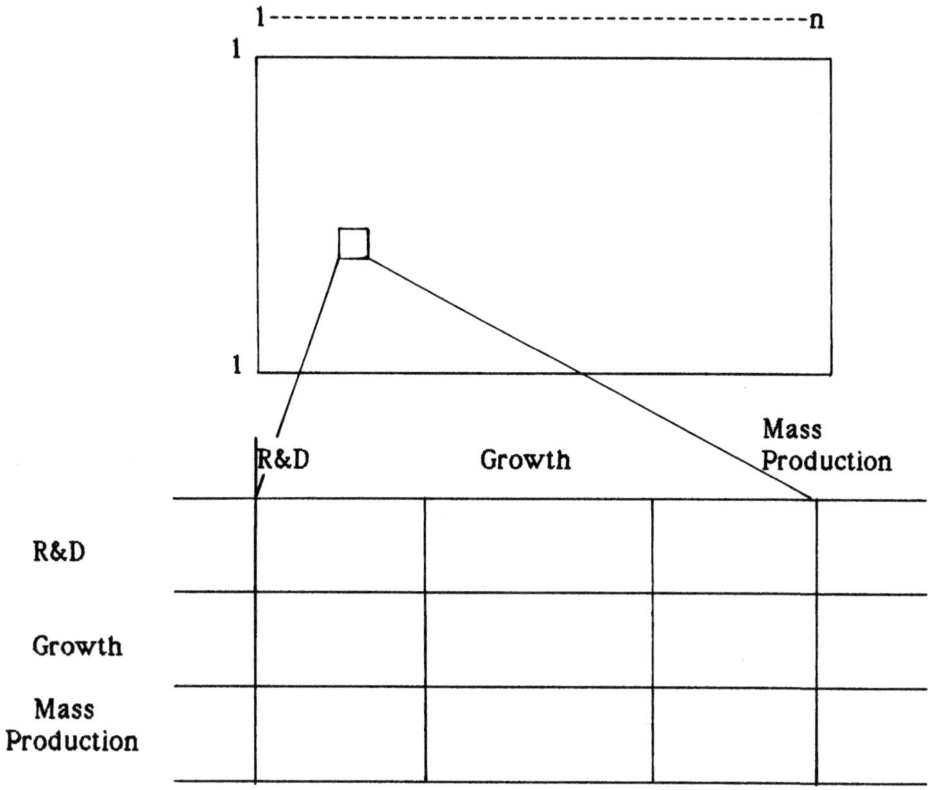

Diagram 19 A possible micromodel for one firm to be linked with the macromodel (Source: Eliasson 1978)

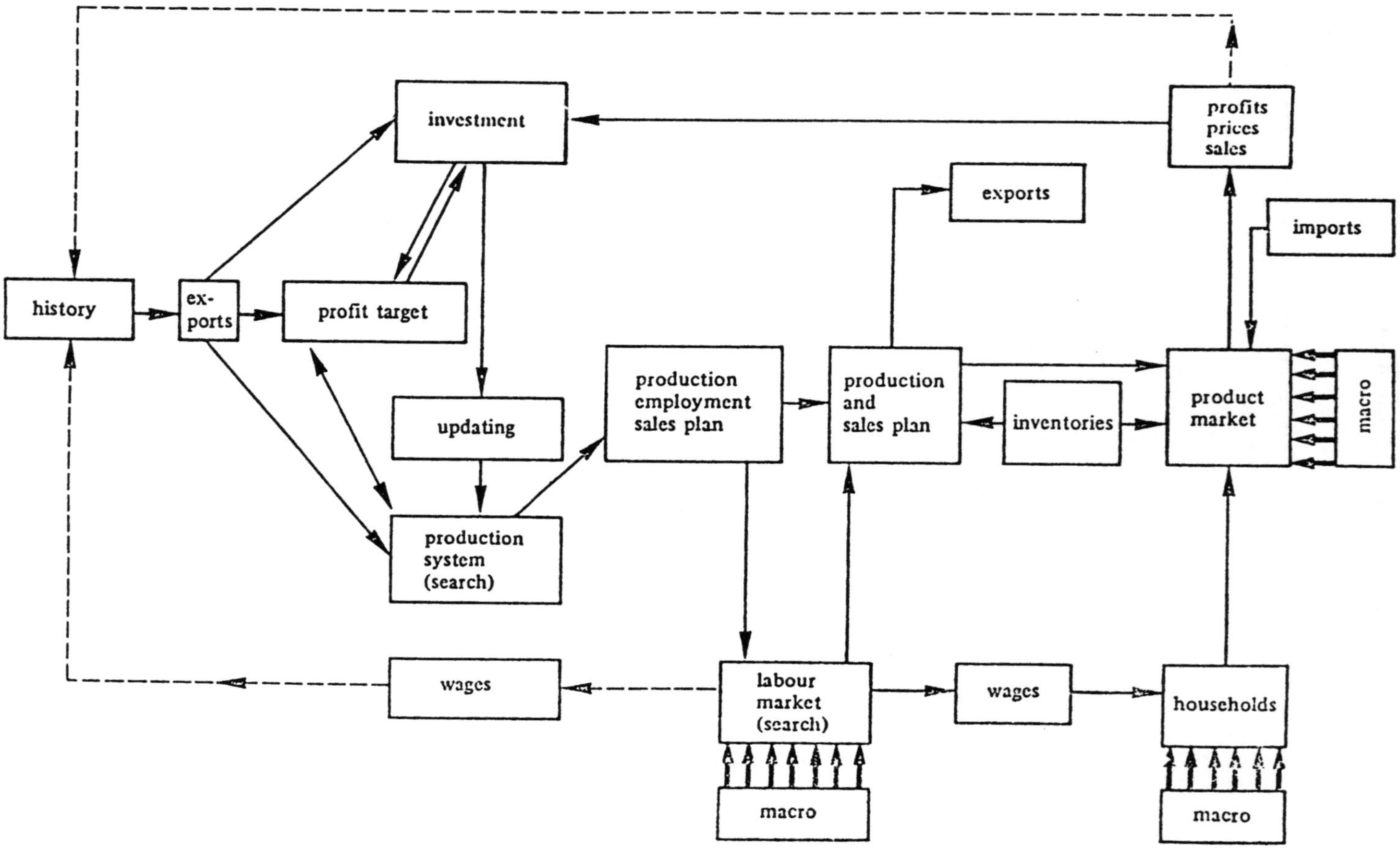

Diagram 20 A micro-macro link with location considerations

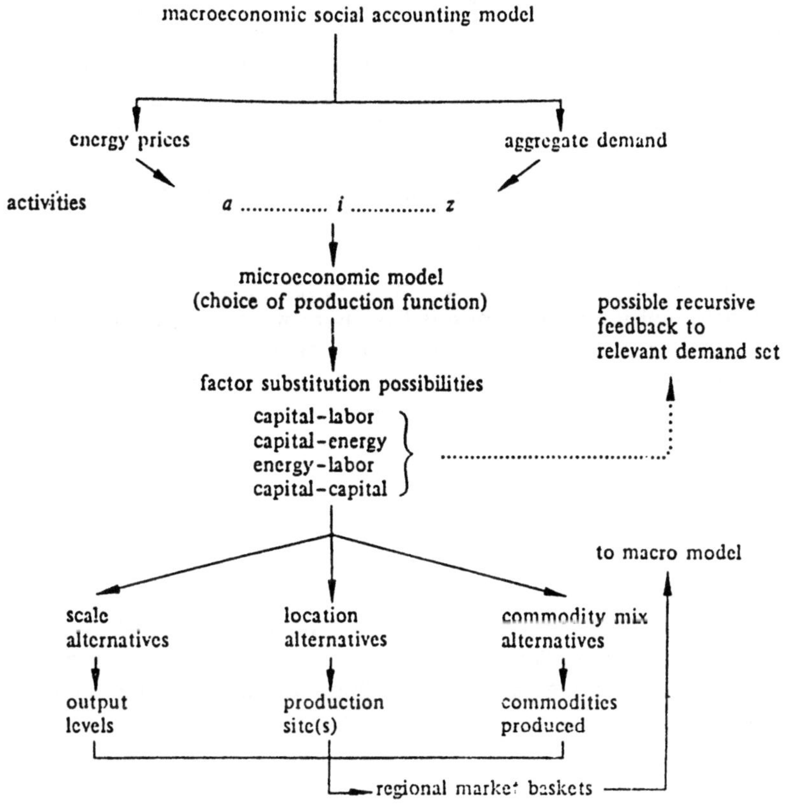

Diagram 20 suggests one possible way in which the issues of micro-to-micro links, process changes and location changes could be considered in an integrated way; elements of the earlier diagrams could thus be incorporated within this framework which would include, as its base, the fundamental economic structure of the system under consideration.

6. CONCLUSIONS

The input-output model has proved to be a valuable tool for analysis of 'traditional' problems - impact analysis, forecasting, and so forth. However, the pace of technical change in the economy suggests that some adaptation of this framework will be necessary to accommodate the striking changes taking place in the structure of production. Markussen (1986) has commented that a great deal of new technology adopted in the US may be directly attributable to defence-initiated spending. This raises a further issue of the degree to which non-defence related R&D has the capability of 'competing' and whether different R&D might be expected to produce a different 'field of influence'.

In the final analysis, some attempt needs to be made to link some of the substantial literature on technological change with an analytical framework capable of handling the direct, indirect and induced income effects of this change. Technical innovation will also have an impact on consumer behaviour; the increase in catalogue shopping in the US is evidence for the potential for change initiated by improvements in communications. Many of the technological changes may thus influence the consumption-industry relationships to a greater extent than the interindustry linkages. If we are able to identify a fundamental economic structure, we may be able to focus our research energies on other components of our economic system and proceed to uncover to a greater extent than previously the full dimension of technological change.

ACKNOWLEDGEMENT

Funding for this research was provided, in part, by the National Science Foundation (Hewings), the Fulbright Commission and the George A. Miller Committee of the University of Illinois (Sonis) and a Development Fund Grant from the University of Queensland (Jensen).

NOTES

[1] It is interesting to note that Thompson considered the possibility of service activities being exported; recent empirical evidence for service firms in the state of Washington suggests that these activities are engaged in interregional trade almost to the degree associated with the manufacturing sector.

[2] In reality, some of the same cells will appear as 'bottlenecks' in more than one round; hence, the actual number of nonzero transactions will usually be (kn where k is the number of rounds and n the number of sectors.

REFERENCES

Bullard, C.W. and A.V. Sebald, Effects of Parametric Uncertainty and Technological Change in Input-Output Models, Review of Economics and Statistics 59, 1977, pp. 75-81.

Carter, A.P., Structural Change in the American Economy, Harvard University Press, Cambridge, 1970.

Eliasson, G. (ed), A Micro-to-Micro Model of the Swedish Economy, Almqvist and Wicksell, Stockholm, 1978.

Hamilton, J.R. and R.C. Jensen, Summary Measures of Interconnectedness for Input-Output Models, Environment and Planning A 15, 1983, pp. 55-65.

Hewings, G.J.D., Regional and Interregional Interdependencies: Alternative Accounting Frameworks, Environment and Planning A 14, 1982 pp. 1587-1600.

Hewings, G.J.D., A Decomposition Approach to the Analysis of Changes in Regional Economic Structure, Modeling and Simulation 14, 1983, pp. 197-199.

Hewings, G.J.D., The Role of Prior Information in Updating Regional Inout-Output Models, Socio-Economic Planning Sciences 18, 1984, pp. 319-336.

Hewings, G.J.D., R.C. Jensen and G.R. West, Holistic Matrix Descriptors of Regional Input-Output Systems, Working Paper in Economics, No. 60, University of Queensland, 1987.

Hewings, G.J.D. and M. Sonis, An Empirical Evaluation of Approaches to the Measurement of Change in Input-Output Tables, mimeo, 1986.

Jackson, R.W. and G.J.D. Hewings, Structural Change in a Regional Ecnomy: An Entropy Decomposition Approach, Modeling and Simulation 15, 1984, pp. 241-246.

Jensen, R.C., West G.R. and G.J.D. Hewings, On the Study of Regional Economic Structure Using Input-Output Tables, Regional Studies, 1988 (forthcoming).

Kuznets, S., Economic Growth of Nations: Total Output and Production Structure, Harvard Univesity Press, Cambridge, 1971.

Lahiri, S., Input-Output Analysis with Scale-Dependent Coefficients, Econometrica 44, 1976, pp. 947-962.

Simpson, D. and J. Tsukui, The Fundamental Structure of Input-Output Tables: An International Comparison, Review of Economics and Statistics 47, 1965, pp. 434-446.

Sonis, M. and G.J.D. Hewings, Error and Sensitivity Input-Output Analysis: A New Approach, 1988, mimeo.

Szyrmer, J.M., Measuring Connectedness of Input-Output Models: Part 1 Survey of Measures, Environment and Planning A 17, 1985, pp. 1591-1612.

Szyrmer, J.M., Measuring Connectedness of Input-Output Models, Part II Total Flow Concept, Environment and Planning A 18, 1986, pp. 857-867.

Thompson, W., A Preface to Urban Economics, Free Press, Glencoe, Illinois.

OPTIMAL PRICING OF TELECOMMUNICATIONS SERVICE IN AN ADVANCED INFORMATION-ORIENTED SOCIETY

Hirotada Kohno and Hitoshi Mitomo

1. INTRODUCTION

In Japan, the telecommunications market has been developed with the monopolistic supply by the Nippon Telegraph and Telephone Public Corporation (NTTPC), which is now privatised. In early 1985 the NTTPC was placed under private management in order to introduce market mechanisms. This market will become highly developed and diversified not only because of the advancement of telecommunications technology but also because of the free entry of competitive firms. In addition, telecommunications systems will be more important as an infrastructure which will sustain the social and economic growth hereafter.

The society with highly advanced telecommunications technology is called the *Advanced Information-Oriented Society*. One way to realise such a society is the development of Information Network Systems (INS) planned by Nippon Telegraph and Telephone Co. Ltd., (NTT), which is the Japanese version of Integrated Service Digital Network (ISDN).

It is anticipated that the INS technology will enable us to enjoy better services with lower costs and that the differentials of charge between short-distance and long-distance communications will be abolished. It is considered that user charges will not be imposed according to seconds, minutes or hours of occupancy of a transmission circuit but proportional to the volume of information transmitted.

We have organised our contribution from this point of view. Our purpose is to analyse the supply side of the telecommunications market. In Section 2, we give a perspective of the pricing of telephone calls in the context of the privatisation of the NTTPC, entry of competitive firms and the innovation of the relevant technology. We explain the pricing of the NTT and the entrants graphically without any mathematical formulations. In Section 3, we analyse the optimal two-part tariff in an advanced information-oriented society in which no distance discrimination exists in the supply of telecommunication services.

2. A PERSPECTIVE ON THE PRICING OF TELECOMMUNICATION SERVICES

After the NTTPC was privatised, several enterprises entered into the supply of telecommunication services between the two metropolises, Tokyo and Osaka. They constructed optical fibre cable transmission systems in this section independently. The entrants intended to supply communications services by leasing the NTT terminal facilities.

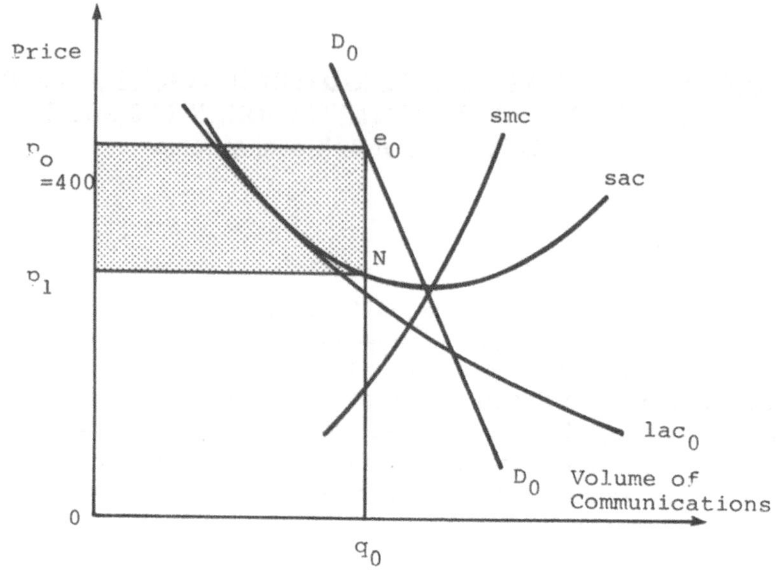

Figure 1: Present demand and cost curves for the NTT telecommunications service between Tokyo and Osaka

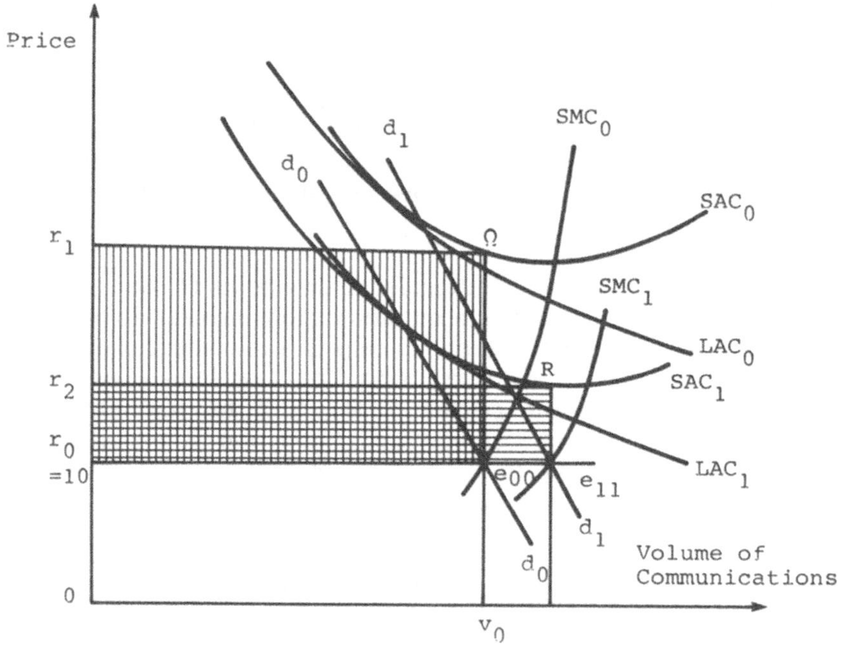

Figure 2: Demand and cost curves for the local telecommunications service

The cost of the structure of the supply of the service in this section can be hypothetically represented as in Figure 1, in which we assume that D_oD_o is the present demand curve, and smc_o, sac_o and lac_o are the present short-run marginal, short-run average and long-run average cost surves, respectively. We also assume, for simplicity, that the NTT supplies only two types of communications service, i.e. the long-distance (between Tokyo and Osaka) and local communications services. The cost curves for local communications services are shown in Figure 2. d_od_o is the present demand curve and SMC_o, SAC_o and LAC_o is the present short-run marginal, short-run average and long-run average cost curves., respectively.

Since the local call rate, r_o, is officially fixed in Japan (10 yen per 3 minutes), the NTT will set the production capacity so that the marginal cost is equal to the price in order to maximise the profit. In this case, the equilibrium will be given by $e_{oo}(r_o,v_o)$ in Figure 2, where the average cost is obviously greater than r_o. On the other hand, the long-distance call rate, p_o, can be determined arbitrarily by the NTT, since it is a kind of monopolistic price. Thus the equilibrium will be given by $e_o(p_o, q_o)$ in Figure 1. Note that p_o is not a completely monopolistic price since the Government regulates it slightly. The NTT obtains the profit, $p_oe_oNp_1$, and incurs the loss, $r_1Qe_{oo}r_o$. Therefore, it should adopt a strategy so that the deficit caused by local calls is made up by the surplus from long-distance calls. This is the so called *cross-subsidisation*. At present, the local call and long-distance call (more than 320 km) rates are set a ten yen and four hundred yen per three minutes, respectively, which yield, in effect, large profits.

Suppose that some firms can enter into the supply of long-distance telecommunications services. In fact, several enterprises are intending to enter. However, we would like to aggregate them. Then, let DD be the demand for the long-distance calls after the entry, which is assumed to be composed of the demand for the NTT, D_1D_1 and for the entrants, D_2D_2. It means that we assume that both services are not completely homogeneous. Therefore, the market price of the services can be written as $p(q_1, q_2)$, where q_1 and q_2 are the supply by the NTT and the entrants, respectively.

After an innovation technology is introduced, cost functions will change drastically. The cost curves for long-distance calls after the technology is introduced will be represented as in Figure 3. In this case, the equilibria for the NTT and the entrants will be given by $e_1(p^*, q_1)$ and $e_2(p^*, q_2)$. The equilibrium price p^* is of course less than p_o. The respective profits from long-distance calls of the NTT and the entrants can be given by $p^*e_1Sp_1$ and $p^*e_2Tp_2$. On the other hand, the local telecommunications service will be supplied at e_{11} in Figure 2. The cost curves are assumed to shift downward to SMC_1, SAC_1 and LAC_1. The deficit will be reduced to $r_2Re_{11}r_o$.

In this case, the NTT behaves as if it maximises the profit from long-distance services, $p^*e_1Sp_1$, plus the access charge imposed on the entrants, net of the deficit from local call services, $r_2Re_{11}r_o$. This will raise an important problem of

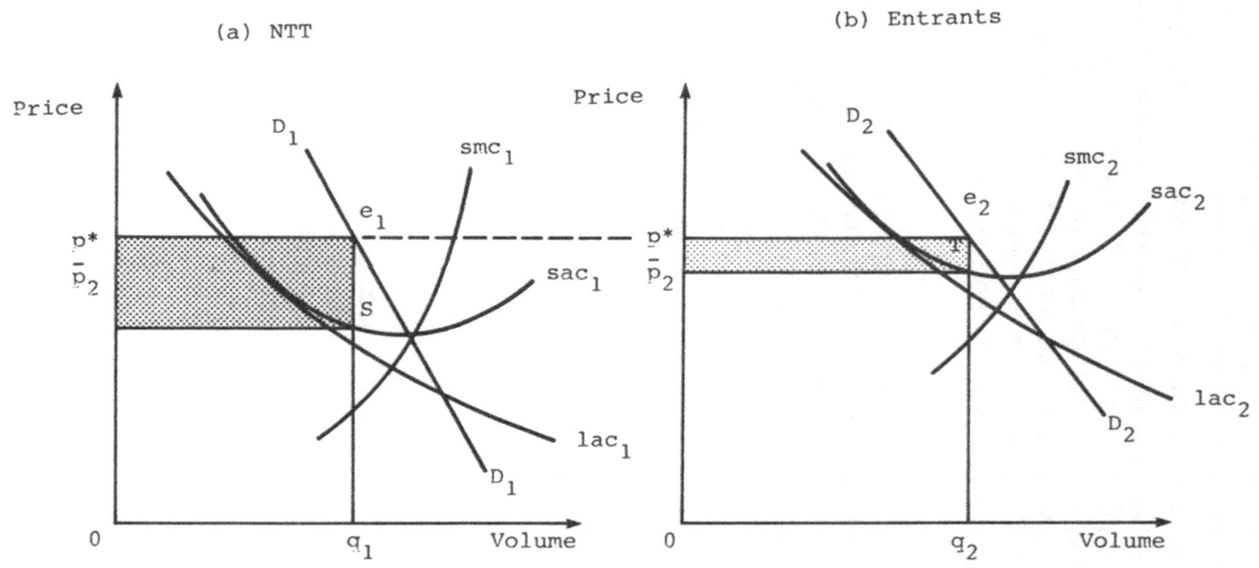

Figure 3: Demand and cost curves for the NTT and Entrants' Telecommunications Service in the near future

determining the optimal *access charge* which the entrants have to pay to the NTT in connecting their transmission systems to local terminal systems of the NTT, because the NTT monopolistically supplies terminal services. If the NTT imposes it according to the volume transmitted from(to) the entrants' transmission system to(from) NTT's terminal system, it could function for them as a specific tax. Assuming that the short-run cost curves in Figure 3(b) are derived from a currently efficient production technology for the entrants, if p^* were the zero profit price for NTT in the context of the total profit function shown above, NTT could deter them from entering only if it sets the access charge larger than p^*p_2. If the charge proposed is too large for the entrants to yield profits, they might bargain the charge down to be feasible. Alternatively, in order to promote the entrants, the Government has to direct the NTT to set the access charge low. This kind of intervention should be necessary not only to make the entrants profitable (i.e. lower than p^*p_2) but also to facilitate consumers to join the new system. The higher price will give consumers less incentive to subscribe to the new system. However, if this charge is low enough for the entrants to yield profits, they might reduce the price so as to bid customers away. For this process, a game theoretic approach will give a clear interpretation.

In the long run, innovative technology will change the system of supplying telecommunications services. If the technology such as an optical fibre network or satellite link comes into use, discrimination between local and long-distance telecommunications will diminish. We analyse the extreme case in the following section.

3. OPTIMAL TWO-PART TARIFF IN AN ADVANCED INFORMATION-ORIENTED SOCIETY

Communications systems are usually supplied under a two-part tariff system. Two-part tariff is the system in which users must pay a marginal charge, m, according to their occupancy or communication volume, v, in addition to a monthly fixed charge, C_0. That is,

$$C(v) = C_0 + mv. \tag{3.1}$$

As the telecomunications technology advances, it is expected that the charge will not be imposed proportionally to the distance between caller and recipient but to the volume transmitted. In this case, v in Equation (3.1) is just the volume of communications.

Most of the communications systems have demand (consumption) externalities in that the benefit of a subscriber depends on the number of subscribers to the system. As the number of subscribers increases, the benefit which a subscriber can obtain from the service also increases. This characteristic is essential to analysing the demand and supply of communications services and is discussed repeatedly by several authors. On the premise of the existence of the externalities, Rohlfs (1974) and Artle and Averous (1975) analysed the demand for telecommunications service, and Squire (1973), Littlechild (1975) analysed the supply side. Oren and Smith (1981) analysed both, on which the definition of the demand function in our model is based. However, they ignored the benefit from receiving calls and did not consider how the criteria of pricing would affect the firms' profit and social welfare.

When a new communications system is to be set up, even an establishment that feels it is very convenient and is willing to subscribe will not do so alone. It will either subscribe with others simultaneously or agree to subscribe in anticipation of others joining.

We now consider a region in which establishments constitute a complete set with respect to the potential inter-establishment communications. An establishment is defined as a unit such as an individual, household, office, etc., that is willing to communicate regardless of whether they join the telecommunications system. Assume that each establishment is identified with some unique index ξ , and without loss of generality that ξ is within the interval [0, 1]. That is, all the establishments in the region are assumed to distribute in this interval. Any establishment is assumed to have the potential to communicate with other establishments within this set. Suppose that ξ distributes in [0, 1] continuously. Then, the total potential volume of communications of an establishment ξ is defined as

$$V(\xi) - \int_0^1 s(\xi, \eta)d\eta + \int_0^1 s(\eta, \xi)d\eta \tag{3.2}$$

where h is the index of an establishment in the same set, $s(\xi,\eta)d\eta$ is the potential volume of communications sent from an establishment with index ξ to all establishments with indices in the range $[\eta, \eta + d\eta)$ and $s(\eta, \xi)d\eta$ is that received by the establishment ξ sent from all establishments in $[\eta, \eta + d\eta)$.

Each establishment has his own total potential volume $V(\xi)$. Then, we can arrange the ranking of establishments in the region according to the magnitude of $V(\xi)$. If we assume the continuity of the distribution of ξ in [0, 1] after the arrangement, the complete order of all establishments in the region is made with respect to the total potential volume of communications. In this case, all establishments need not subscribe, and the subscribers' set will be a subset of the complete establishments' set. Suppose that the preference order of joining the system is monotone decreasing in ξ. If not, we must specify which establishment is going to subscribe at each price level. Let the index of the subscriber who has the minimum total potential volume be y and that of the subscriber who has the maximum volume be 0, then the realisable potential volume of a subscriber with index $\xi \leq y$ is defined as:

$$S(\xi, y) - \int_0^y s(\xi, \eta)d\eta + \int_0^y s(\eta, \xi)d\eta. \tag{3.3}$$

Note that y is not exogenous to the region but to an establishment. From the assumption, $S(\xi, y)$ is monotone decreasing in ξ.

Let $B(m, \xi, y)$ be the benefit of the establishment ξ for the charge m. We can realise this definition from the fact that the benefit from sending would be the function of the charge m and the realisable potential volume $S(\xi, y)$, i.e. $B(m, \xi, y) = B(m, S(\xi, y))$. It is plausible to assume that the benefit of communications is derived both from sending and from receiving:

$$B(m, \xi, y) = B_s(m, \xi, y) + B_r(m, \xi, y),$$

where B_s and B_r are the benefits derived from sending and receiving, respectively. The benefit from sending can be defined as the relevant area under the communications demand function, assuming that each establishment determines its optimal volume from utility maximisation. That is:

$$B_s(m, \xi, y) = \int_0^{V_m} D^{-1}\, dv,$$

where $V_m = D(m, \xi, y)$ is the demand function. However, the benefit from receiving can hardly be formulated meaningfully. We assume for simplicity that it could also be a function of m, ξ and y in the same way as the benefit from sending.

For a subscriber set to be viable, the benefit must be equal to the total charge paid, with respect to the minimum subscriber, $\xi = y$, i.e.

$$B_N(m,y,y) \equiv B(m,y,y,) - C(m,y,y) = 0, \qquad (3.4)$$

where $B_N(m,y,y)$ is the net benefit of the smallest subscriber and $C(m,y,y)$ is the total charge paid according to the volume sent. From the monotonicity of $B(m, \xi, y)$ in ξ and y, for any y^* such that $B_N(m,y,y) = 0$, the set $[0, y^*]$ is an equilibrium users set. If the derivative of $B_n(m,y,y)$ is negative at the point y^*, the equilibrium is stable.

In the following subsection, we will derive the optimal two-part tariff. A subscribers' set, y, can be determined by the total charge composed of the fixed charge C_0 and marginal charge m. Thus, the policy variables for the supplier or policy maker are C_0 and m. He can attain any subscribers' set by combining arbitrarily C_0 and m. However, we do not adopt this conventional method. We do not ask the size of the subscribers' set which is derived from C_0 and m. Our purpose is to derive the optimal C_0 and m. The process we adopt is as follows. First, we consider C_0 as a free variable. A subscribers' set, y, is independent of marginal charge m, because we can attain a subscribers' set by setting C_0 appropriately for any level of m. Then, we maximise profit or total surplus with respect to m. We also maximise it with respect to y, so that the optimal subscribers' set can be derived which will bring about the maximum profit or total surplus. Given the optimality conditions for both y and m, we can derive the optimal C_0 which will also give the maximum profit or surplus.

Optimal Two-Part Tariff

We now consider the following two rules of optimal pricing:

(i) profit maximisation, and
(ii) total surplus maximisation.

We use the following notation:

C_0 : fixed charge per subscriber
m : marginal charge per unit of volume
v : volume of communications sent from an establishment ξ, i.e.,

$$v = D(m, \xi\, y).$$

We assume that

$$\partial D/\partial m \lesseqgtr 0, \quad \partial D/\partial y \gtreqless 0.$$

with:
k : fixed cost per subscriber
c : constant marginal cost per unit of volume
$\phi(m,\xi,y)$: consumer surplus of the establishment ξ in case of subscribers set y and marginal charge m

$$\phi(m,\xi, y) = \int_m^\infty D(p, \xi, y)d \tag{3.5}$$

so that $\Phi(m, y)$, the total consumers surplus of all subscribers in case of subscribers set y is:

$$\begin{aligned}\Phi(m, y) &= \int_0^y \phi(m, \xi, y)d\xi \\ &= \int_0^y \int_m^\infty D(p, \xi, y)\, dp\, d\xi\end{aligned} \tag{3.6}$$

$D_R(m,y)$, the total demand for communications services is equal to

$$D_T(m, y) = \int_0^y D(m, \xi, y)d\xi \tag{3.7}$$

From the above definitions, the following equations hold:

$$\partial\phi(m, \xi, y)/\partial m = - D(m, \xi, y) \tag{3.8}$$

$$\partial \Phi(m, y)/\partial m = - D_T(m, y). \tag{3.9}$$

$\psi(m, \xi, y)$ is the benefit of the establishment ξ from receiving. We assume for simplicity that

$$\partial \psi/\partial m \lesssim 0, \qquad \partial \psi/\partial y \gtrsim 0.$$

so that $\Psi(m, y)$, the total benefit from receiving is

$$\Psi(m, y) = \int_0^y \psi(m, \xi, y) d\xi \tag{3.10}$$

Since each subscriber must pay the fixed charge, C_0, regardless of his volume of communications, the net benefits left to the establishment ξ and all the subscribers is

$$\phi(m, \xi, y) + \psi(m, \xi, y) - C_0 \tag{3.11}$$

$$\Phi(m, y) + \Psi(m,y) - yC_0 = \int_0^y \phi(m, \xi, y)d\xi + \int_0^y \psi(m, \xi, y)d\xi - yC_0 \tag{3.12}$$

respectively.

Furthermore, for $[0, y]$ to be the equilibrium users set, the benefit of the smallest subscriber, $B(m,y,y)$ must be equal to his total charge paid:

$$B(m,y,y) = C_0 + m\, D(m,y,y). \tag{3.4'}$$

By the way, $B(m,y,y)$ can be represented as the sum of the consumer surplus plus the benefit from receiving of the smallest subscriber, $\phi(m,y,y) + \psi(m,y,y)$, and his total marginal charge paid, $mv_y = mD(m,y,y)$, which depends on his volume, $v_y = D(m,y,y)$, so that Equation (3.4') can be rewritten as:

$$\phi(m, y, y) + \psi(m, y, y) = C_0. \tag{3.13}$$

Net profit of the supplier is composed of two factors: net profit per subscriber and per unit of volume supplied. Thus, the total net profit of the supplier, R, is the sum of total net revenue from subscribers and from the supply of communications services. That is:

$$\begin{aligned} R &= (C_0 - k)y + (m-c)\, D_T(m,y) \\ &= (C_0 - k)y + (m-c) \int_0^y (m, \xi, y)\, d\xi \end{aligned} \tag{3.14}$$

From Equations (3.12) and (3.14) the total surplus derived from this communications services, W, can be represented as

$$\begin{aligned} W &= (\Phi(m,y) + \Psi(m,y) - yC_0) + R \\ &= \Phi(m,y) + \Psi(m,y) - yk + (m-c)\, D_T \\ &= \int_0^y (\phi(m,\xi,y) + \psi(m,\xi,y))\, d\xi - yk + (m-c) \int_0^y D(m,\xi,y)\, d\xi . \end{aligned} \tag{3.15}$$

Profit Maximisation

The profit, R, is given by Equation (3.14) so that the profit maximisation problem is formulated as the maximisation of (3.14) subject to (3.13). Substituting (3.13) for C_0, the problem can be rewritten as the unconstrained maximisation:

$$\max.\ R = (\phi(m,y,y) + \psi(m,y,y) - k)y + (m-c)\, D_T(m,y) . \tag{3.16}$$

The first order conditions are:

$$\partial R/\partial m = y(-D(m,y,y) + \psi(m,y,y)/\partial m) + D_T + (m-c)\, \partial D_T/\partial m = 0 . \tag{3.17}$$

$$\begin{aligned} \partial R/\partial y &= y(\partial\phi(m,y,y)/\partial y + \partial\psi(m,y,y)/\partial y) \\ &\quad + (\phi(m,y,y) + \psi(m,y,y) - k) + (m-c)\, \partial D_T(m,y)/\partial y = 0 . \end{aligned} \tag{3.18}$$

Rewriting Equation (3.17), we have

$$(m-c)/m = (1 - v_y/\bar{v} - (1/\bar{v})(\partial\psi/\partial m))/e_m \tag{3.19}$$

or

$$m = ce_m/(e_m - 1 + v_y/\bar{v} + (1/\bar{v})(\partial\psi/\partial m)) \tag{3.19'}$$

where

$$v_y = D(m,y,y) \text{ and } \bar{v} = D_T(m,y)/y$$

and e_m is the price elasticity of total demand, D_T, with respect to marginal charge, m,

$$e_m = -(\partial D_T / \partial m)(m/D_T) \gtrless 0 .$$

Since, from the assumption, the average demand, v, is greater than the demand of the smallest subscriber, v_y, that is

$$v_y/\bar{v} \lessgtr 1,$$

and

$$\partial\psi(m, \xi, y)/\partial m \lessgtr 0,$$

the inequality, m > c, must hold. The marginal charge should be proportional to the marginal cost and set greater than it. If we ignore the benefit from receiving, the profit margin (m-c)/m is obviously equal to

$$(1 - v_y/\bar{v})e_m.$$

The existence of the benefit from receiving increases it by the amount,

$$(1/\bar{v})(\partial\psi/\partial m)/e_m,$$

which denotes the marginal reduction of the benefit of the smallest subscriber from receiving per the average volume of demand.

In order to consider the most profitable size of the system, we solve implicitly Equation (3.18) with respect to y by substituting Equation (3.19') for m. Rewriting Equation (3.18) we obtain

$$C_0 = \{k-(m-c)\,\partial D_T / \partial y\}/(1-e_y) \qquad (3.20)$$

whereby e_y is the elasticity of the benefit of the smallest subscriber with respect to the scale of subscribers set:

$$e_y = \frac{\partial\{\phi(m,y,y)+\psi(m,y,y)\}}{\partial y}\,\frac{y}{\phi(m,y,y)+\psi(m,y,y)} \gtrless 0 .$$

$\partial D_T/\partial y$ is the increase in demand of all subscribers derived from the marginal subscriber's joining. The fixed charge, C_0, diverges from the fixed cost, k, by the two factors. The first is $1/(1-e_y)$. As we know from the definition, e_y is the index relevant to the benefit which the marginal subscriber can enjoy through joining the system. Since $e_y \gtrless 0$, the fixed charge, C_0, will be set greater than the fixed cost by the benefit of the smallest subscriber. The second is $(m-c)\,\partial D_T/\partial y$. It is obvious that this term is the increase in the net revenue of the operator which results from the increase in total demand caused by the marginal subscriber joining the system. The fixed charge will be set lower than the fixed cost by the this amount. Therefore, it will be determined by the relative strength of these opposing factors whether the fixed charge C_0 is actually greater or lower than the fixed cost, k.

Surplus Maximisation

The sum of the consumers benefit and producer surplus is given by Equation (3.15). Since the total surplus does not depend on the fixed charge, C_0, the maximisation problem can be solved by differentiating directly Equation (3.15). The first order necessary conditions are:

$$\partial W/\partial m = \partial\Phi(m,y)/\partial m + \partial\Psi(m,y)/\partial m + D_T + (m-c)\,\partial D_T/\partial m$$

$$= \partial\Psi(m,y)/\partial m + (m-c)\,\partial D_T/\partial m = 0\,. \tag{3.21}$$

$$\partial W/\partial y = \partial\Phi/\partial y + \partial\Psi/\partial y - k + (m-c)\,\partial D_T/\partial y = 0\,. \tag{3.22}$$

Equation (3.21) is reduced to

$$m = c - \frac{\partial\Psi}{\partial m} \Big/ \frac{\partial D_T}{\partial m}$$

$$= c - \partial\Psi \,/\, \partial D_T\,. \tag{3.23}$$

Since both $\partial D_T/\partial m$ and $\partial\Psi/\partial m$ are nonpositive, $(\partial\Psi/\partial m)/(\partial D_T/\partial m) \gtrless 0$. Equation (3.23) suggests that the marginal charge, m, must be smaller than the marginal cost, c, by the change in the total benefit from receiving induced by the marginal increase in total demand.

From Equation (3.22), we can derive the optimal size of the system which maximises the total surplus. At the optimum, $m-c \neq -\partial\Psi/\partial D_T$, so that we have

$$\partial\Phi/\partial y - k = 0\,. \tag{3.24}$$

We know from Equation (3.6) that $\partial\Phi/\partial y$ is not equal to the benefit of the smallest subscriber. Thus, $\partial\Phi/\partial y = C_0$, and the equation, $C_0 = k$, does not hold, which will result from the fact that the benefit of establishment ξ explicitly depends on the size of subscribers set y. If the existence of such externalities is not assumed, the fixed charge should be equal to k obviously.

By the way, the total consumer surplus function

$$\Phi(m,y) = \int_0^y \phi(m, \xi, y) d\xi$$

is continuous in [0, y]. Applying the mean value theorem for integrals, there exists $\omega \in [0, y]$ such that

$$\int_0^y \phi(m, \xi, y) d\xi = \phi(m, \omega, y)(y-0) . \tag{3.25}$$

Thus, we have approximately

$$\begin{aligned} \partial\Phi/\partial y &= \phi(m, \omega, y) + y\, \partial(\phi(m, \omega, y))/\partial y \\ &= \phi(m, \omega, y) + C_0 - \phi(m, y, y) \\ &\quad + y\, \partial\phi(m, \omega, y) / \partial y \end{aligned}$$

and substituting this for Equation (3.24) yields

$$\begin{aligned} C_0 &= k - [\phi(m, \omega, y) - \phi(m, y, y)] \\ &\quad - y\, \partial\phi(m, \omega, y) / \partial y . \end{aligned} \tag{3.26}$$

Let us define ω, which satisfies Equation (3.25), as the 'average subscriber'. The second term of the right hand side of Equation (3.26) (in brackets) is the difference between the consumer surplus of the average subscriber and of the smallest subscriber. The last term is the total benefit of the existing subscribers derived from the marginal subscriber's joining the system, which is measured at the average subscriber. Both of them result from the existence of consumption externalities and have nonnegative values from the definition. Therefore, in order to maximise the total surplus, the fixed charge, C_0, must be set lower than the fixed cost, k, by the amount of the above two terms.

Under the optimal pricing for total surplus maximisation, the deficit per subscriber

$$[\phi(m, \omega, y) - \phi(m, y, y)] + y\, \partial\phi(m, \omega, y) / \partial y ,$$

and per volume,

$$\partial\Psi / \partial D_T ,$$

will occur at the operator. Thus, this deficit should be made up by subsidies and so on, in the same way as in the case of marginal cost pricing of public utility rates in the presence of decreasing average cost. Table 1 summarises the previous results.

Numerical Example

In order to analyse further, we give a numerical example. We show a very particular case where the benefit from receiving does not exist. This is because we cannot define meaningfully the benefit function of receiving though such a benefit exists.

Let the realisable potential volume sent and the linear demand function be

$$S(\xi, y) = \alpha/2(1 - \xi)(2 - y)y$$

$$D(m, \xi, y) = (1 - m)\, S(\xi, y)$$

$$= \alpha/2(1 - m)(1 - \xi)(2 - y)y\,.$$

In this case, $D(0, \xi, y) = S(\xi, y)$. The total demand is given by

$$D_T(m, y) = \alpha/4(1 - m)(2 - y)^2\, y^2.$$

The consumer surplus of the establishment ξ and the total consumer surplus at price m are represented as

$$\phi(m, \xi, y) = \alpha/4(1 - m)^2\,(1 - \xi)(2 - y)y,$$

$$\Phi(m, y) = \alpha/8(1 - m)^2\,(2 - y)^2\, y^2\,,$$

respectively. An example of the value of parameters is given in Table 2.

Profit Maximisation

From Equations (3.16)-(3.20), we derive the optimal two-part tariff in case of profit maximisation. At first, from Equation (3.19), we know

$$m = c + (1 - c)y/2\,,\ 1 - m = (1 - c)(2 - y)/2\,.$$

Substituting them into Equation (3.18) yields the quartic equation

$$y(2 - y)^2\,(4 - 5y) = 16k/\alpha(1 - c)^2\,. \qquad \text{(a)}$$

Let $c = 0.2$, $k = 5.0$ and $\alpha = 106.29$. The equilibrium subscribers set is given by one of the roots in [0, 1] of the above equation, $y^* = 0.6$, where the asterisk denotes optimal. Thus, we obtain the marginal charge, $m = 0.44$, and the fixed

TABLE 1
Optimal Two-Part Tariff

	Profit maximisation	Total surplus maximisation
Marginal Charge (m)	$m = ce_m/\{e_m - 1 + v_y/\bar{v} + (1/\bar{v})(\partial\psi/\partial m)\}$ where $v = D(m,y,y)$, $\bar{v}_y\ D_T(m,y)/y$ $e_m = -(\partial D_T/\partial m)(m/D_T)$	$m = c - \dfrac{\partial\Psi}{\partial D_T}$
Fixed charge(C_0)	$C_0 = \{k - (m-c)\,\partial D_T/\partial y\}/(1-e_y)$ where $e_y = -\dfrac{\partial\{\phi(m,y,y)+\psi(m,y,y)\}}{\partial y}\ \dfrac{y}{\phi(m,y,y)+\psi(m,y,y)}$	$C_0 = k - [\phi(m,\omega,y) - \phi(m,y,y)]$ $-y\ \dfrac{\partial\phi(m,\omega,y)}{\partial y}$

charge $C_0 = 2.80$.

Total Surplus Maximisation

If the benefit from receiving does not exist, the marginal charge, m, is obviously equal to the constant marginal cost, c. Thus, $m = c = 0.2$. In order to derive the equilibrium subscribers set, substituting it into Equation (3.23) yields

$$34y^3 - 102y^2 + 68y - 5 = 0 \qquad \text{(b)}$$

Thus, we obtain $y^* = 0.85$. The fixed charge per subscriber is given by $C_0 = 2.49$.

The indices derived are represented in Table 3.

We know from the value of y^* that 60 and 85 per cent of total establishments join the system in case of profit maximisation and surplus maximisation, respectively. The other solution, y_c, of Equations (a) and (b) in [0, 1] is called the 'critical mass', which represents the minimum subset of subscribers needed for the service to become viable. Once this level is attained, establishments will prefer to join the system. 9.2 per cent of subscription level is required for profit maximisation and 8.4 per cent for surplus maximisation. It is evident from these values that more subscribers are necessary for the system to be set up and the final subscription level is lower in case of profit maximisation.

In this example, the supplier can obtain the profit 0.24 per volume of communication in case of profit maximisation, though the fixed charge per subscriber must be set lower than the fixed cost in case of profit maximisation. As we have shown, the fixed charge diverges from the fixed cost by two factors. In this example, $1-e_y = 0.07$ and $(m-c)\, \partial D_T/\partial y = 4.80$, so that the net increase in revenue by the increase in total demand induced by the subscription of the marginal establishment overcomes the inverse of his own subscription benefit.

In the case of surplus maximisation, although the supplier has to bear the deficit 2.13, the total consumer surplus and the total surplus derived are 2.8 and 1.6 times as large as in profit maximisation.

For the supplier to adopt the criterion of total surplus maximisation, it will be enough to make sure of the profit 1.20 which will be attained in profit maximisation. If we assume that a lump sum tax system which does not break marginal conditions can be utilised then the loss (= 3.33) which the supplier will suffer from surplus is greater than in profit maximisation ($2.94 < 8.13 - 3.33$). Thus, this simple example gives the case where the surplus maximisation is socially superior.

Therefore, in supplying a communications service, not only to achieve the efficiency by introducing the law of competition such as privatisation, free entry, etc., it is desirable in some cases to adopt the total surplus maximisation criterion through the intervention of the authority.

TABLE 2
Parameters

Constant marginal cost (c)	0.2
Fixed cost per subscriber (k)	5.0
Parameter (α)	106.29

TABLE 3
The Indices Derived

	Profit Maximisation	Total surplus maximisation
Equilibrium subscribers set (y^*)	0.60	0.85
Critical mass (y_C)	0.092	0.084
Marginal charge per volume (m)	0.44	0.20
Fixed charge per subscriber (C_0)	2.80	2.49
Total demand (D_T)	10.50	20.31
Profit (R)	1.20	-2.13
Total consumers surplus (Φ)	2.94	8.13
Total surplus	2.46	3.88

4. CONCLUSION

Introduction of a competition policy is now considered more suitable for securing a certain grade of communications services. Japanese policy gets along with this argument. We have discussed the pricing for telecommunications services in Japan in the context of deregulation, privatisation and free entry.

As the technology advances, the factor of distance will become less important and the pricing will be determined according to the volume transmitted. On the premise of consumption (demand) externalities, we have derived the optimal two-part tariff both for profit maximisation and for total surplus maximisation. In the former case, the constant marginal charge per volume is set higher than the constant variable cost, while the fixed charge per subscriber diverges from the fixed cost according to the two opposing factors which result from the externality effects. In the latter case, the constant marginal charge is set lower than the variable cost by the benefit from receiving induced by the marginal increase in total demand. Also the fixed charge must be set lower than the fixed cost because of the externality effects. These results are, of course, derived from considering the demand and tariff structures in equilibrium.

In the numerical example, we have shown the case where a competition policy is not necessarily superior to regulation.

For further extension, a more general nonlinear cost structure should be introduced because increasing returns to scale are essential to the telecommunications industry. Competing suppliers will bring about more interesting results. Finally, the analysis of another pricing rule such as the Ramsey pricing might be more suggestive.

REFERENCES

Artle, R. and C. Averous, The Telephone System as a Public Good: Static and Dynamic Aspects, The Bell Journal of Economics and Management Science, Vol. 6, No. 2, Autumn 1975, pp. 89-100.

Feldstein, M.S., Equity and Efficiency in Public Sector Pricing: The Optimal Two-Part Tariff, The Quarterly Journal of Economics, Vol. LXXXVI, No. 2, May 1972, pp. 175-187.

Hazlewood, A., Optimum Pricing as Applied to Telephone Service, The Review of Economic Studies, Vol. XVIII, 1950-51, pp. 67-78.

Kohno, H., Advanced Information-Oriented Society and Regional Development, Expressways and Automobiles, Vol. 28, No. 1, January 1985, pp. 8-15 (in Japanese).

Littlechild, S.C., Common Costs, Fixed Charges, Clubs and Games, The Review of Economic Studies, Vol. XLII(1), No. 129, January 1975, pp. 117-124.

Littlechild, S.C., Two-Part Tariffs and Consumption Externalities, The Bell Journal of Economics, Vol. 6, No. 2, Autumn 1975, pp. 661-670.

Littlechild, S.C., Peak-Load Pricing of Telephone Calls, The Bell Journal of Economics and Management Science, Vol. 1, No. 2, Autumn 1970, pp. 191-210.

Mitomo, H., Optimal Pricing of Telecommunications in the Presence of Externalities, The 23rd Annual Domestic Meeting of the Japan Section of the Regional Science Association, October 1986, (in Japanese).

Mitomo, H., A Managerial-Economic Analysis of Communications Markets, Expressways and Automobiles, Vol. 28, No. 5, May 1985, pp. 23-33, (in Japanese).

Ng, Y. and M. Weisser, Optimal Pricing with a Budget Constraint - The Case of the Two-Part Tariff, The Review of Economic Studies, Vol. XLI(3), No. 127, pp. 337-345.

Oren, S.S. and S.A. Smith, Critical Mass and Tariff Structure in Electronic Communications Markets, The Bell Journal of Economics, Vol. 12, No.2, Autumn 1981, pp. 467-487.

Rohlfs, J., A Theory of Interdependent Demand for a Communications Service, The Bell Journal of Economics and Management Science, Vol. 5, No. 1, Spring 1974, pp. 16-37.

Squire, L., Some Aspects of Optimal Pricing for Telecommunications, The Bell Journal of Economics and Management Science, Vol. 4, No. 2, Autumn 1973, pp. 515-525.

EVALUATION OF TELECOMMUNICATION SYSTEMS WITH MULTIPLE CRITERIA DECISION ANALYSIS: A GAME THEORETIC APPROACH

Fumiko Seo and Masatoshi Sakawa

1. INTRODUCTION

In this contribution, we present a method based on multiple criteria decision analysis for evaluating the formation of a new integrated telecommunications system. Our method is a game theoretic approach based on fuzzy multiattribute utility analysis. Game theory, which has been developed for multiple agents decision making, is used to evaluate the efficiency of forming an integrated information network. First, the construction of alternative integrated systems for existing individual communication networks is evaluated from the point of view of utility exchanges, and here fuzzy multiattribute utility analysis is applied. For considering a diversity in the evaluation due to multiperson decision making, a fuzzy preference relation is introduced into the process in order to assess the multiattribute utility function (MUF). This device is used for numerically assessing agreement levels in constructing MUFs. The fuzzy MUF (FMUF) is assessed for each service of the telecommunications systems. Second, the characteristic function of an n-person cooperative game is assessed in terms of an incremental value of FMUF. The payoff value based on the incremental value of FMUF is calculated for each service treated as a player who will participate in an integrated network to be regarded as a coalition. Alternative concepts of the nucleolus are used as the solution concepts of a game. Third, we will provide a device to measure these alternative solutions in comparable terms. On the one hand, it is known that the nucleolus as a solution concept can be generated by repeatedly solving mathematical programming problems. On the other hand, it is asserted that, based on the sensitivity theorem, the dual optimal solutions generated from mathematical programming can be interpreted as the opportunity costs or the shadow prices for systems evaluation, and thus be used as the basic evaluation factor of multiple criteria decision problems. We will use the dual optimal solutions generated from mathematical programming to evaluate numerical results of alternative nucleolus concepts in comparable terms. After this process, the judgemental phase of multiple criteria decision making is introduced as the final step of the assessment. Numerical examples for some steps are also presented.

2. MULTIATTRIBUTE UTILITY ANALYSIS WITH A FUZZY PREFERENCE RELATION

2.1 Formulation of integrated service networks

Modern telecommunications systems are formed as a digital network based on recent progress in electronics such as the Very Large Scale Integrated Circuit

(VLSI), digital switching systems, and optical communications systems. Formation of the digital network opens a way to consolidate existing individual networks such as telephone, facsimile, telex, data and video communications, and computer systems into an integrated information network. Thus, the integrated service network (ISN), such as the Integrated Service Digital Network (ISDN), has multiple functions, which were previously operated in an individual network for each service. New construction of ISN is performed by converting existing transmission lines and equipment into a new digital network. This conversion can be assessed as a utility exchange from a multiobjective point of view. The change of utility levels due to the new construction of ISN can be assessed in terms of alteration in the degrees of performance by the existing networks., which can be evaluated on multiple attributes for each service. Fuzzy multiattribute utility analysis can then be applied for the evaluation of the alteration in the information systems.

Multiattribute utility analysis (Keeney and Raiffa 1976) for each communication service has four steps: (i) selection of attributes $(X_1,\dots,X_m)$ with their numerical ranges from the worst to the best, (ii) evaluation of the single attribute utility function (UNIF) $u_i(x_i)$, $i=1,\dots,m$, (iii) assessment of the scaling constant k_i for UNIF, and (iv) derivation of the multiattribute utility function (MUF). In the following subsections, we will briefly discuss (i) and (iii) where fuzzification devices are introduced for treating collective choice problems in terms of the cognitive ambiguity.

2.2 Selection of attributes for ISN

Let A be a set of existing networks of individual services and B be a set of newly constructed systems of ISN. Let x_{pq} be the traffic intensity in transmission lines that are used by $q \in B$ converted from $p \in A$ and y_q be the traffic in newly constructed transmission lines that are used by $q \in B$, where p and q denote services such as telephone, data, video, and facsimile communications. The traffic is the number of calls multiplied by the average hold-on time per hour. Denote a new network of ISN constructed in any level of an integration to be S, and call it a coalition. Let $x_S \triangleq (x_{pq})$, where $p \in S \cap A$, $q \in S \cap B$, and $y_S \triangleq (y_q)$, where $q \in S \cap B$. A utility function of a coalition S due to the new formation of ISN is represented as $u_S(x_S, y_S)$, and a utility function for an existing service p is $u_p(x_{pq})$. These utility functions are evaluated in terms of MUF. The incremental value of utility for a coalition S is defined as

$$\Delta u_S = u_S(x_S, y_S) - \sum_{p \in S} \omega_p u_p(x_{pq}),$$

where ω_p is a weight for a normalisation,

$$\sum_{p \in S} \omega_p = 1, \omega_p > 0.$$

This incremental value Δu_S is used as the coalition value in a game.

The main attributes to be considered in MUF for a new construction of ISN are the costs for developers, the traffic potential as a measure of user's benefit, and the impacts on the regional economy.

The individual cost $C_p(x_{pq})$ and the coalition cost

$$C_S(x_S, y_S) \triangleq \sum_{p \in S} C_p(x_{pq}) + \sum_{q \in S} C_q(y_q)$$

are now considered from the point of view of developers (suppliers), which include new construction costs and OMR costs and are measured in long terms as well as short terms.

The user's benefits are assessed in terms of the traffic potential $\Pi_p(x_{pq})$ and $\Pi_S(x_S, y_S)$ by redefining the gravity concept (Isard 1960) as:

$$\Pi_p(x_{pq}) \triangleq G \frac{n_p n_q}{d_{pq}(x_{pq})}, \tag{2.1}$$

$$\Pi_q(y_q) \triangleq G' \frac{n_q}{d_{0q}(y_q)}, \tag{2.2}$$

$$\Pi_S(x_S, y_S) \triangleq \sum_{p \in S} \Pi_p(x_{pq}) + \sum_{q \in S} \Pi_q(y_q), \tag{2.3}$$

where n_p and n_q are numbers of subscribers for services p and q, $p \in A$, $q \in B$, respectively; $d_{pq}(x_{pq})$ is the psychological 'distance' (resistance) of the user to the conversion of an existing service p into a new service q, in which a propagation ('demonstration') effect is taken into account and thus

$$\frac{\partial d_{pq}}{\partial x_{pq}} < 0, \text{ and } \frac{\partial d_{0q}}{\partial y_q} < 0 .$$

Let

$$\log \frac{T_{pq}}{E_{pq}} = a - b \log d_{pq}(x_{pq}) \tag{2.4}$$

where T_{pq} is the actual traffic (erlangs, erl.) in $q \in B$ converted from $p \in A$, and E_{pq} is the predicted traffic. Then,

$$\frac{T_{pq}}{E_{pq}} = \frac{c}{d^b_{pq}} \tag{2.5}$$

where $c \triangleq$ antilogue a. Putting as

$$E_{pq} \triangleq k_p \frac{n_p n_q}{n} \tag{2.6}$$

derives

$$T_{pq} = \frac{ck_p}{n} \frac{n_p n_q}{d^b_{pq}} = G \frac{n_p n_q}{d^b_{pq}} \tag{2.7}$$

where n is the number of users for the existing networks and k_p is the calling rate (the traffic per subscriber) in a service p. By putting b = 1 in (2.7), one may derive the traffic potential Π_p in (2.1). Putting $p \triangleq 0$ in (2.4)-(2.6) leads to the traffic potential Π_q in (2.2) with a parameter G'.

The impact on regional economy $R_p(x_{pq})$ and $R_S(x_S, y_S)$ can be assessed on a subjective scale ranging from 0 to 10 as a composite attribute.

Then the MUF for the existing service p, $p \in A$, to be converted into q, $q \in B$, is represented as $u_p(x_{pq}) = u_p(C_p(x_{pq}), \Pi_p(x_{pq}), R_p(x_{pq}))$, and the MUF for a coalition S is represented as $u_S(x_S, y_S) = u_S(C_S(x_S, y_S), \Pi_S(x_S, y_S), R_S(x_S, y_S))$. These functions can be the nested MUFs. For each attribute, a single attribute utility function (UNIF) is evaluated with the standard procedure. We will provide a method to treat the MUF as the FMUF with some fuzzification devices. In the next section, attributes are denoted by X_i, X_j, $i,j = 1,...,m$, $i \neq j$, for convenience.

2.3 Construction of FMUF

Fuzzy multiattribute utility function (FMUF) can be constructed on fuzzy set theory developed by Zadeh (1965). Although the multiattribute utility function (MUF) is constructed as if a single decision maker has assessed it, the authors intend to introduce collective choice into the evaluation process of MUF. Although the collective choice problem with fuzzy preference relations has been discussed by Blin (1974) and Blin and Whinston (1974), based on Zadeh (1971), they do not regard the construction of the utility function. In our device, fuzzification for MUF is performed twofold: before and after the value tradeoff experiments among attributes. First, before the experiments, attributes X_i, $i = 1, ...,m$, are compared with each other and a fuzzy preference ordering among the attributes is found. With a defuzzification device, a nonfuzzy collective preference ordering is derived. Then a numerical ordering of the scaling constants k_i is determined corresponding to the nonfuzzy preference ordering among X_i. The relative values

k_i/k_r, $i \neq r$, of the scaling constants are found with the value tradeoff experiments based on the preference ordering of the attributes. Second, after the value tradeoff experiments, a numerical value of the fuzzy scaling constant $\tilde{k}_r$ for UNIF $u_r(x_r)$ of the most preferable attribute X_r is assessed as a fuzzy number. Then all values of the fuzzy scaling constants $\tilde{k}_i$, $i = 1, \ldots, m$, can be numerically determined. Finally for the representation check, fuzzy comparisons among fuzzy numbers are also performed.

In the first step of the fuzzification, the fuzzy preference ordering is defined with the membership function $\mu_R(X_i, X_j)$ for all $X_i \in X_i$ and $X_j \in X_j$, where X_i and X_j are fuzzy sets. The membership function $\mu_R(X_i, X_j)$ associates with each pair $(X_i, X_j) \in X_i \times X_j$ its 'grade of membership' μ_R, where R is a fuzzy binary relation $(>, \sim)$ for preference defined on an ordered pair of attributes. The numerical values of $\mu_R(X_i, X_j)$ that takes a range of the interval [0, 1] represents a strength of the preference relation R between X_i and X_j.

Definition 1 (Fuzzy Weak Ordering): Fuzzy weak ordering is defined with connectivity and transitivity as follows.

1. Connectivity:

$$X_i \neq X_j \Rightarrow \mu_R(X_i, X_j) > 0 \text{ or } \mu_R(x_j, X_i) > 0 . \tag{2.8}$$

2. Transitivity:

$$\mu_R(X_i, X_k) \geq \bigvee_{xj} \mu_R (X_i, X_j) \wedge \mu_R (X_i, X_k) \tag{2.9}$$

where where $\mu_R \vee \mu'_R$ denotes max (μ_R, μ'_R) and $\mu_R \wedge \mu'_R$ denotes min (μ_R, μ'_R).

A hierarchical structure of the fuzzy preference ordering can be considered in resolution of the fuzzy binary relation R into a union of several nonfuzzy sets. For a number α in [0, 1], an α-level set R_α of a fuzzy relation R is defined by

$$R_\alpha = \{(X_i, X_j) \mid \mu_R (X_i, X_j) \geq \alpha\} . \tag{2.10}$$

The R_α is a nonfuzzy set of $X_i \times X_j$ and those sets form a nested sequence of nonfuzzy relations with

$$\alpha_i \geq \alpha_j \Rightarrow R_{\alpha_i} \subset R_{\alpha_j} .$$

The α is used for representing an agreement level of collective choice.

According to Zadeh's proposition (1971), any fuzzy relation R defined on $X \in (\tilde{X}_1 \times \ldots \times \tilde{X}_m)$ admits the resolution

$$R = \sum_{\alpha} \alpha R_{\alpha}, 0 < \alpha \leq 1 \tag{2.11}$$

where $\sum_{\alpha}$ stands for the union $\cup_{\alpha}$ and αR_{α} denotes a nonfuzzy set defined by

$$\mu_{\alpha R_{\alpha}}(X_i, X_j) \triangleq \alpha \mu_{R_{\alpha}}(X_i, X_j), \tag{2.12}$$

or equivalently,

$$\mu_{\alpha R_{\alpha}}(X_i, X_j) = \begin{cases} \alpha, \text{for } (X_i, X_j) \in R_{\alpha} \\ 0, \text{otherwise,} \end{cases} \tag{2.13}$$

For the resolution of a fuzzy preference relation R into the nonfuzzy subsets as the α-level set R_{α}, the relation matrix whose elements are composed of U_k are constructed. The class C_i of the nonfuzzy weak-ordered set if defined corresponding to the α-level decomposition (2.10), which includes a set of all preference ordering compatible with new elements appeared in the R_{α_i}. Taking the intersection, we can obtain the weak-ordered nonfuzzy relation in an indicated level, which can be used as the indicator of an agreement level of the preference order constructed in the collective choice (see Appendix for an example of a fuzzification process).

In the second step of fuzzification, the fuzzy multiattribute utility function (FMUF) is assessed. The numerical values of the scaling constants k_i, $i = 1,..., m$, whose numerical ordering has already been determined corresponding to the nonfuzzy preference ordering for the attributes X_i, $i = 1, ..., m$, are assessed as the fuzzy number.

After the value tradeoff experiment that determines the relative values of the scaling constants, the FMUF can be derived with fuzzy scaling constants $\tilde{k}_i$, $i = 1, ..., m$, which are treated as fuzzy numbers such as the L-R type (Dubois and Prade 1978, 1980). An L-R-type fuzzy number n is represented in the following form

$$\tilde{n} \triangleq (\bar{n}, \alpha, \beta), \tag{2.14}$$

where $\bar{n}$ is a 'mean' value, and α and β show left and right side dispersion. A membership function of the fuzzy number $\tilde{n}$ is

$$\mu_{\tilde{n}} = \begin{cases} L((\bar{n} - z)/\alpha), & z \leq \bar{n}, \alpha > 0 \\ R((z - \bar{n})/\beta), & \bar{n} \leq z, \beta > 0 \end{cases} \tag{2.15}$$

where $L(0) = R(0) = 1$. We can assess the value of n, α and β from a distribution pattern of diversification in assessing the scale constants k_r for the most preferable attribute X_r and of the corresponding utility value u_r. With these fuzzy numbers $\tilde{k}_r$ and $\tilde{u}_r$, all fuzzy scaling constants $\tilde{k}_i$, $i = 1,\ldots, m$, $i \neq r$, can be obtained from $\tilde{k}_i = \tilde{k}_r\tilde{u}(x_r)$ by the definition of MUF.

The fuzzification of the scaling constants will have some effects on choosing the representation forms (multiplicative or additive) of the MUF. For this reason, the following representation check should be performed.

$$\begin{aligned} &\text{a) If } \sum_{i=1}^{m} \tilde{k}_i > 1, \text{ then } -1 < K < 0 \text{ (multiplicative form).} \\ &\text{b) If } \sum_{i=1}^{m} \tilde{k}_i < 1, \text{ then } K > 0 \text{ (multiplicative form).} \\ &\text{c) If } \sum_{i=1}^{m} \tilde{k}_i = 1, \text{ then } k = 0 \text{ (additive form).} \end{aligned} \tag{2.16}$$

Because the scaling constant $\tilde{k}_i$, $i = 1, \ldots, m$, is a fuzzy number, the assertion (> and <) for that is still fuzzy. Thus it should be asked whether the assertion

"$\sum_{i=1}^{m} \tilde{k}_i$

is greater (or smaller) than 1" is true. The separation theorem for two fuzzy sets can be applied to the comparison of the fuzzy numbers,

$$\sum_{i}^{m} \tilde{k}_i \text{ and } \tilde{1} = (\bar{1}, 0, 0).$$

The separation theorem asserts that when M is the maximal grade of the intersection of two bounded convex fuzzy sets, the degree of separation D of those sets is obtained by $D = 1-M$. To give an answer to the above question, we choose a threshold level β, $1 > \beta > 0$. If $M > \beta$, then it can be asserted that

$$\sum_{i=1}^{m} \tilde{k}_i = \tilde{1}$$

in the level β. K in (2.16) is a nonzero solution to

$$1 + K = \prod_{i=1}^{m} (1 + K\tilde{k}_i). \tag{2.17}$$

It has been proven that the K-value can be determined uniquely in any high-order equation (2.17) (Keeney and Raiffa 1976).

The u_i-value as UNIF can also be assessed in terms of the fuzzy number as a result of collective choice. In the result, the FMUF can be derived as a fuzzy number of in a sophisticated form:

additive

$$\tilde{U}(x_1, \ldots, x_m) = \sum_{i=1}^{m} (\tilde{k}_i \tilde{u}_i(x_i)), \tag{2.18}$$

or multiplicative

$$1 + K\tilde{U}(x_1, \ldots, x_m) = \sum_{i=1}^{m} (K\tilde{k}_i \tilde{u}_i(x_i) + 1). \tag{2.19}$$

The FMUF can be used for u_p and u_S in the preceding section.

3. NUCLEOLUS OF AN N-PERSON COOPERATIVE GAME IN THE CHARACTERISTIC FUNCTION FORM

The FMUF is evaluated for each service p of a telecommunication system, which is included in an integration of existing individual networks into a new information system. The integration is treated as a formation of a coalition by players in terms of an n-person cooperative game. The characteristic function v(S) for a coalition S is defined on an incremental value of utility as follows:

$$v(S) = u_S(x_S, y_S) - \sum_{p \in S \cap A} \omega_p u_{(p)}(x_{pq}) \tag{3.1}$$

The u_S and $u_{(p)}$ can take the mean values of the assessed FMUFs for a coalition S and a player (service) p, respectively, and then can be treated as the nonfuzzy numbers for simplicity in numerical operations hereafter. These utility assessments can be presented along with the evaluation of the agreement levels in the collective choice. ω_p is a weight for a player p in a coalition S, and $\omega_p > 0$,

$$\sum_{p \in S \cap A} \omega_p = 1.$$

The ω_p is a preassigned value of reflecting a policy of the decision maker (DM) in constructing an integrated information system (coalition) S, $S \subseteq N$, where $N \triangleq \{1, ..., n\}$ denotes the set of all players, and represents a particular consideration on services to be promoted in the integrated system. The coalition value v(S) indicates a social surplus of utility due to the formation of the coalition (integration) S.

Now the decision maker (DM) intends to conduct the development of a new ISN in various forms so as to 'maximise' the social surplus of the coalition S to be reallocated to each player. Define a payoff vector as $z \triangleq (z_1, ..., z_n)$, whose elements are incremental values of utility for a player (service) p, p = 1, ..., n, due to the construction of an ISN system. In terms of an n-player cooperative game in the characteristic function form, the excess of the value of a game for a coalition S over the total payoff is defined as

$$e(S, z) \triangleq v(S) - z(S), \quad S \subset N, \tag{3.2}$$

where $v(\Phi) = 0$. N is a set of n players in a new ISN system, and

$$z(S) \triangleq \sum_{p \in S} z_p.$$

The excess is regarded as a measure of dissatisfaction of a coalition S at the payoff z. The core is defined as a set of all payoff vectors that cannot be improved by any coalition, and is shown by

$$e(S, z) \leq 0 \text{ (coalitional rationality)} \tag{3.3}$$

along with $z(N) - v(N) = 0$, where

$$z(N) \triangleq \sum_{p \in N} z_p$$

The existence and uniqueness of the core are not necessarily assured in all cases. Thus, by relaxing the definition of the core (3.3), the concept that defines the quasi-core is introduced (Shapely and Shubik 1966, Schmeidler 1969, Maschler, Peleg and Shapley 1979).

Define the (strong) ε-core as a quasi-core concept relaxed with a parameter ε as

$$e(S, z) \triangleq v(S) - z(S) < \varepsilon, \text{ for all } S \neq \phi, N, \tag{3.4}$$

along with $v(N) = z(N)$. It means that the payoff vector cannot be improved by any coalition S, when a tax transfer or a subsidy of ε is imposed on the payoff z(S). Based on this concept, the smallest ε-core that maximises the excess is constructed, which is defined as

$$\varepsilon_o(z) = \min_{z \in \chi} \max_{S \neq \phi, N} e(S, z) \tag{3.5}$$

where χ is a set of preimputation that satisfies the collective rationality, $z(N) = v(N)$. $\varepsilon_o(z)$ shows the payoff vector that minimises the maximum dissatisfaction of the coalition S, and is called the least core, which provides the nucleolus (z) of the game $\Gamma(N, v)$ via a lexicographic ordering of the excess. The lexicographic ordering is defined as follows. Let $\theta(z) \triangleq (\theta_1(z), \theta_2(z), ..., \theta_{2^n}(z))$ be the 2^n-vector whose elements are the number $\theta_k \triangleq e(S_k, z)$, $k = 1, ..., 2^n$, on $S \subset N$, arranged in a nonincreasing order. The lexicographic order is given by the relation $\theta(z) \leq_L \theta(y)$, which holds when $\theta_i(z) = \theta_i(y)$ for all $i < j$ and $\theta_j(z) < \theta_j(y)$. It means that if there exists equality between the maximal values of the excess $\theta_i(z)$ and $\theta_i(y)$, $i = 1,2, ...,$ that are arranged in a nonincreasing order, then the next greatest values of the excess, $\theta_j(z)$ and $\theta_j(y)$, are compared with each other, and so on. The comparison continues sequentially until the inequality is found. Then, the nucleolus of a game is defined as the set of payoff vectors such that

$$\mathcal{N}(z) \triangleq (z \in \chi \mid \theta(z) <_L \theta(y) \text{ for all } y \in \chi). \tag{3.6}$$

Naturally, the payoff vector z is more acceptable than y. In other words, the nucleolus is defined as the payoff vector that minimises the maximum excess.

The nucleolus as the solution concept for the quasi-core is obtained by solving at most n-1 linear programming problems (Kopelowitz 1967, Littlechild 1974, Owen 1974). Redefine the concept of ε-core (3.4) augmented with a parameter μ as

$$e_\mu(S, z) \triangleq v(S) - z(S) < \mu\varepsilon, \tag{3.7}$$

along with $v(N) = z(N)$. The nucleolus $\mathcal{N}(\mu)$ defined on the augmented ε-core is obtained as a solution by repetitively running a linear programme. Consider an 0-normalisation that is defined with $v(\{p\}) = 0$ for all $p \in N$. The augmented nucleolus $\mathcal{N}(\mu)$ is obtained by solving the following linear programme, and the $\varepsilon_o(z)$-value (3.5) is found.

(P)

Minimise ε
z_p, ε
subject to

$z_p \geq 0$ for all $p \in N$

$v(S) - (z(S) + \mu\varepsilon) \leq 0$ for all $S \subset N$

$$v(N) - z(N) = 0 \tag{3.8}$$

The interpretation of the primal problem (3.8) with the augmenting parameter μ is clear. When $\mu = 1$, the solution of (P) provides the nucleolus. When $\mu = s$, the weak nucleolus is obtained, where s denotes the number of players in S (Shapley and Shubik 1966). When $\mu = v(S)$, the proportional nucleolus is obtained (Young, Okada and Hashimoto 1982). Sakawa et al. (1983) proposed the concession nucleolus when

$$\mu = \sum_{p \Phi S} \Phi_p,$$

is the Shapley value. The Shapley value is defined as

$$\Phi_p(v) \triangleq \sum_{\substack{S \subseteq N \\ S \ni p}} \frac{(s-1)!(n-s)!}{n!} [v(S)-v(S-\{p\})] \tag{3.9}$$

The second term of the Shapley value represents the marginal amount of contribution of a player p to the value of coalition S. The first term represents a total of the relative frequency for a player p to appear in every coalition S. Thus

$$\sum_{p \in S} \Phi_p$$

shows the total marginal contributions by each player to every coalition S weighted by the relative frequencies of appearance of each player. The concept of the concession nucleolus defined in terms of (3.7) shows that the excess or the dissatisfaction of a coalition S should be divided by the sum of marginal contributions of each player in the coalition S. In this concept, some kind of externality or 'opportunity cost' for participation of each player p is taken into account for every coalition S. Alternatively, when $\mu = v(N) - v(N - S)$, the contribution nucleolus, as we will call it here, is found for a coalition S. These concepts enlarge the quasi-core concept in alternative ways.

4.COMPARATIVE EVALUATION OF ALTERNATIVE NUCLEOLI

Alternative solutions $z^\dagger \triangleq (z_1^\dagger, \ldots, z_n^\dagger)$ of the augmented nucleolus provide alternative payoff values for each player (service). These solutions depend on alternative criteria and thus are not unique for the final selection. The obtained utility value for a player p in an ISN system is shown as

$$w_p^\dagger = u_{(p)} + z_p^\dagger = \begin{cases} u_{(p)} + z_p^\dagger & p \in N, p \in A \\ z_p^\dagger & p \in N, p \in B \end{cases} \tag{4.1}$$

where

$$w_p, \sum_{p \in N} w_p = \hat{u}_N,$$

represents an allocation of total utility generated from the construction of ISN to each player (service) p.

For choosing the preferred solution z^* from among alternative solutions $z_i^\dagger$ we examine the dual optimal solutions of y_S and y_N that are generated from alternative programming formulations for the augmented nucleoli.

The interpretation of the dual variables can be made clear by forming the Lagrangian function of the primal problem (3.8):

$$L \triangleq \varepsilon + \sum_{S \subset N} y_S (v(S) - (z(S) + \mu\varepsilon)) + y_N (v(N) - z(N)). \quad (4.2)$$

Then, according to the sensitivity theorem. considering that ε, z_p, y_S, and y_N are all functions of v(S) and v(N), from the Kuhn-Tucker conditions, we can derive

$$\frac{\partial \varepsilon}{\partial v(S)} = y_S \quad \text{for} \quad y_S > 0, \; S \subset N, \quad (4.3)$$

$$\frac{\partial \varepsilon}{\partial v(N)} = y_N \quad (4.4)$$

as the optimalising conditions. It is known, from the first order optimality conditions, that

$$\sum_{\substack{S \subset N \\ S \ni p}} y_S = y_N \text{ and } \sum_{S \subset N} y_S \mu = 1.$$

The dual variable y_S represents a tradeoff between the 'tax' transfer ε and the coalition value v(S) for every coalition. This property also holds for the grand coalition N. In other words, the evaluation prices y_S, $S \subset N$, for each coalition, and y_N are imputed inversely corresponding to the marginal changes of the coalition values v(S) and v(N) in terms of a marginal increment of the "tax" transfer ε. It means that y_S and y_N indicate marginal evaluations of the coalition values in terms of the 'tax' transfer ε. Larger values of y_S and y_N show relative inefficiency of v(S) and v(N), because a smaller value of the maximum ε is more desirable in this case. Thus y_S and y_N indicate the opportunity costs of the coalition values measured commonly in terms of the 'tax' transfer ε. These values y_S and y_N can be used inversely as the measure of satisfaction with (or efficiency of) the coalition (integration) S and N. The augmenting parameter μ denotes a discount factor that indicates a deviation from the balanced game. When $\mu = 1$, the nucleolus implies that the game is balanced. Table 1 represents a summary of these results.

5. EXAMPLE

Consider an ISN system which is composed of conversions from existing services for telephone, facsimile, data and video communications and telex networks. Suppose that the utility assessment u_P and u_S in terms of the mean values of FMUF has already been performed with the agreement levels. The assessed u-values are shown in Table 2. Then, by solving the linear program (3.8) at most n-1 times, the payoff values are obtained and shown with the obtained u-values in Table 3. It is known that this game has a core. The dual solutions that are derived as the simplex multiplier are shown in Table 4. It is known that the nucleolus is the most preferable and the weak nucleolus is second preferable, and so on, in the order shown in Table 4 However, some additional considerations for final selection can be introduced discretionally and judgementally of these numerical results from the mediator's point of view.

6. CONCLUDING REMARKS

As applications of new telecommunication systems in Japan, we may mention the construction of integrated communication networks for new urban areas (such as the Tokyo Bay Coastal Area Network), the Future Information City Plan (TUKUBANET, and the Mitaka-Musashino Model). Alternative programmes for construction of these networks can be considered in relation to alternative regional development policies. For these alternative programmes, assessment should be undertaken not only from an economic point of view, but also from a multiobjective point of view. In addition, an evaluation should be made of how the benefit for each communication service in an existing individual network can be raised due to the transition to a new ISN. This is a multiple actor decision problem. The game theory that embodies FMUF in the characteristic function will be able to provide an assessment to meet these requests. As a further methodological development along these lines, a fuzzy game can be introduced for consistently extending the fuzzy evaluation with FMUF, although some computational complexity may make the application of the method rather cumbersome. Computer assistance can facilitate the work for this assessment in the various steps. Based on alternative policy aims for developing new information systems, alternative construction programmes can be assessed comparably for each service and the most preferable programmes can be selected.

ACKNOWLEDGEMENT

This research is supported by the grant from the Kajima Foundation and the Japan Ministry of Education, Science and Culture.

REFERENCES

Blin, J.M., Fuzzy Relations in Group Decision Theory, Journal of Cybernetics, Vol. 4, No. 2, 1974, pp. 17-22.

Blin, J.M. and A.B. Whinston, Fuzzy Sets and Social Choice, Journal of Cybernetics, Vol. 3, No. 4, 1974, pp. 28-36.

Dubois, D. and H. Prade, Operations on Fuzzy Numbers, International Journal of Systems Sciences, Vol. 9, No. 6, 1978, pp. 613-626.

Dubois, D. and H. Prade, Systems of Linear Fuzzy Constraints, Fuzzy Sets and Systems, Vol. 3, 1980, pp. 37-48.

Isard, W., Methods of Regional Analysis: An Introduction to Regional Science, The MIT Press, Cambridge, 1960.

Keeney, R.L. and H. Raiffa, Decisions with Multiple Objectives, Preferences and Value Tradeoffs, Wiley, New York, 1976.

Kopelowitz, A., Computation of the Kernels of Simple Games and the Nucleolus of N-Person Games, R.M. 31, Department of Mathematics, Hebrew University, Jerusalem, 1967.

Littlechild, S.C., A Simple Expression for the Nucleolus in a Special Case, International Journal of Game Theory, Vol. 3, No. 1, 1974, pp. 21-29.

Maschler, M., B. Peleg and L.S. Shapley, Geometric Properties of the Kernel, Nucleolus, and Related Solution Concepts, Mathematics of Operations Research, Vol. 4, No. 4, 1979, pp. 303-338.

Owen, G., A Note on the Nucleolus, International Journal of Game Theory, Vol. 3, No. 2, 1974, pp. 101-103.

Sakawa, M., K. Tada and I. Nishizaki, A New Solution Concept in a Cooperation N-Person Game and Its Applications, Journal of Electronics and Communication Society, J.66-A(12), 1983, (in Japanese).

Schmeidler, D., The Nucleolus of a Characteristic Function Game, SIAM Journal of Applied Mathematics, 17(6), 1969, pp. 1163-1170.

Seo, F. and M. Sakawa, Fuzzy Multiattribute Utility Analysis for Collective Choice, IEEE Transactions on Systems, Man, and Cybernetics, Vol. SMC-15, No.1, 1985, pp. 45-53.

Shapley, L.S. and M. Shubik, Quasi-Cores in a Monetary Economy with Nonconvex Preferences, Econometrica, Vol. 34, No. 4, 1966, pp. 805-827.

Young, H.P., N. Okada and T. Hashimoto, Cost Allocation in Water Resources Development, Water Resources Research, Vol. 18, No. 3, 1982, pp. 463-475.

Zadeh, L.A., Fuzzy Sets, Information and Control, Vol. 8, 1965, pp. 338-353.

Zadeh, L.A., Similarity Relations and Fuzzy Orderings, Information Sciences, Vol. 3, 1971, pp. 177-200.

TABLE 1
Evaluation for nucleolus

cases	y_S for $v(S)$	y_N for $v(N)$	equilibrium conditions
nucleolus	$\frac{\partial \varepsilon}{\partial v(S)} = y_S$ $y_S > 0$	$\frac{\partial \varepsilon}{\partial v(N)} = y_N$	$-\sum_{\substack{S \subset N \\ S \ni p}} y_S = y_N$ $\sum_{S \subset N} y_S = 1, \quad y_S > 0$
augmented nucleolus	$\frac{\partial \varepsilon}{\partial v(S)} = y_S$ $y_S > 0$	$\frac{\partial \varepsilon}{\partial v(N)} = y_N$	$-\sum_{\substack{S \subset N \\ S \ni p}} y_S = y_N$ $\sum_{S \subset N} y_S \mu = 1, \quad y_S > 0$
disruption nucleolus	$\frac{\partial r}{\partial v(S)} = (1+r) y_S$ $y_S > 0$	$\frac{\partial r}{\partial v(N)} = y_N$	$-(1+r) \sum_{\substack{S \subset N \\ S \ni p}} y_S = y_N$ $-\sum_{S \subset N} y_S (v(S) - x(S)) = 1,$ $y_S > 0$

Note: $\mu = 1$: nucleolus. $\mu = s$: weak nucleolus $\mu = v(S)$: proportional nucleolus.

$\mu = \sum_{p \in S} \Phi_p$: concession nucleolus.

$\mu = v(N) - v(N - S)$: contribution nucleolus.

TABLE 2
Values of the characteristic function

$$v(S) \,\Delta\, 100\Big(u_S(x_S, y_S) - \sum_{p \in S \cap A} \omega_p u_{\{p\}}(x_{pq})\Big) \quad S \subset N$$

$$N \,\Delta\, (1, 2, 3, 4, 5)$$

$v(\{1\}) = 0,$	$u_{\{1\}} = 0.45$	(p = 1: Telephone)
$v(\{2\}) = 0,$	$u_{\{2\}} = 0.35$	(p = 2: Facsimile)
$v(\{3\}) = 0,$	$u_{\{3\}} = 0.40$	(p = 3: Data, communication)
$v(\{4\}) = 0,$	$u_{\{4\}} = 0.25$	(p = 4: Video, communication)
$v(\{5\}) = 0,$	$u_{\{5\}} = 0.30$	(p = 5: Telex)

v(1, 2) = 46 - 38 = 8;	$\omega_1 = 0.3$, $\omega_2 = 0.7$
v(1, 3) = 53 - 42 = 11;	$\omega_1 = 0.3$, $\omega_3 = 0.7$
v(1, 4) = 48 - 31 = 17;	$\omega_1 = 0.3$, $\omega_4 = 0.7$
v(1, 5) = 45 - 35 = 10;	$\omega_1 = 0.3$, $\omega_5 = 0.7$
v(2, 3) = 49 - 38 = 11;	$\omega_2 = 0.4$, $\omega_3 = 0.6$
v(2, 4) = 44 - 29 = 15;	$\omega_2 = 0.4$. $\omega_4 = 0.6$
v(2, 5) = 43 - 33 = 10;	$\omega_2 = 0.6$, $\omega_5 = 0.4$
v(3, 4) = 53 - 31 = 22;	$\omega_3 = 0.4$, $\omega_4 = 0.6$
v(3, 5) = 50 - 36 = 14;	$\omega_3 = 0.6$, $\omega_5 = 0.4$
v(4, 5) = 45 - 27 = 18;	$\omega_4 = 0.6$, $\omega_5 = 0.4$
v(1, 2, 3) = 58 - 39 = 19;	$\omega_1 = 0.2$, $\omega_2 = 0.4$, $\omega_3 = 0.4$
v(1, 2, 4) = 57 - 33 = 24;	$\omega_1 = 0.2$, $\omega_2 = 0.4$, $\omega_4 = 0.4$
v(1, 2, 5) = 55 - 37 = 18;	$\omega_1 = 0.3$, $\omega_2 = 0.4$, $\omega_5 = 0.3$
v(1, 3, 4) = 64 - 35 = 29;	$\omega_1 = 0.2$, $\omega_3 = 0.4$, $\omega_4 = 0.4$
v(1, 3, 5) = 58 - 37 = 21;	$\omega_1 = 0.2$, $\omega_3 = 0.4$, $\omega_5 = 0.4$
v(1, 4, 5) = 59 - 31 = 28;	$\omega_1 = 0.2$, $\omega_4 = 0.4$, $\omega_5 = 0.4$
v(2, 3, 4) = 63 - 34 = 29;	$\omega_2 = 0.3$, $\omega_3 = 0.4$, $\omega_4 = 0.3$
v(2, 3, 5) = 58 - 36 = 22;	$\omega_2 = 0.3$, $\omega_3 = 0.4$, $\omega_5 = 0.3$
v(2, 4, 5) = 56 - 30 = 26;	$\omega_2 = 0.3$, $\omega_4 = 0.4$, $\omega_5 = 0.3$
v(3, 4, 5) = 62 - 32 = 30;	$\omega_3 = 0.4$, $\omega_4 = 0.4$, $\omega_5 = 0.2$
v(1, 2, 3, 4) = 74 - 35 = 39;	$\omega_1 = 0.1$, $\omega_2 = 0.3$, $\omega_3 = 0.3$, $\omega_4 = 0.3$
v(1, 2, 3, 5) = 70 - 38 = 32;	$\omega_1 = 0.2$, $\omega_2 = 0.3$, $\omega_3 = 0.3$, $\omega_5 = 0.2$
v(1, 2, 4, 5) = 69 - 33 = 36;	$\omega_1 = 0.2$, $\omega_2 = 0.3$, $\omega_4 = 0.3$, $\omega_5 = 0.2$
v(1, 3, 4, 5) = 75 - 33 = 42;	$\omega_1 = 0.1$, $\omega_3 = 0.3$, $\omega_4 = 0.3$, $\omega_5 = 0.3$
v(2, 3, 4, 5) = 72 - 32 = 40;	$\omega_2 = 0.1$, $\omega_3 = 0.3$, $\omega_4 = 0.4$, $\omega_5 = 0.2$
v(1, 2, 3, 4, 5) = 86 - 34 = 52;	$\omega_1 = 0.1$, $\omega_2 = 0.2$, $\omega_3 = 0.3$, $\omega_4 = 0.3$, $\omega_5 = 0.1$

TABLE 3
Numerical results for nucleolus

Player: P	1	2	3	4	5
Individual utility: $u_{\{p\}}$	0.45	0.35	0.40	0.25	0.30
Payoff vector: z_p (× 100)					
Nucleolus: $\mu = 1$	8.20	6.20	12.20	16.20	9.20
Weak nucleolus: $\mu = s$	8.20	6.20	12.20	16.20	9.20
Proportional nucleolus:					
$\mu = v(S)$	7.98	5.78	12.38	16.78	9.08
Concession nucleolus:					
$\mu = \sum_{p \in S} \Phi_p$	8.03	5.95	12.29	16.61	9.14
Contribution nucleolus:					
$\mu = v(N) - v(N-S)$	8.20	6.20	12.20	16.20	9.20
Obtained utility value:					
w_p (× 100)					
Nucleolus: $\mu = 1$	53.20	41.20	52.20	41.20	39.20
Weak nucleolus: $\mu = s$	53.20	41.20	52.20	41.20	39.20
Proportional nucleolus:					
$\mu = v(S)$	52.98	40.78	52.38	41.78	39.08
Concession nucleolus:					
$\mu = \sum_{p \in S} \Phi_p$	53.03	40.95	52.29	41.61	39.14
Contribution nucleolus:					
$\mu = v(N) - v(N-S)$	53.20	41.20	52.20	41.20	39.20

TABLE 4
Simplex multipliers for coalitions and maximal ε-value

	Nucleolus	Weak nucleolus	Proportional nucleolus	Concession nucleolus	Contribution nucleolus
y_S for v(S):					
v(1,2,3,4)					
v(1,2,3,5)					
v(1,2,4,5)	0.2	0.05	0.00529	0.00481	0.00385
v(1,3,4,5)					
v(2,3,4,5)					
y_N for v(N):					
v(1,2,3,4,5)	−0.80	−0.20	−0.02116	−0.01923	−0.01538
maximum ε-value	−3.8	−0.95	−0.10053	−0.09135	−0.07308

ANNEX

Construction of a nonfuzzy preference orfer from fuzzy preference relations

Define the strength-of-preference rule (Seo and Sakawa 1985):

$$\mu_R(x_i, x_j) - \frac{1}{m} \sum_k w^k N^k(0_{ij}) - S(0_{ij})/m \qquad (A.1)$$

where $N^k(0_{ij})$ denotes a total score (e.g. the number of votes) for a preference ordering 0_{ij} to be weighted by $w^k \in w$, $k = 1, ..., K$. A weighting coefficient w^k represents the strength of preference for each ordered pair (X_i, X_j) of attributes. m is the number n of voters multiplied by a maximum value of w^k, viz. $m \Delta \max (w^k n)$. For instance, suppose that $n - 20$ and $w\ W\ (w^1, w^2, w^3) - (3, 2, 1)$, then $m - 60$.

Suppose that we have diversified evaluation for the preference order among the attributes, $X_1, X_2, ..., X_5$, as a result of collective choice and obtained the following score sheet:

$$\begin{array}{ll}
0^1 - (X_1, X_2, X_3, X_4, X_5), & N(0^1) - 4 \\
0^2 - (X_1, X_2, X_5, X_4, X_3), & N(0^2) - 2 \\
0^3 - (X_2, X_1, X_3, X_5, X_4), & N(0^3) - 2 \\
0^4 - (X_2, X_1, X_4, X_3, X_5), & N(0^4) = 1 \\
0^5 - (X_3, X_5, X_1, X_2, X_4) & N(0^5) - 2 \\
0^6 - (X_3, X_1, X_5, X_4, X_2), & N(0^6) - 1 \\
07 = (X_1, X_3, X_2, X_5, X_4), & N(0^7) = 3 \\
0^8 - (X_4, X_1, X_2, X_3, X_5), & N(0^8) = 2 \\
0^9 - (X_4, X_5, X_1, X_3, X_2), & N(0^9) - 1 \\
0^{10} - (X_2, X_4, X_3, X_5, X_1), & N(0^{10}) - 2 \\
\hline
 & 20
\end{array} \qquad (A.2)$$

Then the following scores for the binary relations can be obtained from the original score sheet (A.2).

$$
\begin{array}{llll}
O_{12} = (X_1, X_2), & N(O_{12}) = 15, & S(O_{12}) = 38 \\
O_{13} = (X_1, X_3), & N(O_{13}) = 15, & S(O_{13}) = 37 \\
O_{14} = (X_1, X_4), & N(O_{14}) = 14, & S(O_{14}) = 35 \\
O_{15} = (X_1, X_5), & N(O_{15}) = 15, & S(O_{15}) = 38 \\
O_{21} = (X_2, X_1), & N(O_{21}) = 5, & S(O_{21}) = 13 \\
O_{23} = (X_2, X_3), & N(O_{23}) = 13, & S(O_{23}) = 32 \\
O_{24} = (X_2, X_4), & N(O_{24}) = 16, & S(O_{24}) = 42 \\
O_{25} = (X_2, X_5), & N(O_{25}) = 16, & S(O_{25}) = 33 \\
O_{31} = (X_3, X_1), & N(O_{31}) = 5, & S(O_{31}) = 12 \\
O_{32} = (X_3, X_2), & N(O_{32}) = 7, & S(O_{32}) = 16 \\
O_{34} = (X_3, X_4), & N(O_{34}) = 12, & S(O_{34}) = 28 \\
O_{35} = (X_3, X_5), & N(O_{35}) = 17, & S(O_{35}) = 39 \\
O_{41} = (X_4, X_1), & N(O_{41}) = 5, & S(O_{41}) = 10 \\
O_{42} = (X_4, X_2), & N(O_{42}) = 4, & S(O_{42}) = 8 \\
O_{43} = (X_4, X_3), & N(O_{43}) = 8, & S(O_{43}) = 21 \\
O_{45} = (X_4, X_5), & N(O_{45}) = 10, & S(O_{45}) = 21 \\
O_{51} = (X_5, X_1), & N(O_{51}) = 5, & S(O_{51}) = 12 \\
O_{52} = (X_5, X_2), & N(O_{52}) = 4, & S(O_{52}) = 9 \\
O_{53} = (X_5, X_3), & N(O_{53}) = 3, & S(O_{53}) = 7 \\
O_{54} = (X_5, X_4), & N(O_{54}) = 10, & S(O_{54}) = 22
\end{array}
\qquad (A.3)
$$

The set of preference ordering $O \, \Delta \, \{O^j\}$ that appears in the original score sheet (A.2) is a fuzzy set. The binary score sheet (A.3) is also a fuzzy set, and derives a 5x5 relation matrix $[\mu_R]$ (A.4) whose elements are values of the membership function $\mu_R(X_i, X_j)$ (A.1) for the fuzzy binary preference relation R on $(X_i, X_j) \in X_i \times X_j$, $i, j = 1, \ldots, 5$, $i \neq j$.

$$
[\mu_R] \quad \begin{bmatrix} 0 & 0.63 & 0.62 & 0.58 & 0.63 \\ 0.22 & 0 & 0.53 & 0.70 & 0.55 \\ 0.20 & 0.27 & 0 & 0.47 & 0.65 \\ 0.17 & 0.13 & 0.35 & 0 & 0.35 \\ 0.20 & 0.15 & 0.12 & 0.37 & 0 \end{bmatrix} \qquad (A.4)
$$

The problem is to find a nonfuzzy collective preference ordering from the fuzzy set (A.4). In general, the relation matrix can represent connectivity, but intransitivity will occur in some triples $(X_i, X_j, K_k) \in X_i \times X_j \times X_k$.

For example, the relation matrix (A.4) includes intransitivity in triples (X_1, X_2, X_4), (X_3, X_2, X_1), (X_4, X_1, X_2), (X_4, X_3, X_1), $(X_4, X_3\ X_2)$, (X_4, X_5, X_1), (X_4, X_5, X_2), (X_5, X_1, X_2), (X_5, X_1, X_3), (X_5, X_2, X_3), and (X_5, X_4, X_3). For ensuring the transitivity for every binary preference relation, according to the definition of fuzzy transitivity (2.9), there are alternative ways to revise the original relation matrix: 1) to augment the value of $U_R(X_i, C_k)$, 2) to lessen the value of $\mu_R(X_i, X_j)$

$\wedge\ \mu_R(X_j, X_k)$ and 3) to lessen the value of $\mu_R(X_i, X_j)$ or the value of $\mu_R(X_j, X_k)$ discretionally. With those alternative devices, different revised relation matrices with the transitivity can be obtained. An effective computer program. ICOPSS/FR is available for the transitivity checks to obtain the weak-ordered preference relations.

The revised matrices which embody the transitivity are presented to the assessors as candidates for acceptance. Elements that appear in the matrices can be regarded as relative weights for preferences revealed in the pairwise comparison in collective choice under the selection rule. In practice, it is asked whether the changed values of the weights on preference would be acceptable for the assessors. If the revised values in one of all the obtained matrices with transitivity are more acceptable than the others, a fuzzy set representing a weak-ordered, collective preference relation has been obtained. For example, a revised matrix (A.5) with transitivity is finally obtained by reconciliation among the planners in the second way.

$$[\mu'_R] = \begin{bmatrix} 0 & 0.58 & 0.62 & 0.58 & 0.63 \\ 0.20 & 0 & 0.53 & 0.70 & 0.55 \\ 0.13 & 0.13 & 0 & 0.47 & 0.65 \\ 0.13 & 0.13 & 0.35 & 0 & 0.35 \\ 0.12 & 0.12 & 0.12 & 0.12 & 0 \end{bmatrix} \tag{A.5}$$

The procedure for deriving a nonfuzzy preference ordering among the attributes is to decompose the fuzzy set of preference ordering in (A.3) into a union of the α-level sets based on the finally obtained transitive relation matrix (A.5). The α-level decomposition is:

$$\begin{aligned}
R_{\alpha=0.7} &= (X_2, X_4) \\
R_{\alpha-0.6} &= R_{\alpha=0.7} \cup ((X_1, X_3), (X_1, X_5), (X_3, X_5)) \\
R_{\alpha=0.5} &= R_{\alpha=0.6} \cup ((X_1, X_2), (X_1, X_4), (X_2, X_3), (X_2, X_5)) \\
R_{\alpha=0.4} &= R_{\alpha=0.5} \cup ((X_3, X_4)) \\
R_{\alpha=0.3} &= R_{\alpha=0.4} \cup ((X_4, X_3,), (X_4, X_5)) \\
R_{\alpha=0.2}\ & R_{\alpha=0.3} \cup (X_2, X_1) \\
R_{\alpha=0.1}\ & R_{\alpha=0.2} \cup ((X_3, X_1), (X_3, X_2), (X_4, X_1), (X_4, X_2), (X_5, X_1), \\
& (X_5, X_2), (X_5, X_3), (X_5, X_4)).
\end{aligned} \tag{A.6}$$

The classes of the nonfuzzy weak-ordered set is defined corresponding to the α-level decomposition (A.7) as follows:

$$
\begin{array}{lll}
C_1: & (X_2, X_4) & \text{..... level .7} \\
C_2: & ((X_1, X_3), (X_1, X_5), (X_3, X_5)) & \text{..... level .6} \\
C_3: & ((X_1, X_2), (X_1, X_4), (X_2, X_3), (X_2, X_5) & \text{..... level .5} \\
C_4: & (X_3, X_4) & \text{..... level .4}
\end{array}
\tag{A.7}
$$

where the class Ci is a set of all orderings for the pentamerous relations are compatible with the above-described binary relations. Taking the intersection, we find the collective ordering

$$C1 \cap C2 \cap C3 \cap C4 = (X1, X2, X3, X4, X5), \tag{A.8}$$

or in another expression,

$$X1 \quad X2 \quad X3 \quad X4 \quad X5 \,. \tag{A.9}$$

Taking the minimum α-level, we can call (A.9) the weak-ordered nonfuzzy relation in the level 0.4 for our decision problem. Or preferably, using the membership function $\mu_{C1 \cap C2 \cap C3 \cap C4}(X_i, X_j) = 0.47$, we can say about the collective preference ordering (A.9) 'the degree of agreement is 0.47'.

COMPUTER-AIDED MULTIOBJECTIVE DECISION MAKING UNDER RISK

Hiroyuki Tamura

1. INTRODUCTION

Recent advances in information technologies and system science enable us to build mathematical models of complex human preferences under risk with the aid of interactive computers (either TSS terminals of a main frame, a work station or even a personal computer). Once we obtain such a model we may use this model for analysing and/or supporting decision making under risk. In this chapter we describe a theoretical background and a method of computer-aided modelling of human preferences. After briefly describing a single attribute utility function based on von Neumann-Morgenstern's hypothesis (1947) of expected utility, additive, multilinear and convex decompositions are described for multiattribute utility functions. These decompositions are based on Fishburn's additive independence (1970), Keeney and Raiffa's utility independence (1976) and our convex dependence (Tamura and Nakamura 1983) conditions, respectively. The concept of convex dependence is a generalised concept of utility independence where we consider the change of a person's risk attitude on one attribute to be dependent upon the conditional level of the other attribute. To clarify the interpretation of this concept an example of a tradeoff between urban environment and economic consumption is discussed.

As an application of the concept of convex dependence to a decision making problem with multiple persons we describe convex dependence between two conflicting persons. This concept can describe the change of attitude of each person toward the group utility depending upon the utility level of the other person. To clarify the interpretation of this concept a hypothetical example for siting a major airport in a suburban area is included.

2. UTILITY THEORY

2.1 Preliminaries

Let

$$A = \{a, b, \ldots\}$$

be a set of alternative actions from which a decision maker must choose one action. Suppose the choice of $a \in A$ will result in consequence x_i with probability p_i, and the choice of $b \in A$ will result in consequence x_i with probability q_i, and so forth. Let

$$X = \{x_1, x_2, ...\}$$

be a set of all possible consequences. In this case

$$p_i \geq 0, q_i \geq 0, ... \text{ for all } i$$

$$\Sigma_i p_i = \Sigma_i q_i = ... = 1.$$

Let the real function u be a utility function on X. Then the expected utilities of actions a,b,... are given, respectively, by

$$E_a = \Sigma_i p_i u(x_i), \quad E_b = \Sigma_i q_i u(x_i) ... \tag{2.1}$$

The assertion that the decision maker chooses an alternative action as if he maximises his expected utility is called the ***expected utility hypothesis*** of von Neumann and Morgenstern (1947). In other words the decision maker chooses an action according to the normative rule

$$a \succ b \iff E_a > E_b, \qquad a \sim b \iff E_b = E_b \tag{2.2}$$

where $a \succ b$ denotes "a is preferred to b", and $a \sim b$ denotes "a is indifferent to b". This rule is called the ***expected utility rule***. A utility function which satisfies Equations (2.1) and (2.2) is uniquely obtained within the class of positive linear transformations.

Figure 1 shows a decision tree and lotteries which explain the above mentioned situation, where ℓ_a, ℓ_b, ... denote ***lotteries*** which the decision maker comes across when he considers the actions a, b, ..., respectively. A ***certainty equivalent*** of lottery ℓ_a is now defined as an amount x such that the decision maker is indifferent between the amount x for certain and the lottery ℓ_a. From the expected utility hypothesis we obtain

$$u(x) = E_a = \Sigma_i p_i u(x_i). \tag{2.3}$$

In a set X of all possible consequences, let x^0 and x^* be the worst and the best consequences, respectively, Since utility function is unique within the class of positive linear transformations, let us normalise the utility function as

$$u(x^0) = 0, \qquad u(x^*) = 1. \tag{2.4}$$

Let $\langle x^*, p, x^0 \rangle$ be a lottery yielding consequences x^* and x^0 with probabilities p and (1-p), respectively. Especially when p=0.5, this lottery is called the ***fifty-fifty lottery*** and this is denoted as $\langle x^*, x^0 \rangle$. Let x be a certainty equivalent of lottery

$$x \sim \langle x^*, p, x^0 \rangle \tag{2.5}$$

then

$$u(x) = pu(x^0) + (1 - p)u(x^0) = p. \tag{2.6}$$

It is easy to identify a single attribute utility function of a decision maker by asking the decision maker about the certainty equivalents of some fifty-fifty lotteries (see Keeney and Raiffa 1976). The attitude of a decision maker towards risk can be described in the following way. A decision maker is ***risk averse*** if he prefers the expected consequence $x(=\Sigma\ p_i x_i)$ of any lotteries to that lottery. In this case

$$u(x) > \Sigma_i\ p_i u(x_i). \tag{2.7}$$

If a decision maker is risk averse, his utility function is concave. The reverse is also true. A decision maker is ***risk neutral*** (prone) if and only if his utility function is linear (convex).

Additive and utility independence based on utility decomposition has been described extensively by Keeney and Raiffa (1976). Let a specific consequence $x \varepsilon X$ be characterised by two attributes (performance indices) Y and Z. For example, price and performance of cars, natural environment and economy of a nation, and so forth. In this case, as a specific consequence $x \varepsilon X$ is represented by an ordered pair

$$x = (y, z), \qquad y \varepsilon Y, z \varepsilon Z. \tag{2.8}$$

A set of all possible consequences X can be written as a rectangular subset of a two-dimensional Euclidean space as $X = YxZ$. This consequence space is called ***two-attribute space***. Although Y and Z could represent vector attributes, both of them are regarded as single attribute spaces here. A two-attribute utility function is defined on $X = YxZ$ as $u{:}YxZ \to Re$. Thus we introduce the following definition of utility independence. Attribute Y is ***utility independent*** of attribute Z denoted as Y(UI)Z, if the conditional preferences for lotteries on Y given $z\varepsilon Z$ do not depend on the condition level z. Let us now assume that y^0 and z^0 are the worst level of the attributes Y and Z, respectively, and y^* and z^* are the best level of Y and Z, respectively. Then we may use the following definition. Given an arbitrary $z\varepsilon Z$ a ***normalised conditional utility function*** $u_1(y|z)$ on Y is defined by

$$u_1(y|z) = [u(y,z) - u(y^0,z)]/[u(y^*z) - u(y^0,z)] \tag{2.9}$$

where it is assumed that $u(y^*,z) > u(y^0,z)$. Similarly, $u_2(z|y)$ on Z may also be

Now we can derive:

$$u_1(y^o|z) = u_2(z^o|y) = 0, \quad u_1(y^*|z) = u_2(z^*|y) = 1. \tag{2.10}$$

$$u_1(y|z) = u_1(y|z^o), \text{ for all } z \varepsilon Z, \text{ if } Y(ur)Z. \tag{2.11}$$

In other words, utility independence implies that the normalised conditional utility functions do not depend on the different conditional levels.

Attributes Y and Z are defined as ***additive independent***, if, for arbitrarily chosen values of $y' \varepsilon Y$ and $z' \varepsilon z$,

$$\langle (y,z),(y',z') \rangle \sim \langle (y,z'),(y',z) \rangle, \text{ for all } y \varepsilon Y,\ z \varepsilon Z. \tag{2.12}$$

Consequently, attributes y and Z are additive independent, if and only if

$$u(y,z) = a u_1(y|z^o) + b u_2(z|y^o) \tag{2.13}$$

where

$$a + b = 1. \tag{2.14}$$

The additive independence is a special case of mutual utility independence (Keeney and Raiffa 1976).

2.2 Utility decomposition based on convex dependence

The following results are due to Tamura and Nakamura (1983). This section deals with the case where

$$u_1(y|z) \neq u_1(y|z^o), \qquad \text{for some } z \varepsilon Z$$

$$u_2(z|y) \neq u_2(z|y^o), \qquad \text{for some } y \varepsilon Y$$

that is, utility independence does not hold between the attributes Y and Z.

Attribute Y is ***n-th order convex dependent*** on attribute Z, denoted as $Y(CD_n)Z$, if there exists a distinct $z_0, z_1, \ldots, z_n \varepsilon Z$ and real functions $\lambda_0, \lambda_1, \ldots, \lambda_n$ on Z such that the normalised conditional utility function $u_1(y|z)$ can be written as

$$u_1(y|z) = \sum_{i=0}^{n} \lambda_i(z) u_1(y|z_i), \quad \sum_{i=0}^{n} \lambda_i(z) = 1 \tag{2.15}$$

for all $y \varepsilon Y$ and $z \varepsilon Z$, where

$$\lambda_i(z) = \begin{cases} \delta_{ij}, & z = z_j, \quad j = 0,1,\ldots,n \\ \text{real number}, & z \neq z_j, \quad j = 0,1,\ldots,n \end{cases} \quad i = 1,2,\ldots,n \tag{2.16}$$

where δ_{ij} denotes Kronecker delta and n is the smallest nonnegative integer for which Equation (2.15) holds.

This definition says that if $Y(CD_n)Z$, any normalised conditional utility function on Y can be described as a convex combination of (n+1) normalised conditional utility functions with different conditional levels where the coefficients $\lambda_i(z)$ are not necessarily nonnegative.

For n = 0,1,..., if $Y(CD_n)Z$, then Z is at most (n+1)th order convex dependent on Y. If Y(UI)Z, then $Y(CD_0)Z$, and Z(UI)Y or $Z(CD_1)Y$. In general, if $Y(CD_n)Z$, then Z satisfies one of the three properties $Z(CD_{n-1})Y$, $Z(CD_n)Y$ or $Z(CD_{n+1})Y$.

In Tamura and Nakamura (1983), we have obtained two main *convex decomposition theorems* which can represent a wide range of utility functions. Moreover, when the utility on the arbitrary point (y_n, z_n) has a particular value, we can obtain one more decomposition of utility functions which does not depend on the point (y_n, z_n). This decomposition still satisfies $Y(CD_n)Z$ and $Z(CD_n)Y$, so we call this new property *reduced n-th order convex dependence* and denote it by $Y(RCD_n)Z$.

2.3 Interpretation of Convex Dependence

For describing the interpretation of convex dependence between two different attributes, we discuss a utility problem for a choice between environment and consumption (see Tamura and Nakamura 1978). In this problem, there exists a conflict between these two attributes, because the more we consume the more we pollute. It will be shown that the two attributes, environment and consumption, do not satisfy the utility independence property. Therefore, we may want to take into account the convex dependence property.

Let Y and Z be the attributes of environment and consumption, respectively, and $e \varepsilon Y$ and $c \varepsilon Z$ be the attribute levels. We restrict these attribute levels to $e^0 \lesssim e \lesssim e^*$ and $c^0 \lesssim c \lesssim c^*$ where $e = e^0$ means the environment is polluted and is at its worst level, $e = e^*$ means no pollution exists and the environment is clean, $c = c^0$ means the consumption is at the lowest level, and $c = c^*$ represents consumption at the highest level.

Now we consider how a normalised conditional utility function $u_1(e|c)$ for environment changes depending upon the consumption level c. It is evident that the preference of the environment changes according to the consumption level c. Comparing $u_1(e|c^0)$ this normalised conditional utility function is drawn schematically in Figure 2a. When $c = c^*$ - even if the environment is deteriorating starting from the clean level ($e = e^*$) - the decrease of utility is not so rapid in terms of compensation for high consumption, but as the environment quality level approaches the worst level, the utility for environmental quality decreases rapidly. When $c = c^0$, the decrease of utility for the environment takes place even for any environmental level, because the consumption level is suppressed to a very low level.

Next, we consider how a normalised conditional utility function $u_2(c|e)$ for consumption changes depending upon the environmental level. Comparing

$u_2(c|e^*)$ with $u_2(c|e^0)$, these normalised conditional utility functions are drawn schematically in Figure 2b. When $e = e^*$, the utility for consumption increases according to the law of diminishing marginal utility.

Accordingly, the tradeoff between consumption and environment does not satisfy the utility independence property, but by taking into account the convex dependence property we may construct an appropriate utility function.

3. GROUP UTILITY THEORY

In the previous methods of social choice or group decision making, the preference attitude of each decision maker (individual member of the group) has been described without taking into account the utility level (level of satisfaction) of the other decision makers, and such preference structures have been aggregated by some rule for group decision making. Keeney and Kirkwood's approach (1975) is also in this category. As a result we have often come across contradicting social decisions as seen in the so-called voting paradox. As shown in Arrow's (1963) impossibility theorem, there are no procedures for obtaining a group ordering of the various alternatives from the individual's ordinal rankings of the alternatives that is consistent with five reasonable criteria.

In real situations, the preference attitude of each decision maker depends heavily on the outcomes or utility levels obtained by the other decision makers. For example, a decision maker is satisfied with his low income and he feels that the group utility is relatively high even if his own utility level is low, when the other decision maker's utility level or outcome is lower than or equal to his outcome. On the other hand, the same decision maker is not satisfied with his high outcome when the other decision maker's outcome is higher than his outcome. Hence, the utility independence assumption among the multiple decision makers is not appropriate.

In this section, a group utility theory is described based on the concept of convex dependence. The group decision making by two (conflicting) decision makers is considered, where we discuss a systematic way of describing each decision maker's preference which depends on the utility level of the other decision maker. In other words, change of attitude of each decision maker towards the group utility is described depending upon the utility level of the other decision maker. The group utility function is then constructed by aggregating such preferences of each decision maker. The following development is due to Tamura and Yukimura (1983).

Let $U_1 \times U_2$ denote the utility function space, and let $u_1(x_1) \in U_1$, $u_2(x_2) \in U_2$ denote the utility function of decision makers 1 and 2 (DM1 and DM2) on the multiattribute consequence spaces X_1 and X_2, respectively, where $x_i \in X_i (i = 1,2)$ denotes a specific consequence for DMi. A group utility function $W(x_1, x_2)$ is assumed to be described as $w[u_1(x_1), u_2(x_2)]$. We shall now simplify the notation as follows:

$$w(u_1, u_2) = w[u_1(x_1), u_2(x_2)] \tag{3.1}$$

$$u_i^o = u_i(x_i^o), u_i^* = u_i(x_i^*), \quad i = 1,2 \tag{3.2}$$

where x_i^o and x_i^* denote the worst and the best consequences of DMi, respectively, and hence u_i^o and u_i^* denote the utility level of DMi for the worst and the best consequences, respectively. We will describe how to construct $w(u_1, u_2)$.

Given an arbitrary $u_2 \varepsilon U_2$, a Normalised Conditional Group Utility Function (NCGUF) $w_1(u_1|u_2)$ of DM1 on U_1 is defined as:

$$w_1(u_1|u_2) = [w(u_1,u_2)-w(u_1^o,u_2)]/[w(u_1^*,u_2)-w(u_1^o,u_2)] \tag{3.3}$$

where it is assumed that $w(u_1^*,u_2) > w(u_1^o, u_2)$, $u_1 0 = 0$, $u_1^* = 1$.
Then, $w_1(u_1|u_2)$ is normalised as

$$w_1(u_1^o|u_2) = 0, w_1(u_1^*|u_2) = 1, \quad \text{for all } u_2 \varepsilon U_2. \tag{3.4}$$

Similarly, NCGUF of DM2 $w_2(u_2|u_1)$ can be defined by

$$w_2(u_2|u_1) = [w(u_1,u_2)-w(u_1,u_2^o)]/[w(u_1,u_2^*)-w(u_1,u_2^o)] \tag{3.5}$$

where $w(u_1,u_2^*) > w(u_1,u_2^o)$, $u_2^o = 0$, $u_2^* = 1$. It is also assumed that the group utility function $w(u_1,u_2)$ is normalised so that

$$w(u_1^o,u_2^o) = 0, \quad w(u_1^*,u_2^*) = 1. \tag{3.6}$$

From a mathematical point of view, formulas of group utility functions are identical with those of multiattribute utility functions.

NCGUF (3.3) of DM1 represents his subjective preference structure for the group utility as a function of his own utility level under the condition that the utility level of DM2 is given. NCGUFs (3.3) and (3.5) will play an important role for constructing a group utility function. Convex dependence between two decision makers is now defined as follows. Utility of DM1 is said to be n-th order convex dependent of the utility of DM2, denoted by $U_1(CD_n)U_2$, if NCGUF of DM1 $w_1(u_1|u_2)$ can be described as a convex combination of (n+1) NCGUFs of DM1 $w_1(u_1|u_2^i)$, $i = 0,1,\dots, n$ with different conditional levels.

To clarify the interpretation of convex dependence between two (conflicting) decision makers, we deal with a decision making problem for siting a major airport, where we describe how to represent NCGUFs of each decision maker taking into account the situation of the other decision maker.

Let DM1 be the representative of the regional inhabitants and DM2 the representative of the developer of the airport. Existence of a benevolent dictator

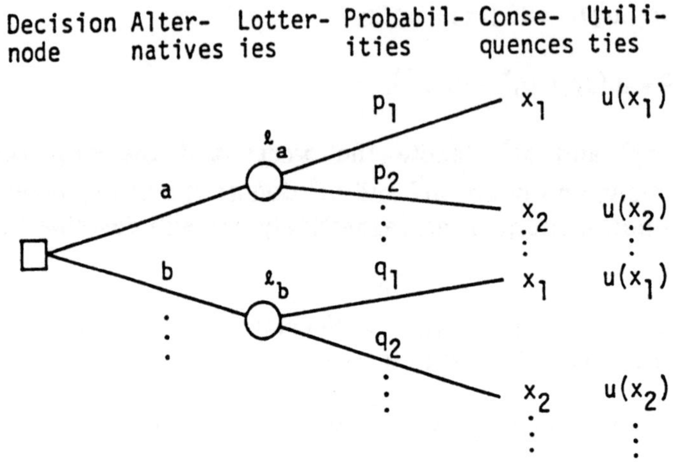

Figure 1: Decision Tree and Lotteries

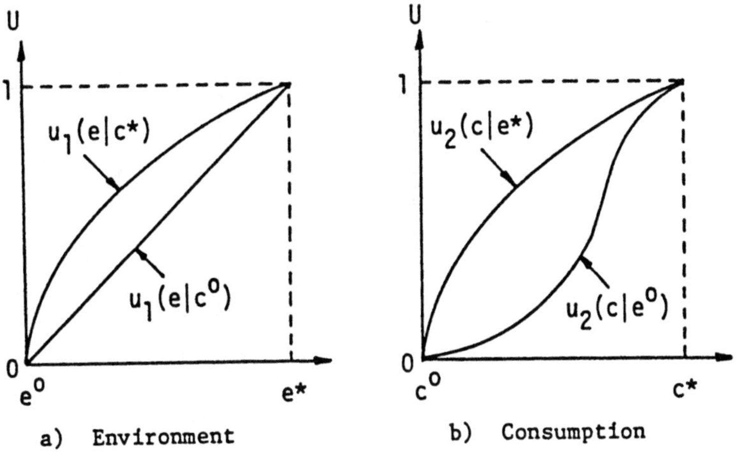

Figure 2: Normalised conditional utility function for environment and consumption.

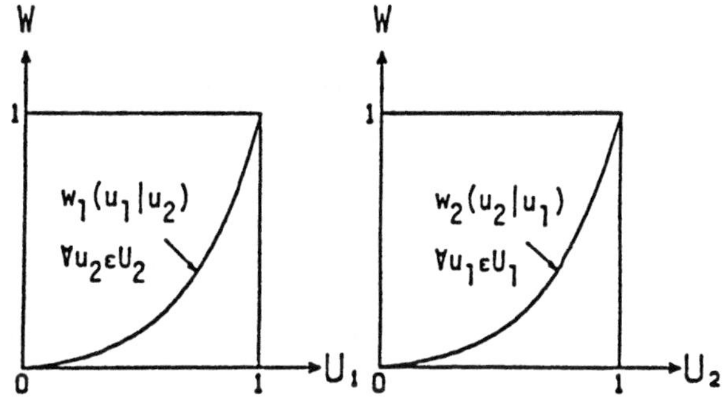

$(u_1^{.25}, u_1^{.5}, u_1^{.75}) = (0.7, 0.8, 0.9)$ $(u_2^{.25}, u_2^{.5}, u_2^{.75}) = (0.7, 0.8, 0.9)$

$$u_i^{.5} \sim \langle u_i^*, u_i^o \rangle, \quad u_i^{.25} \sim \langle u_i^{.5}, u_i^o \rangle$$

$$u_i^{.75} \sim \langle u_i^*, u_i^{.5} \rangle, \quad i = 1,2$$

Figure 3: NCGUFs for Case A.

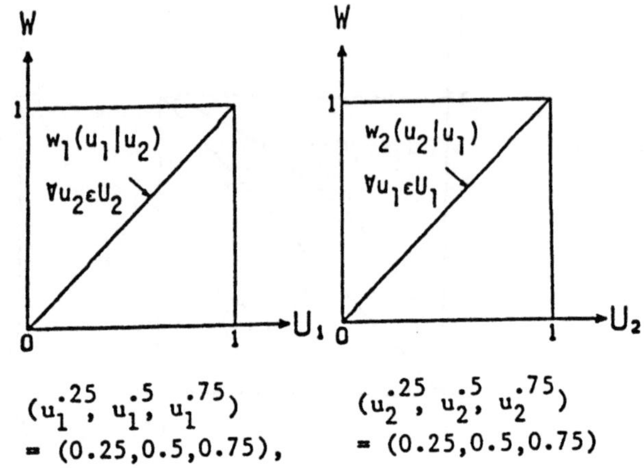

Figure 4: NCGUFs for Case B.

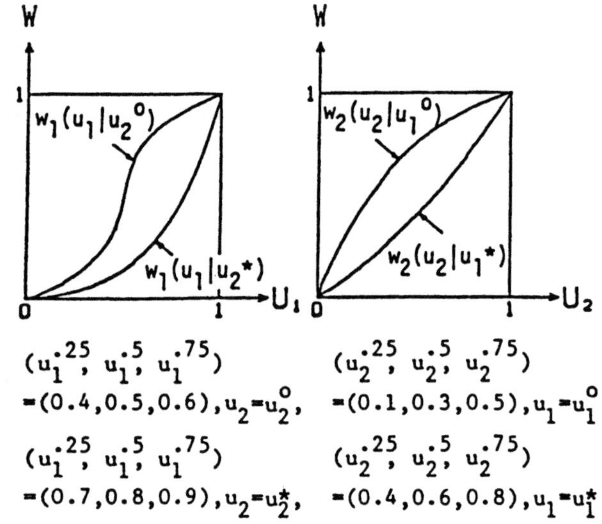

Figure 5: NCGUFs for Case C.

who mediates DM1 and DM2 by assessing the scaling coefficients, is postulated. We can regard that DM1 wishes to construct the airport as far from the regional area as possible to reduce the environmental negative effect of the airport. On the other hand, DM2 wishes to construct the airport at a closer location to the city for convenience and efficiency of the airport. Therefore, DM1 and DM2 are obviously conflicting.

We now consider two mutually utility independent cases and one mutually first order convex dependent case, and will interpret each case.

Case A: $U_1(MUI)U_2$

Suppose the certainty equivalents and the resulting NCGUFs of DM1 and DM2 are assessed as shown in Figure 3. Convex NCGUFs in this figure show that both DM1 and DM2 do not think that the group utility is high unless the utility levels of their own are very high, and that each DM's attitude towards the group utility does not depend on the utility level of the other DM. In other words, each DM is mutually utility independent and the attitude is selfish and stubborn.

In this case the group utility function is described as

$$w(u_1,u_2) = aw_1(u_1|u_2^o) + bw_2(u_2|u_1^o)$$
$$+ (1 - a - b)w_1(u_1|u_2^o)w_2(u_2|u_1^o). \quad (3.7)$$

Case B: Keeney-Kirkwood model

Suppose the certainty equivalents and the resulting NCGUFs of DM1 and DM2 are assessed as shown in Figure 4. Linear NCGUFs in this figure show that NCGUF of each DM is equal to his own utility level. In this case each DM is again mutually utility independent and his attitude towards the group utility is stubborn but not as selfish as in Case A.

In this case $w_1(u_1|u_2^o) = u_1$, $w_2(u_2|u_1^o) = u_2$ in Equation (3.7) and the group utility function is described as

$$w(u_1,u_2) = au_1 + bu_2 + (1 - a - b)u_1u_2. \quad (3.8)$$

Case C: $U_1(CD_1)U_2$ and $U_2(CD_1)U_1$

Suppose the certainty equivalents and the resulting NCGUFs of DM1 and DM2 are assessed as shown in Figure 5. Furthermore, suppose the first order convex dependence between DM1 and DM2 is assured. This means that the preference attitude of DM1 (DM2) to the group utility varies depending upon the utility level of DM2 (DM1). Even when the utility level of DM2 is at the worst level ($u_2 = u_2^o$), the attitude of DM1 towards the group utility is selfish for low u_1, because the environmental impact of the airport to DM1 is straightforward. But for higher u_1 the attitude of DM1 is changed to be more gentle.

On the other hand, when the utility level of DM2 is at the best level ($u_2 = u_2^*$), the attitude of DM1 towards the group utility is always selfish. In other words, when the utility level of DM2 is high, DM1 does not feel that group utility is high unless his own utility level is very high. This can be interpreted that in the group decision DM1 is claiming equity by comparing his own utility level with that of DM2. When the utility level of DM1 is at the worst level ($u_1 = u_1^o$), the attitude of DM2 is gentle and sympathetic, but when the utility level of DM1 is at the best level ($u_1 = u_1^*$), the attitude of DM2 is changed to be slightly self-centred.

As shown in Case C the concept of convex dependence makes it possible to describe in NCGUFs the change of attitude of each decision maker depending upon the utility level of the other decision maker. By using the group utility theory based on the concept of convex dependence, it is possible to offer clear information on various preference orderings for the alternatives depending upon the various attitudes of each decision maker in the group and various cases for the values of scaling coefficients assessed by a benevolent dictator.

4. CONCLUDING REMARKS

Centering around the concept of convex dependence multiattribute utility theory and group utility theory, we have briefly surveyed as multiobjective decision making. A major advantage of the convex decomposition is that it includes many previous decompositions such as additive, multiplicative, bilateral and interpolation decompositions as special cases. Therefore, depending upon the complexity of tradeoffs the convex decompositions could provide more flexible multiattribute and/or group utility functions for modelling preferences of a decision maker or multiple (conflicting) decision makers.

Since the convex decompositions need only single-attribute utility functions even for high-order convex dependent cases, it is relatively easy to identify the multiattribute utility functions. Graphic terminals of a large-scale computer could be effectively used for this purpose.

We did not include the value theoretic approach (Dyer and Sarin 1979 and Sarin 1983) in this paper, however, riskless and/or risky preference representation based on the value theoretic approach is an important topic for further research. Under this approach it might be possible to discriminate a decision maker's strength-of-preference and the attitude towards risk.

The approach described in this paper is based on the expected utility hypothesis of von Neumann and Morgenstern (1947). Many paradoxes (Allais and Hagen 1979, and Kahneman and Tversky 1979) have been observed which violate particular axioms. For overcoming this difficulty nonlinear utility analysis (Fishburn 1984) is being investigated.

REFERENCES

Allais, M. and O. Hagen, Expected Utility Hypotheses and the Allais Paradox, Reidel Publishing Company, Dordrecht, Holland, 1979.

Arrow, K.J., Social Choice and Individual Values, 2nd Ed., Wiley, New York, 1963.

Dyer, J.S. and Sarin, R., Measurable Multiattribute Value Functions, Opns. Res., 27, 1979, pp. 810-822.

Fishburn, P.C., Utility Theory for Decision Making, Wiley, New York, 1970.

Fishburn, P.C., Multiattribute Nonlinear Utility Theory, Mgmt. Sci., 30, 1984, pp. 1301-1310.

Kahneman, D. and A. Tversky, Prospect Theory: An Analysis of Decision Under Risk, Econometrica, 47, 1979, pp. 263-291.

Keeney, R.L. and C.W. Kirkwood, Group Decision Making Using Cardinal Social Welfare Functions, Mgmt. Sci., 22, 1975, pp. 430-437.

Keeney, R.L. and H. Raiffa, Decisions with Multiple Objectives: Preferences and Value Tradeoffs, Wiley, New York, 1976.

Sarin, R.K., Measurable Value Function Theory: Survey and Open Problems, in: Hansen, P. (ed.), Essays and Surveys on Multiple Criteria Decision Making, Springer-Verlag, Berlin, 1983.

Tamura, H. and Y. Nakamura, Constructing a Two-Attribute Utility Function for Pollution and Consumption Based on a New Concept of Convex Dependence, in: Myoken, H. (ed.), Information, Decision and Control in Dynamic Socio-Economics, Bunshindo, Tokyo, Japan, 1978.

Tamura, H. and Y. Nakamura, Decompositions of Multiattribute Utility Functions Based on Convex Dependence, Opns. Res., 31, 1983, pp. 488-506.

Tamura, H. and K. Yukimura, Identification of Group Utility Functions for Group Decision Making Based on Convex Dependence, Proceedings, 3rd IFAC/IFORS Symposium on Large Scale Systems, Warsaw, Poland, 1983, pp. 513-518.

Von Neumann, J. and O. Morgenstern, Theory of Games and Economic Behavior, 2nd Ed., Princeton University Press, Princeton, N.J., 1947.

DEVELOPMENT OF INFORMATICS AND POSSIBLE CHANGES IN URBANISATION PROCESSES

Isao Orishimo

1. DEVELOPMENT OF INFORMATICS

Usually informatics is defined as computer and information science (Gorn 1983, p.121). It is concerned with symbolic expressions and their manipulations and hence also with the study, design and use of data structures and their transformation by mechanical means (Gorn 1983, pp.130-131). A similar concept of computers and communication sciences can be found in Kobayashi (1982).

In order to illustrate the technical development of informatics very roughly we can depict its framework on the basis of the mechanical structure of an ordinary computer. As is well known, the speed of CPU and its memory capacity is increasing very rapidly, given the constant price. The working of robotics, cybernetics, or artificial intelligence can be understood in the same way by means of the simple structure of the computer.

Here is it most important to realise what kind of information is transmitted by informatics, though apparently the speed of CPU and memory capacity is increasing extraordinarily rapidly as mentioned above. In general, information itself contains two kinds of meaning. The one is descriptive or parametric information, and the other is structural - non-mechanic, morphogenetic or qualitative information (Langlois 1983, p.594; Nijkamp 1985, p.215). In the case of descriptive information, it is easy for us to transmit it through telecommunications, and to store it through memory in computers. But in the case of non-mechanic information, it is not easy to transmit it through telecommunications, because this kind of information operates on parameters of the system which may adjust the working of the system. Face-to-face communication should be more adequate in this case, because in case of this kind of information, without face-to-face contact, it takes a lot of time to communicate with each other. We will denote in this chapter, the former type of information as Information I and the latter type as Information II.

If we shift our attention from information to knowledge, sometimes both meanings of knowledge and information are intermingled. For instance, when the information sector and knowledge-producing sector (Machlup 1972, 1984, Jonscher 1983) are discussed, both concepts are used very ambiguously. And sometimes, knowledge and information are distinguished from each other based on the characterisation that the former is a stock of the latter and the latter is a flow (Machlup 1984). As is well known, Machlup breaks down the content of knowledge into five kinds, such as practical knowledge, intellectual knowledge, small talk and past-time knowledge, spiritual knowledge, and unwanted knowledge (Machlup 1972). However, in our understanding, his breakdown is not necessarily adequate for us to make clear the concept of knowledge as being distinguishable from information. From our point of view, it is also reasonable to break down two kinds of meanings of knowledge. One is termed *parametric* knowledge which means the stock of descriptive information - or more or less screened stock of descriptive information - which is originally conceptualised as human capital (Machlup 1984), some part of which may be constructed as artificial intelligence such as an expert system. Another is named *structural* knowledge, which is more deeply rooted in the cultural context, recognised as the integral of traditional cultural heritages. We denote the former as Knowledge I and the latter as Knowledge II. Compared with the case of information, the weight of Knowledge II should be greater.

As we can see, knowledge is not merely the stock of descriptive Information I. Information I is based on mechanistic development, which is in some sense antagonistic towards Knowledge II. Knowledge is often gained through the orderly loss of Information I and restructuring it, filtering it; piling Information I merely produces noise (Boulding 1984).

In the development of informatics, it is necessary to consider the mechanistic development of technology, which especially relates to the computer, data processing. In contrast, there exists a non-mechanistic development of a cultural structure such as the urban system. There are two ways of recognising the urbanisation process. Also there are two sides of the effect on the urbanisation process caused by the development of informatics, one is through Information I and the other is through Information II. The aspect recognised by the former is a mechanistic one, and the aspect recognised by the latter is non-mechanistic, and more organisational. Also there is influence in the effect brought about by Information I, and another influence is the effect brought about by Information II.

In the terminology of a system, a human system is the open and self-organising system, which is not isolated from exchanging information with an outside environment, and is able to change its structure in response to the environment. The urban system is the aggregate human system, which is very much tied to the biologically and culturally evolved structure of the human organism, being affected in its structural knowledge. So, an urban system is not merely a cybernetic system but a non-mechanic and self-organising system, though some aspect of the system is simplified as a mechanic system.

Non-mechanistic and organisational processes of urbanisation such as clearance processes according to the technological development suggested by Jacobs (1985) will be one of the most important aspects even in the case of informatics development. The organisational process of urbanisation is based on the accumulation of the structural self-organising knowledge, which is based on culturally idiosyncratic heritage. It is very difficult to analyse this aspect theoretically.

We break down two kinds of urbanisation processes, Urbanisation Processes I and II, which we can recognise respectively based on Information and Knowledge I and II. Urbanisation Process I is recognised as developing mechanistically or in a morphostatic way, as a causal system. The other, Urbanisation Process II, is recognised as developing non-mechanistically or in a morphogenetic way. Also, descriptive information would naturally have more effect on Urbanisation Process I. However, in the case of structural information, when it affects the system, which is metamorphosing or self-organising, it is reasonable to consider that this kind of information should affect Urbanisation Process II. Also, in the case of knowledge, parametric knowledge is more naturally reflected in Urbanisation Process I, and structural knowledge in Urbanisation Process II.

The development of informatics unavoidably affects the urban system through the flow of information by telecommunications networks as well as the accumulation of knowledge. Information flow of high density as a result of the development of informatics brings with it to the urban system various kinds of information systems for planning, such as road pricing systems, environmental pricing systems, etc. There are several aspects of the effect of information. Agglomerations of knowledge as human capital such as research institutes and universities bring with it different kinds of accessibility rather than hitherto acknowledged in location theory. This is the third aspect of the impact of Information II on the urbanisation process.

Knowledge II in this context may be called the *ultimate* genetic resource which may be understood as management capability and research capability; without exchange of these kinds of recognition of information and knowledge, we cannot expect a reasonable understanding of urbanisation. Agglomeration necessitates face-to-face contact to exchange this kind of Information II or Knowledge II.

From the point of view of the difference between information and knowledge and between two kinds of information and knowledge respectively, we distinctly experience the non-mechanistic nature of the human system. So, the real issues of information and knowledge actually cut across the mechanism/antimechanism dichotomy (Langlois 1983, p.587).

In the following sections, we pick up the main characteristics of the impact of the development of informatics on recent urbanisation processes, which is recognised to affect Urbanisation Process I in our context, and then we try to apply traditional location theory to one of these characteristics in which the mechanistic approach is influential.

2. RECENT REALISTIC TRENDS IN THE URBANISATION PROCESS

We investigate fundamental characteristics of the changing urbanisation process, with respect to the development of informatics and check the main points of the investigated characteristics based on research carried out on them. Among them, there are many topics such as the change in industrial structure, and the change in the characteristics of accessibility including the change in sensitivity of the environmental quality.

We would like to distinguish two kinds of impact of telecommunications development on the urbanisation process which will be recognised either mechanistically or non-mechanistically. One is the change of the characteristics of accessibility and the other is the rapid decrease in the telecommunications price. We recognised that the former is generally related to Information II and the latter is related to Information I.

1. There are many research efforts and essays on the change of the industrial structure. Software oriented knowledge industry, as well as hardware oriented industry such as telecommunications facilities and various kinds of computers are emerging as the information industry. Accompanying this, the other service industry is occupying one of the main factors of recent industrial development; this change in the industrial structure is having severe impacts on the urbanisation process.

1.1 With respect to traditional location theory explicitly, the points of market and resource supply in the Weberian model are to be changed to the points of knowledge accumulation such as institutes and universities, R&D investment accumulation, as well as international nodal points such as international airports (Andersson 1981). The spatial meaning of the Schumpeterian hypothesis (Levin 1984) should be verified in this process in which the accessibility to these institutions mentioned above is highly regarded.

Furthermore, the increasing speed and cheapness of telecommunications reduces the former external economies of physical proximity. Corporate headquarters and major white collar concentrations like the insurance industry disperse from the decaying central cities to the suburbs. The location of research laboratories, new universities, and large hospital complexes is less dependent on the traditional factors of economic geography and more influenced by the nearness of educational facilities, easier life-styles and political factors (Bell 1980).

1.2 Improvement in the sensitivity to environmental quality as location factor both in the case of the firm and of the individual.

Seeking more favourable environmental conditions, especially in the case of the so called high technology industry, one of the main location factors, the amenity favourability of the middle size cities, is regarded as more important than the advantages of big metropolitan agglomerations. Quality of life, especially residential life, appears to be a major attraction of California, particularly of the Bay Area. Environmental questions such as open space and air quality are considered to be key factors in location decisions (Feldman 1985).

As technology makes centres more attractive and city transport less onerous, it will also be making the private car more desirable and low-density living more available.

2. Rapid decrease in price of telecommunications (including data processing), and a remarkable improvement in its quality.

2.1 Substitutability versus complementarity of telecommunications with transportation. Main features of the aspect are as follows:

(i) intranational aspect: intraurban aspect and interurban aspect.
(ii) international aspect.

In the case of telecommunications, there are two kinds of impact on the location behaviour for urban residents. Commuting by bus or train can be effectively substituted by quite large amounts of telecommunications and computing (Meier 1985). On the other hand, there will be little tradeoff between communications and transportation, but rather an increase in both (Dickey 1985).
The dispersion in the metropolitan area becomes more extensive. In the case of the Tokyo metropolitan area, the dispersion is said to be extending to more than 150 km from the CBD. On the other hand, from the interurban point of view information technologies should help to spread the interconnections between cities (and nationally). This would mean that many more of the factors which influence growth and change in cities will come not from within but from without (Dickey 1985). As this will occur not merely from a local but from a national and international nodal point of view; the meaning of agglomeration should be regarded as more important.

2.2 Development of the application of a monitoring system for urban planning such as road pricing systems and environmental pricing systems. One of the most remarkable effects on the urban system might be the effective traffic simulators (Gorn 1983) in real time, though the realisation of the system would depend on the cultural background of the system.

Also, the opportunities for distributed road pricing, road user advice, and communications have now converged to make effective use of the road system an economic practical proposition within a short handful of years. Automation and continuous central acquisition of vehicle movement data at marginal cost provide an economic means of continuously monitoring flows and their composition. Road pricing would be more flexible, however, and charges would be tailored to respond to changes in demand on different parts of the road network in quite a detailed way, with drivers being informed how much the choices of route open to them were likely to cost (Bly 1985). For example, INSYRON not only integrates land use classifications, dwelling details and public utility access points, but also covers traffic flow, road accidents and other activities (Nijkamp 1985).

We have summarised two remarkable characteristics in the recent realistic trend of the urbanisation process. Here we would like to consider the different kinds of effect of Information I and II on the realistic trend of the urbanisation process.

3. THEORETICAL CONSIDERATIONS ON THE REALISTIC TREND

Information II is morphogenetic and therefore has a self-organising function as previously mentioned. Thus, it is difficult to communicate this only by means of telecommunications. Face-to-face contact should be indispensable to communicate this kind of information even as a complement to telecommunications.Information II might have a complex effect on the location choice. As a matter of fact, R&D activities and the institutes and universities disperse by themselves. But on the other hand, the necessity of its way of contact forces individuals to exhibit more agglomeration oriented location behaviour.

Therefore we confine the following theoretical formulation to the effect of Information I which is adequate to communicate by telecommunications.

We would like to address ourselves to the latter characteristic mentioned above, theoretically based on the most common formulation of the Alonso type of location and land use theory, which is already popularly established. The formulation is confined in the intraurban location context with respect to telecommunication of Information I.

We formulate the residential equilibrium model the purpose of which is to deal with the effect of telecommunications representing the development of informatics as a whole on location behaviour. We presuppose, as usual, a von Thünen type of homogeneous spatial structure (Alonso 1964).

The time for telecommunication calling is recognised for the individual as the amount of utility augmenting service, similar to goods and services. Then, it is recognised as the amount of utility reducing service, which is the same as the time for working. First, the equilibrium of individual location behaviour is expressed by the following equations:

$$\max \quad U = u(r, q, L, x) \tag{3.1}$$

$$\text{s.t.} \quad k(r) + p_L(r)L + pq + p_c(x) \leq y \tag{3.2}$$

where:

r	:	distance from CBD
L	:	quantity of land
q	:	quantity of composite goods other than land
x	:	total time of telephone calling
$p_L(r)$	:	land price of location, r
p_c	:	price of telephone calling per unit duration
$k(r)$	:	price for commuting distance, r

As a realistic approximation, we suppose that $k(r) = k\, r$, where k is the price of commuting of unit distance $p_c = p_o + p_1 r x$, where p_o is the price of the subscription (installation) of the telephone, p_1 is the price per call of unit duration per unit distance. As usual, we suppose:

$$\frac{\partial u}{\partial r} < 0.$$

About the sign of

$$\frac{\partial U}{\partial x}$$

we temporarily suppose that

$$\frac{\partial u}{\partial x} > 0,$$

based on our presupposition.

For simplification, using a Cobb-Douglas utility function, we set $U = Ar^{-\alpha}q^{\beta}L^{\gamma}x^{\delta}$, where $\alpha, \beta, \gamma, \delta > 0$.

Drawing on theoretical and empirical researches carried out worldwide, we suppose that

$$p_l = \frac{a}{r}, \text{ where } a > 0.$$

From the data in our country, within about a seventy kilometer radius in the metropolitan area, we suppose $p_c = p_l r x$ as an approximation. For simplification, we concentrate our attention on the relationship between the commuting, residential area and telecommunications. So, we exclude the consumption of composite commodities, q.

Now, we solve the equations (3.1) and (3.2) through a Lagrangian equation as in (3.3):

$$\mu = Ar^{-\alpha}L^{\gamma}x^{\delta} - \lambda\,[k\,r + \frac{a}{r}L + p_c r x - y] \tag{3.3}$$

With respect to the endogenous variables, x, L, r, and λ we are now solving the necessary condition:

$$\frac{\partial L}{\partial r} = -\alpha\frac{U}{r} - \lambda(k - \frac{a}{r_2}L + P_c x) = 0 \tag{3.4}$$

$$\frac{\partial \mu}{\partial L} = \beta\frac{U}{L} - \lambda\frac{a}{r}L = 0 \tag{3.5}$$

$$\frac{\partial \mu}{\partial x} = \gamma\frac{U}{x} - \lambda p_c r = 0 \tag{3.6}$$

$$\frac{\partial \mu}{\partial \lambda} = -\,(k\,r + \frac{a}{r}L + P_c x\,r - y) = 0 \tag{3.7}$$

Solving these equations with respect to r, L and x, we get the following

$$r = c_1 \frac{y}{k} \tag{3.8}$$

$$L = c_2 \frac{Y^2}{\kappa} \tag{3.9}$$

$$x = c_3 \frac{k}{p_c} \tag{3.10}$$

where:

$$c_1 = \frac{\beta - \alpha - \gamma}{2\beta - \alpha} \qquad c_2 = \frac{\beta(\beta - \alpha - \gamma)}{a(2\beta - \alpha)} \qquad c_3 = \frac{\gamma}{\beta - \alpha - \gamma}$$

By equation (3.8)-(3.10), the equilibrium condition for an individual location is expressed as a function of exogenous variables, k, y, and p_c. As travel costs for commuting per distance decreases, the equilibrium location of the consumer will be dispersed from CBD. Also the increase in income will positively affect the dispersion of the consumer's location. With respect to telecommunications, the decrease in value of p_c according to the technical innovation of informatics also brings the dispersion from the CBD.

In the second stage, we suppose that the development of informatics makes the working system in the home more popular. In this case, the time for telephone calling, x, should be counted as a minus effect on the utility function.

$$U = Ar^{-\alpha} q^{\beta} L^{\gamma} x^{-\delta} \tag{3.11}$$

In this case, the firm should pay a wage rate, w_1, per unit hour of work and calling in the home for the individual, whereas y is the other payment for the work in the firm. Accordingly, total income for the individual would be $y + w_1 x$.

For simplification similar to the first model, we suppose that explanatory variables of the utility function are confined to distance from the CBD, quantity of residential land and the amount of telecommunications. Namely,

$$U = r^{-\alpha} L^{\beta} x^{\gamma} \tag{3.11'}$$

where $\alpha, \beta, \gamma > 0$.

The budget constraint is as follows:

$$k\, r + p_1 L + p_c x < w_2 x + y \tag{3.12}$$

We formulate the Lagrangian equation as follows:

$$\mu = r^{-\alpha} L^{\beta} x^{-\gamma} - \lambda \ (k + \frac{a}{r} L + p_c x - w_1 x - y) \tag{3.13}$$

And we solve the equation with respect to r, L, x and λ.

$$\frac{\partial \mu}{\partial r} = - \alpha \frac{U}{r} - \lambda \ k - \frac{p_L L}{r} = 0 \tag{3.14}$$

$$\frac{\partial \mu}{\partial l} = \beta \frac{U}{l} - \lambda_{p_2} - 0 \tag{3.15}$$

$$\frac{\partial \mu}{\partial x} = - \gamma \frac{U}{x} - \lambda p_c w_1) = 0 \tag{3.16}$$

$$\frac{\partial \mu}{\partial \lambda} = k \ r + p_L L + p_c x - w_1 x - y = 0 \tag{3.17}$$

Rearranging the equations mentioned above, we get the following:

$$r = c_4 \frac{y}{k} \tag{3.18}$$

$$x = c_5 \frac{y}{w_1 - p_c} \tag{3.19}$$

where:

$$c_4 = \frac{-\alpha + \beta}{-\alpha + 2\beta - \gamma}, \ c_5 = \frac{\gamma}{-\alpha + 2\beta - \gamma} \tag{3.20}$$

In the latter case mentioned above, the decrease in the price of telephone calling causes an increase in individual telephone calling for work in the home.

In the third stage of our presupposition, we formulate the following model, in order to consider the time constraint along with the budget constraint.

$$\max.\ U = u(r, q, L, t_W, x) \tag{3.21}$$

$$\text{s.t. } kt_t(r) + pq + p_L(r)L + p_O + p_1rx \leqq y(t_W, x) \tag{3.22}$$

$$t_t(r) + t_W + x \leqq T \tag{3.23}$$

Where t_W is the duration time which the individual stays in his office, t_t is the time for the individual to commute to the office, and T is the time limitation for his work including commuting, staying in the office, and calling from his home to the office.

We suppose that $y = w_1t_W + w_2x$, where w_2 is the wage rate for his work in this office, and w_1 is the compensated wage rate for his work calling in his home.

In the model, we intend to clarify the individual location equilibrium conditions, under the situation that individuals regard more seriously the time constraint than the income constraint according to the development of informatics, and also, individuals become more sensitive to time spent commuting. Based on the monitoring system of transportation, the information on the velocity is to be given for the individuals through the facility installed in the car.

The major question is the evaluation of time and the opportunity cost of spending time in one way or another. In general, it is not entirely appropriate to include time as a cost constraint in any utility function, because even the time spent in commuting can be used in a way which increases the utility for the individual. The use of the car telephone is one way. But another example, is the case where after one has left his busy job, it might be relaxing just to wait half an hour sitting quietly in a traffic jam. That is a positive instead of a negative contribution to utility, because many people do not like to jump immediately from the office into the home. So, there are many alternative opportunities for time consumption. Clearly, here also are competitive elements of private transport (the car, for instance, including the telephone usage in the car) vis a vis the train where you can read a newspaper; all such evaluations for transportation with respect to time consumption have to be made. That places time evaluation in a much broader perspective than the traditional economic approach in which time was merely regarded as a cost component (Nijkamp, Comment at the Toyohashi Symposium 1986).

Regardless of the complexities related to time consumption, as a first approximation, we formulated the model mentioned above. However, it is very difficult to get a direct meaningful result. We have also tried to formulate and solve G.S. Becker's type of time allocation model (Becker 1965). Based on this model, we try to conduct comparative static analysis with respect to the parameters, p_1, k, w_1, w_2, p_1. We will show here the idea of the model and summarise the result of the solution.

We denote the following:

N_T : total time for the consumer to be able to spend his time, say in a month
N_x : time to work in a month
T_{tw} : times to commute and to work in the office in a month
t_w : mean time of the work once in his office
$\frac{r}{v}$: mean time of commuting to the office
$\bar{x}$: mean duration time of the call to his office.

We specify the utility function:

$$U - A\, q^{\alpha} L^{\beta} T_L^{\gamma} \tag{3.25}$$

The budget constraint is

$$K\, rN_{tw} + pq + p_L(r)\, 1 + \bar{x} N_x P_c \lesssim y \tag{3.26}$$

where:

$$T_L = N_T - xN_x - (t_w + \frac{2r}{v})\, N_{tw} \tag{3.27}$$

$$y - wN_x^{\delta} N_{tw}^{1-\delta} \tag{3.28}$$

$$y_d - w\, f(N_{tw}, N_x) - p_c N_x \tag{3.29}$$

The Lagrangian equation is formulated as follows:

$$m - Aq^{\alpha} L^{\beta} T_L^{\gamma} - l(KrN_{tw} + pq + p_L(r)L + xN_x p_c - wN_x^{\delta} N_{tw}^{1-\delta}) \tag{3.30}$$

Differentiating (3.30) with respect to q, L, N_x, N_{tw} gives:

$$\frac{\partial \mu}{\partial q} - \alpha \frac{U}{q} - \lambda p - 0 \tag{3.31}$$

$$\frac{\partial\mu}{\partial\lambda} = \beta\frac{U}{L} - \lambda p_L = 0 \tag{3.32}$$

$$\frac{\partial\mu}{\partial N_x} = -\gamma x \frac{U}{T_L} - \lambda\left(-\delta\frac{y}{N_x} + x p_c\right) = 0 \tag{3.33}$$

$$\frac{\partial L}{\partial N_{tw}} = -\gamma\left(t_w + \frac{r}{t_w}\right) \frac{U}{T_c} - \lambda\left(Kr - (1 - \delta)y/N_{tw}\right) \tag{3.34}$$

Given the distance from the CBD, we solve N_{tw}, N_x and y_d with respect to p_c, r and w in the general form of the functions. Thus, through the indirect utility function we obtained, we seek the parametric dynamics. As a result of the comparative static analysis, we obtain the following final results:

$$\frac{\partial p_L}{\partial p_c} < 0, \frac{\partial L}{\partial p_L} < 0, \frac{\partial L}{\partial p_c} < 0. \tag{3.35}$$

Thus, in certain locations, as the price of telecommunications decreases, the price of the residential land will increase; as the price of residential land increases, the area of individual residence will decrease; and finally as the price of telecommunications decreases, the land area of individual residence will also decrease.

So, to compensate for the decrease of residential area, people will live more closely to the CBD. Also, another result,

$$\frac{dy_d}{dr} < 0$$

tells us that the dispersion from the CBD does not increase the disposable income (see Higano and Orishimo 1987).

Thus, based on three types of models, we considered the effect of the development of informatics on Urbanisation Process I. Several aspects of the basic points of the recent realistic characteristics of the urbanisation process referred to in

Section 2 have been analysed theoretically.

Through commuting, people are able to exchange overall communication. So Information I and II or Knowledge I and II are exchanged by face-to-face contact through communication. However, the substance of the face-to-face communication is only partially substituted by telecommunications. It should be noted that in the simplified model mentioned above, we can just make clear this kind of partial substitution.

4. CONCLUSION

With respect to the development of informatics, there are many cultural critiques such as Toffler's (1980). Most of the critiques stress the discontinuity of the urbanisation process of cultural development according to the development of informatics. Although the recent rapid development of informatics is certainly remarkable, the traditional productive industry exists as the base of the economic development. So, we can predict the continuous development of the economy along the cultural tradition in the short term. On the other hand, general statements on forecasting such developments are very difficult because the characteristics of the impact on society by the development of informatics seems to be very much idiosyncratic in each cultural context.

As the benefit brought about by informatics is also a mechanical one, it seems to be difficult to metamorphose the culture itself based on the informatics. So, we have to make every effort to succeedingly reduce the contradiction between the mechanic aspect and the non-mechanic aspects of our culture by distinguishing the different characters of information itself such as we understand Information I and II.

If we admit that policy means the implementation of planning, which improves our adjustment capability for our environment, apparently the development of informatics with respect to the urbanisation process would imply several kinds of possibilities. One is to improve our spatial adjustment - planning capability through various kinds of information systems such as monitoring systems and so on. We reviewed in our contribution the theoretical framework of the realistic and possible characteristics of the urbanisation process caused by the development of informatics. Based on such a theoretical framework, we could improve our planning capability through information systems.

REFERENCES

Alonso, W., Location and Land Use - Toward a General Theory of Land Rent, Harvard University Press, Cambridge, 1964.

Andersson, A.E., Accessibility and the Economics of Public Goods, in: P. Nijkamp and P. Rietveld (eds.), Cities in Transition - Problems and Policies, Sijthoff and Noordhoff, 1981, pp. 99-117.

Batty, Industrial Futures, United Kingdom

Bell, D., The Social Framework of the Information Society, in: M.L. Dertouzos, M.L. and J. Moss (eds.), The Computer Age - A Twenty-Year View, Massachusetts Institute of Technology, 1980, pp. 163-211.

Becker, G.S., A Theory of the Allocation of Time, The Economic Journal, September 1965, pp. 493-517.

Bly, P., Surface Transport, in: J. Brotchie, P. Newton, P. Hall and P. Nijkamp (eds.), The Future of Urban Form - The Impact of New Technology, Nichols, 1985.

Boulding, K.E., A Note on Information and Production, in: M. Jussawalla and H. Ebenfield (eds.), Communication and Information Economics, New Perspectives, North-Holland, Amsterdam, 1984.

Dickey, D., Urban Impacts of Information Technology, in: J Brotchie, P. Newton, P. Hall and P. Nijkamp (eds.), The Future of Urban Form - The Impact of New Technology, Nichols, 1985.

Feldman, M., Patterns of Biotechnology Development, in: J. Brotchie, P. Newton, P. Hall and P. Nijkamp, (eds.), The Future of Urban Form - The Impact of New Technology, Nichols, 1985.

Gorn, S., Informatics (Computer and Information Science) Its Ideology, Methodology and Sociology, in: F. Machlup and U. Mansfield (eds.), The Study of Information - Interdisciplinary Messages, John Wiley and Sons, Chichester, 1983.

Griliches, Z. (ed.), R&D Patents and Productivity, University of Chicago Press, Chicago, 1984.

Higano, Y. and I. Orishimo, Change of the Residential Location in the City by Telecommunication Development - Differentiation of Labour Market by Work Place, Presented at the 10th Pacific Regional Science Conference, 1987.

Jones, B., Sleepers, Wake!, Harvester Press, 1983.

Jacobs, J., Cities and the Wealth of Nations - Principles of Economic Life, Vintage Books, 1985.

Jonscher, C., Information Resources and Economic Productivity, Information Economics and Policy 1, North-Holland, Amsterdam, 1983, pp. 13-35.

Jussawalla, M. and C. Cheach, Towards an Information Economy - The Case of Singapore, Information Economics and Policy 1, 1983, pp. 161-176.

Kobayashi, K., Computers and Communications. The Software Challenge - A Human Perspective, Simul Press, 1982.

Langlois, R.N., Systems Theory, Knowledge and the Social Sciences, in: F. Machlup and U. Mansfield (eds.), The Study of Information - Interdisciplinary Messages, John Wiley and Sons, Chichester, 1983.

Levin, R.C. and P.C. Reiss, Test of a Schumpeterian Model of R&D and Market Structure, in: Z. Griliches (ed.), R&D Patents and Productivity, University of Chicago Press, Chicago, 1984, pp. 175-208.

Machlup, F., The Economics of Information and Human Capital, Knowledge: Its Creation, Distribution and Economic Significance, Volume 3, Princeton University Press, 1984.

Machlup, F., The Production and Distribution of Knowledge in the United States, Princeton University Press, 1972.

Meier, P., Telecommunication and Urban Development, in: J. Brotchie, P. Newton, P. Hall and P. Nijkamp (eds.), The Future of Urban Form - The Impact of New Technology, Nichols, 1985.

Moss, M.L. (ed.), Telecommunications and Productivity, Addison-Welsey, 1981.

Nelson, R. and S. Winter, The Schumpeterian Tradeoff Revisited, American Economic Review, Volume 72, 1982, pp. 114-133.

Nelson, R. and S. Winter, Forces Generating and Limiting Concentration under Schumpeterian Competition, The Bell Journal of Economics, Volume 9, 1978, pp. 524-548.

Nijkamp, P., Information Technology and Urban Planning, in: J. Brotchie, P. Newton, P. Hall and P. Nijkamp (eds.), The Future of Urban Form - The Impact of New Technology, Nichols, 1985.

Rubin, M.R., The US Information Sector and GNP: An Input-Output Study, Information Processing and Management, Volume 17, 1981, pp. 163-184.

Schuler, R.E., Evolving Telecommunications Markets: When Does Distance Matter?, Paper presented at the 32nd North American Meetings of the Regional Science Association, Philadelphia, 1986, (mimeo).

Toffler, A., The Third Wave, W. Morrow and Co., 1980.

Voge, J., The Political Economics of Complexity - from the Information to the 'Complexity' Economy, Information Economics and Policy 1, North-Holland, Amsterdam, 1983, pp. 97-114.

CONTRIBUTING AUTHORS

H. Akimaru
Department of Information and Computer Sciences
Toyohashi University of Technology
Tempaku-cho, Toyohashi 440
Japan

A. Andersson
Department of Economics
University of Umea
S-90187 Umea
Sweden

M.J. Beckmann
Department of Economics
Brown University
77 Arlington Avenue
Providence, R.I. 02912
U.S.A.

Technische Hochschule München
Institut für Statistik und Unternehmens-
forschung
Arcisstrasse 21
D-8000 München 2
Federal Republic of Germany

D.E. Boyce
Department of Civil Engineering
University of Illinois at Urbana-Champaign
Urbana, Illinois 61801
USA

M. Chatterji
School of Management
State University of New York
Binghamton, New York, 13901
USA

R.H. Funck
University of Karlsruhe
Kollegium am Schloss
Bau IV, Karlsruhe
Federal Republic of Germany

L.J. Gibson
Department of Geography and Regional Development
The University of Arizona
Tuscon, Arizona 85721
USA

G.J.D. Hewings
Department of Geography
University of Illinois at Urbana-Champaign
Urbana, Illinois 61801
USA

H. Inose
President, National Center for Science Information Systems
Ohtsuka 3-20-1
Bunkyouku, Tokyo
Japan

A. Jensen
Institute of Mathematical Statistics and Operations Research
The Technical University of Denmark
2800 Lyngby
Denmark

R.C. Jensen
Department of Economics
University of Queensland
St. Lucia, Queensland 4067
Australia

Y. Kitahara
Executive Vice President
Nippon Telegraph and Telephone Corporation
Uchisaiwaicho 1-1
Chiyodaku, Tokyo
Japan

R. Koblo
University of Karlsruhe
Kollegium am Schloss
Bau IV, Karlsruhe
Federal Republic of Germany

H. Kohno
Institute of Socio-Economic Planning
University of Tsukuba
Sakura, Ibaraki
Japan

J.S. Kowalski
University of Karlsruhe
Kollegium am Schloss
Bau IV, Karlsruhe
Federal Republic of Germany

H. Mitomo
Institute of Socio-Economic Planning
University of Tsukuba
Sakura, Ibaraki
Japan

P. Nijkamp
Department of Economics
Free University
P.O. Box 7161
1007 MC Amsterdam
The Netherlands

I. Orishimo
Department of Planning and Economics
Toyohashi University of Technology
Tempaku-cho, Toyohashi
Japan

Masatoshi Sakawa
Kyoto Institute of Economic Research
Kyoto University
Sakyo-ku, Kyoto 606
Japan

I. Salomon
Department of Geography
Hebrew University
Mount Scopus
Jerusalem
Israel

F. Seo
Kyoto Institute of Economic Research
Kyoto University
Sakyo-ku, Kyoto 606
Japan

B. Segerstahl
Research Institute of Northern Finland
University of Oulu
Oulu
Finland

M. Sonis
Department of Geography
Bar-Ilan University
52100 Ramat Gan
Israel

H. Tamura
Faculty of Engineering
Osaka University
2-1 Yamada-oka
Suita, Osaka 565
Japan

Tibor Vasko
International Institute for Applied Systems Analysis
Schloss Laxenburg
A-2361 Laxenburg
Austria

Vol. 211: P. van den Heuvel, The Stability of a Macroeconomic System with Quantity Constraints. VII, 169 pages. 1983.

Vol. 212: R. Sato and T. Nôno, Invariance Principles and the Structure of Technology. V, 94 pages. 1983.

Vol. 213: Aspiration Levels in Bargaining and Economic Decision Making. Proceedings, 1982. Edited by R. Tietz. VIII, 406 pages. 1983.

Vol. 214: M. Faber, H. Niemes und G. Stephan, Entropie, Umweltschutz und Rohstoffverbrauch. IX, 181 Seiten. 1983.

Vol. 215: Semi-Infinite Programming and Applications. Proceedings, 1981. Edited by A. V. Fiacco and K. O. Kortanek. XI, 322 pages. 1983.

Vol. 216: H. H. Müller, Fiscal Policies in a General Equilibrium Model with Persistent Unemployment. VI, 92 pages. 1983.

Vol. 217: Ch. Grootaert, The Relation Between Final Demand and Income Distribution. XIV, 105 pages. 1983.

Vol. 218: P. van Loon, A Dynamic Theory of the Firm: Production, Finance and Investment. VII, 191 pages. 1983.

Vol. 219: E. van Damme, Refinements of the Nash Equilibrium Concept. VI, 151 pages. 1983.

Vol. 220: M. Aoki, Notes on Economic Time Series Analysis: System Theoretic Perspectives. IX, 249 pages. 1983.

Vol. 221: S. Nakamura, An Inter-Industry Translog Model of Prices and Technical Change for the West German Economy. XIV, 290 pages. 1984.

Vol. 222: P. Meier, Energy Systems Analysis for Developing Countries. VI, 344 pages. 1984.

Vol. 223: W. Trockel, Market Demand. VIII, 205 pages. 1984.

Vol. 224: M. Kiy, Ein disaggregiertes Prognosesystem für die Bundesrepublik Deutschland. XVIII, 276 Seiten. 1984

Vol. 225: T. R. von Ungern-Sternberg, Zur Analyse von Märkten mit unvollständiger Nachfragerinformation. IX, 125 Seiten. 1984

Vol. 226: Selected Topics in Operations Research and Mathematical Economics. Proceedings, 1983. Edited by G. Hammer and D. Pallaschke. IX, 478 pages. 1984.

Vol. 227: Risk and Capital. Proceedings, 1983. Edited by G. Bamberg and K. Spremann. VII, 306 pages. 1984.

Vol. 228: Nonlinear Models of Fluctuating Growth. Proceedings, 1983. Edited by R. M. Goodwin, M. Krüger and A. Vercelli. XVII, 277 pages. 1984.

Vol. 229: Interactive Decision Analysis. Proceedings, 1983. Edited by M. Grauer and A. P. Wierzbicki. VIII, 269 pages. 1984.

Vol. 230: Macro-Economic Planning with Conflicting Goals. Proceedings, 1982. Edited by M. Despontin, P. Nijkamp and J. Spronk. VI, 297 pages. 1984.

Vol. 231: G. F. Newell, The M/M/∞ Service System with Ranked Servers in Heavy Traffic. XI, 126 pages. 1984.

Vol. 232: L. Bauwens, Bayesian Full Information Analysis of Simultaneous Equation Models Using Integration by Monte Carlo. VI, 114 pages. 1984.

Vol. 233: G. Wagenhals, The World Copper Market. XI, 190 pages. 1984.

Vol. 234: B. C. Eaves, A Course in Triangulations for Solving Equations with Deformations. III, 302 pages. 1984.

Vol. 235: Stochastic Models in Reliability Theory. Proceedings, 1984. Edited by S. Osaki and Y. Hatoyama. VII, 212 pages. 1984.

Vol. 236: G. Gandolfo, P. C. Padoan, A Disequilibrium Model of Real and Financial Accumulation in an Open Economy. VI, 172 pages. 1984.

Vol. 237: Misspecification Analysis. Proceedings, 1983. Edited by T. K. Dijkstra. V, 129 pages. 1984.

Vol. 238: W. Domschke, A. Drexl, Location and Layout Planning. IV, 134 pages. 1985.

Vol. 239: Microeconomic Models of Housing Markets. Edited by K. Stahl. VII, 197 pages. 1985.

Vol. 240: Contributions to Operations Research. Proceedings, 1984. Edited by K. Neumann and D. Pallaschke. V, 190 pages. 1985.

Vol. 241: U. Wittmann, Das Konzept rationaler Preiserwartungen. XI, 310 Seiten. 1985.

Vol. 242: Decision Making with Multiple Objectives. Proceedings, 1984. Edited by Y. Y. Haimes and V. Chankong. XI, 571 pages. 1985.

Vol. 243: Integer Programming and Related Areas. A Classified Bibliography 1981–1984. Edited by R. von Randow. XX, 386 pages. 1985.

Vol. 244: Advances in Equilibrium Theory. Proceedings, 1984. Edited by C. D. Aliprantis, O. Burkinshaw and N. J. Rothman. II, 235 pages. 1985.

Vol. 245: J. E. M. Wilhelm, Arbitrage Theory. VII, 114 pages. 1985.

Vol. 246: P. W. Otter, Dynamic Feature Space Modelling, Filtering and Self-Tuning Control of Stochastic Systems. XIV, 177 pages. 1985.

Vol. 247: Optimization and Discrete Choice in Urban Systems. Proceedings, 1983. Edited by B. G. Hutchinson, P. Nijkamp and M. Batty. VI, 371 pages. 1985.

Vol. 248: Plural Rationality and Interactive Decision Processes. Proceedings, 1984. Edited by M. Grauer, M. Thompson and A. P. Wierzbicki. VI, 354 pages. 1985.

Vol. 249: Spatial Price Equilibrium: Advances in Theory, Computation and Application. Proceedings, 1984. Edited by P. T. Harker. VII, 277 pages. 1985.

Vol. 250: M. Roubens, Ph. Vincke, Preference Modelling. VIII, 94 pages. 1985.

Vol. 251: Input-Output Modeling. Proceedings, 1984. Edited by A. Smyshlyaev. VI, 261 pages. 1985.

Vol. 252: A. Birolini, On the Use of Stochastic Processes in Modeling Reliability Problems. VI, 105 pages. 1985.

Vol. 253: C. Withagen, Economic Theory and International Trade in Natural Exhaustible Resources. VI, 172 pages. 1985.

Vol. 254: S. Müller, Arbitrage Pricing of Contingent Claims. VIII, 151 pages. 1985.

Vol. 255: Nondifferentiable Optimization: Motivations and Applications. Proceedings, 1984. Edited by V. F. Demyanov and D. Pallaschke. VI, 350 pages. 1985.

Vol. 256: Convexity and Duality in Optimization. Proceedings, 1984. Edited by J. Ponstein. V, 142 pages. 1985.

Vol. 257: Dynamics of Macrosystems. Proceedings, 1984. Edited by J.-P. Aubin, D. Saari and K. Sigmund. VI, 280 pages. 1985.

Vol. 258: H. Funke, Eine allgemeine Theorie der Polypol- und Oligopolpreisbildung. III, 237 pages. 1985.

Vol. 259: Infinite Programming. Proceedings, 1984. Edited by E. J. Anderson and A. B. Philpott. XIV, 244 pages. 1985.

Vol. 260: H.-J. Kruse, Degeneracy Graphs and the Neighbourhood Problem. VIII, 128 pages. 1986.

Vol. 261: Th. R. Gulledge, Jr., N. K. Womer, The Economics of Made-to-Order Production. VI, 134 pages. 1986.

Vol. 262: H. U. Buhl, A Neo-Classical Theory of Distribution and Wealth. V, 146 pages. 1986.

Vol. 263: M. Schäfer, Resource Extraction and Market Structure. XI, 154 pages. 1986.

Vol. 264: Models of Economic Dynamics. Proceedings, 1983. Edited by H.F. Sonnenschein. VII, 212 pages. 1986.

Vol. 265: Dynamic Games and Applications in Economics. Edited by T. Başar. IX, 288 pages. 1986.

Vol. 266: Multi-Stage Production Planning and Inventory Control. Edited by S. Axsäter, Ch. Schneeweiss and E. Silver. V, 264 pages. 1986.

Vol. 267: R. Bemelmans, The Capacity Aspect of Inventories. IX, 165 pages. 1986.

Vol. 268: V. Firchau, Information Evaluation in Capital Markets. VII, 103 pages. 1986.

Vol. 269: A. Borglin, H. Keiding, Optimality in Infinite Horizon Economies. VI, 180 pages. 1986.

Vol. 270: Technological Change, Employment and Spatial Dynamics. Proceedings 1985. Edited by P. Nijkamp. VII, 466 pages. 1986.

Vol. 271: C. Hildreth, The Cowles Commission in Chicago, 1939–1955. V, 176 pages. 1986.

Vol. 272: G. Clemenz, Credit Markets with Asymmetric Information. VIII, 212 pages. 1986.

Vol. 273: Large-Scale Modelling and Interactive Decision Analysis. Proceedings, 1985. Edited by G. Fandel, M. Grauer, A. Kurzhanski and A.P. Wierzbicki. VII, 363 pages. 1986.

Vol. 274: W.K. Klein Haneveld, Duality in Stochastic Linear and Dynamic Programming. VII, 295 pages. 1986.

Vol. 275: Competition, Instability, and Nonlinear Cycles. Proceedings, 1985. Edited by W. Semmler. XII, 340 pages. 1986.

Vol. 276: M.R. Baye, D.A. Black, Consumer Behavior, Cost of Living Measures, and the Income Tax. VII, 119 pages. 1986.

Vol. 277: Studies in Austrian Capital Theory, Investment and Time. Edited by M. Faber. VI, 317 pages. 1986.

Vol. 278: W.E. Diewert, The Measurement of the Economic Benefits of Infrastructure Services. V, 202 pages. 1986.

Vol. 279: H.-J. Büttler, G. Frei and B. Schips, Estimation of Disequilibrium Models. VI, 114 pages. 1986.

Vol. 280: H.T. Lau, Combinatorial Heuristic Algorithms with FORTRAN. VII, 126 pages. 1986.

Vol. 281: Ch.-L. Hwang, M.-J. Lin, Group Decision Making under Multiple Criteria. XI, 400 pages. 1987.

Vol. 282: K. Schittkowski, More Test Examples for Nonlinear Programming Codes. V, 261 pages. 1987.

Vol. 283: G. Gabisch, H.-W. Lorenz, Business Cycle Theory. VII, 229 pages. 1987.

Vol. 284: H. Lütkepohl, Forecasting Aggregated Vector ARMA Processes. X, 323 pages. 1987.

Vol. 285: Toward Interactive and Intelligent Decision Support Systems. Volume 1. Proceedings, 1986. Edited by Y. Sawaragi, K. Inoue and H. Nakayama. XII, 445 pages. 1987.

Vol. 286: Toward Interactive and Intelligent Decision Support Systems. Volume 2. Proceedings, 1986. Edited by Y. Sawaragi, K. Inoue and H. Nakayama. XII, 450 pages. 1987.

Vol. 287: Dynamical Systems. Proceedings, 1985. Edited by A.B. Kurzhanski and K. Sigmund. VI, 215 pages. 1987.

Vol. 288: G.D. Rudebusch, The Estimation of Macroeconomic Disequilibrium Models with Regime Classification Information. VII, 128 pages. 1987.

Vol. 289: B.R. Meijboom, Planning in Decentralized Firms. X, 168 pages. 1987.

Vol. 290: D.A. Carlson, A. Haurie, Infinite Horizon Optimal Control. XI, 254 pages. 1987.

Vol. 291: N. Takahashi, Design of Adaptive Organizations. VI, 140 pages. 1987.

Vol. 292: I. Tchijov, L. Tomaszewicz (Eds.), Input-Output Modeling. Proceedings, 1985. VI, 195 pages. 1987.

Vol. 293: D. Batten, J. Casti, B. Johansson (Eds.), Economic Evolution and Structural Adjustment. Proceedings, 1985. VI, 382 pages. 1987.

Vol. 294: J. Jahn, W. Krabs (Eds.), Recent Advances and Historical Development of Vector Optimization. VII, 405 pages. 1987.

Vol. 295: H. Meister, The Purification Problem for Constrained Games with Incomplete Information. X, 127 pages. 1987.

Vol. 296: A. Börsch-Supan, Econometric Analysis of Discrete Choice. VIII, 211 pages. 1987.

Vol. 297: V. Fedorov, H. Läuter (Eds.), Model-Oriented Data Analysis. Proceedings, 1987. VI, 239 pages. 1988.

Vol. 298: S.H. Chew, Q. Zheng, Integral Global Optimization. VII, 179 pages. 1988.

Vol. 299: K. Marti, Descent Directions and Efficient Solutions in Discretely Distributed Stochastic Programs. XIV, 178 pages. 1988.

Vol. 300: U. Derigs, Programming in Networks and Graphs. XI, 315 pages. 1988.

Vol. 301: J. Kacprzyk, M. Roubens (Eds.), Non-Conventional Preference Relations in Decision Making. VII, 155 pages. 1988.

Vol. 302: H.A. Eiselt, G. Pederzoli (Eds.), Advances in Optimization and Control. Proceedings, 1986. VIII, 372 pages. 1988.

Vol. 303: F.X. Diebold, Empirical Modeling of Exchange Rate Dynamics. VII, 143 pages. 1988.

Vol. 304: A. Kurzhanski, K. Neumann, D. Pallaschke (Eds.), Optimization, Parallel Processing and Applications. Proceedings, 1987. VI, 292 pages. 1988.

Vol. 305: G.-J.C.Th. van Schijndel, Dynamic Firm and Investor Behaviour under Progressive Personal Taxation. X, 215 pages. 1988.

Vol. 306: Ch. Klein, A Static Microeconomic Model of Pure Competition. VIII, 139 pages. 1988.

Vol. 307: T.K. Dijkstra (Ed.), On Model Uncertainty and its Statistical Implications. VII, 138 pages. 1988.

Vol. 308: J.R. Daduna, A. Wren (Eds.), Computer-Aided Transit Scheduling. VIII, 339 pages. 1988.

Vol. 309: G. Ricci, K. Velupillai (Eds.), Growth Cycles and Multisectoral Economics: the Goodwin Tradition. III, 126 pages. 1988.

Vol. 310: J. Kacprzyk, M. Fedrizzi (Eds.), Combining Fuzzy Imprecision with Probabilistic Uncertainty in Decision Making. IX, 399 pages. 1988.

Vol. 311: R. Färe, Fundamentals of Production Theory. IX, 163 pages. 1988.

Vol. 312: J. Krishnakumar, Estimation of Simultaneous Equation Models with Error Components Structure. X, 357 pages. 1988.

Vol. 313: W. Jammernegg, Sequential Binary Investment Decisions. VI, 156 pages. 1988.

Vol. 314: R. Tietz, W. Albers, R. Selten (Eds.), Bounded Rational Behavior in Experimental Games and Markets. VI, 368 pages. 1988.

Vol. 315: I. Orishimo, G.J.D. Hewings, P. Nijkamp (Eds.), Information Technology: Social and Spatial Perspectives. Proceedings, 1986. VI, 268 pages. 1988.

Batch number: 10838062

Printed by Printforce, the Netherlands